Evidence ~~for Policy~~
~~A Practi~~

the Australia and New Zealand
School of Government

ANZSOG Program on Government, Politics and Public Management

The Australia and New Zealand School of Government (ANZSOG) is a network initiative of seven jurisdictions (the Australian and New Zealand, New South Wales, Victoria, Queensland, Western Australia and South Australia governments) and fourteen universities. Established in 2003, ANZSOG represents a new and exciting prospect for the development of world-class research and teaching in the public and community sectors.

ANZSOG has announced an extensive research program that promotes innovative and cutting-edge research in partnership with academia and the public sector (see <www.anzsog.edu.au>). In association with UNSW Press, ANZSOG has undertaken to publish a series of books on contemporary issues in Australian government, politics and public management. Titles in this program will promote high-quality research on topics of interest to a broad readership (academic, professional, students and general readers) and will include teaching texts relevant to the ANZSOG consortia in the areas of government, politics and public management.

Series editors are Professor John Wanna and Professor RAW Rhodes, Research School of Social Sciences, Australian National University, Canberra.

Recent titles include:

- *Terms of Trust: Arguments over Ethics in Australian Government* by John Uhr
- *Yes, Premier: Political Leadership in Australia's States and Territories* edited by John Wanna and Paul Williams
- *Westminster Legacies: Democracy and Responsible Government in Asia and the Pacific* edited by Haig Patapan, John Wanna and Patrick Weller
- *The Australian Electoral System: Origins, Variation and Consequences* by David M Farrell and Ian McAllister
- *Cabinet Government in Australia, 1901–2006: Practice, Principles, Performance* by Patrick Weller
- *Power without Responsibility: Ministerial Staffers in Australian Governments from Whitlam to Howard* by Anne Tiernan
- *Australian Foreign Policy in the Age of Terror* edited by Carl Ungerer
- *Calculating Political Risk* by Catherine Althaus
- *In Government We Trust: Market Failure and the Delusions of Privatisation* by Warwick Funnell, Robert Jupe and Jane Andrew.

Evidence for Policy and Decision-Making:
A Practical Guide

Edited by George Argyrous

the Australia and New Zealand

School of Government

A UNSW Press book

Published by
University of New South Wales Press Ltd
University of New South Wales
Sydney NSW 2052
AUSTRALIA
www.unswpress.com.au

© UNSW Press 2009
First published 2009

National Library of Australia Cataloguing-in-Publication entry

Title: Evidence for policy and decision-making: a practical guide/editor:
George Argyrous.
ISBN: 978 086840 903 0 (pbk.)
Subjects: Public administration–Decision making.
Public policy.
Other Authors/Contributors: Argyrous, George, 1963–
Dewey Number: 352.33

Cover design Di Quick
Printer Ligare

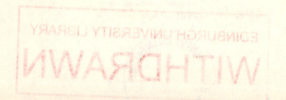

Contents

List of contributors

Peter Abelson is a Visiting Scholar at the University of Sydney, an Adjunct Professor of the Australian and New Zealand School of Government and Managing Director of the economics consultancy Applied Economics P/L

George Argyrous is Senior Lecturer in the School of Social Sciences and International Studies at the University of New South Wales, Australia, and is an Adjunct Faculty member of the Australia and New Zealand School of Government.

Australian Bureau of Statistics (ABS) is Australia's official national statistical agency.

Huw Davies is Professor of Health Policy and Management in the School of Management at the University of St Andrews, and Director of the Social Dimensions of Health Institute at the Universities of Dundee and St Andrews, UK.

Leo Dobes is a Visiting Fellow at the Crawford School of Economics and Government at the Australian National University and Adjunct Associate Professor at the University of Canberra.

Ralph Hall is Professor in the School of Social Sciences and International Studies at the University of New South Wales, Australia.

Sandra Nutley is Professor of Public Management at the University of Edinburgh and Director of the Research Unit for Research Utilisation (RURU) at the Universities of Edinburgh and St Andrews, UK.

Wendy Proctor is an Ecological Economist with the Commonwealth Scientific and Industrial Research Organisation (CSIRO) in Australia and is Secretary of the Australia New Zealand Society for Ecological Economics and the International Society for Ecological Economics.

Gary Saliba is Director of a management consulting company, Strategic Journeys, Visiting Fellow at the Crawford School of Economics and Government at the Australian National University and Adjunct Professor at Charles Sturt University, Albury.

Isabel Walter is Research Fellow in the Social Dimensions of Health Institute at the Universities of Dundee and St Andrews, UK.

Glenn Withers is Chief Executive Officer of Universities Australia. He is also an Adjunct Professor of Public Policy at the Australian National University and a Fellow of the Australia and New Zealand School of Government.

Foreword

Decisions need to be based on evidence, and in recent years the demand for evidence-based policy has grown. In the health sciences, where the term 'evidence-base' first gained wide currency, this has meant the reliance on clinical trials and the accumulation of evidence drawn from these trials. In the fields of policy and management decision-making, however, the evidence base is much wider and more controversial. No single method of gathering evidence or analysing it stands out as providing a more solid base for policy and decision-making. As a result the move to evidence based policy and decision-making has opened up new debates and controversies, rather than providing a conclusive means of arriving at the 'correct' answer.

This book provides a practical guide to these debates and controversies. It does so at a number of different levels. First, it provides practitioners with basic skills in the collection, analysis and presentation of evidence of various kinds. The emphasis is on familiarity with key concepts and how to be an intelligent reader and commissioner of evidence for policy and decision-making. Second, it presents the range of frameworks within which evidence is harnessed to aid decision-making. These frameworks often compete as legitimate decision-making tools, and each has its strengths and weaknesses. This book summarises these strengths and weaknesses so that decision-makers can form their own opinions regarding the relative usefulness of each framework. Last, the emphasis is on the practical use of evidence, rather than understanding the underlying theory behind the concepts. Sometimes this underlying theory is of practical relevance, but it is the latter that is the focus of this book.

This book will become an essential part of a policy practitioner's work. It will help them cut through the maze of information that is presented as evidence for decision-making, and provide them with stronger foundations for their decisions.

Allan Fels

1 Past, present, and possible futures for evidence-based policy

Sandra Nutley, Isabel Walter and Huw Davies

The past decade or so has witnessed widespread interest in the development of policy that is better informed by evidence. Enthusiasm has, however, been tempered by concerns and confusion. Indeed, what is understood by the very phrase 'evidence-based policy' varies considerably, as do evaluations of its relative merits. Hence the objective of this chapter is to provide an overview of what is understood by evidence-based policy, where it has come from, where it has got to, and where it might be headed. In doing so, the chapter:

- sets current discussions of evidence-based policy in historical context;
- discusses different interpretations of evidence-based policy and their implications;
- comments on common critiques of the evidence-based policy agenda;
- outlines the key initiatives associated with efforts to promote and improve evidence-based policy; and
- speculates on some possible futures for evidence-based policy.

Along the way, our discussion will address the thorny issues of what counts as evidence, where policy-making begins and ends, and what it means to 'base' policy on evidence. We have reviewed and summarised many of these issues before for both an Australian (Nutley 2003) and a New Zealand audience (Nutley, Davies & Walter 2003). These reviews have drawn on several studies of developments in the United Kingdom, a country often considered to have led the way in the development of evidence-based policy (Davies, Nutley & Smith 2000; Nutley, Percy-Smith & Solesbury 2003; Walter et al 2004). The present chapter updates and expands these earlier reviews by drawing on our most extensive analysis to date of how research can inform public services (Nutley, Walter & Davies 2007).

Before embarking on this overview, it is important to reflect on our starting point and standpoints. Our understanding of all the above issues is influenced by where we are located and what we do. We are all social science researchers working in UK universities and our understanding and analysis are shaped by this context. There is much that can be learned from the UK experience and we know that many of our observations resonate with experiences in other countries, albeit that they may have different implications in different contexts. Contextual arrangements matter and these include cultural factors (such as attitudes towards large-scale policy experimentation and/or rational policy analysis) and constitutional issues (such as unitary or federal government structures and the degree of subsidiarity). However, although context matters it is not always immutable.

A second important feature of our standpoint is that we are particularly interested in the use of the social research evidence as part of the evidence-based policy agenda. We define *social research* broadly and inclusively as research aimed at understanding the social world, as well as the interactions between this world and public policy/public service. However, we are confident that many of our observations are relevant to other types of research.

Our understanding of what constitutes the *nature of research* is also broad and, like others, we have found it unhelpful to provide any overly specific definition (Court, Hovland & Young 2005). Thus we regard research as any investigation towards increasing the sum of knowledge based on planned and systematic enquiry. This includes any systematic process of critical investigation and evaluation, theory building, data collection, analysis and codification relevant to the development of policy and practice (Court, Hovland & Young 2005). We recognise the importance of other types of evidence, such as routine monitoring data and expert knowledge. However, much of the discussion in this chapter relates particularly to the use of research and research-based evidence.

Third, we tend to take a fairly broad view of policy. In much of our previous work (for example, Davies, Nutley & Smith 2000; Nutley, Walter & Davies 2007) we have adopted the dual phrase of *evidence-based policy and practice*. The reason for this is partly the desire to reflect the parallel debates about evidence use in policy-making and in frontline service delivery. It is also due to an appreciation that in reality there is rarely a clear demarcation between policy and practice. Policy decisions can range from specific issues (decision-making about day-to-day activities) to strategic issues (large-scale decisions between broad policy choices), so policy and practice shade into one another. Policy is made at a local level and even when policy is decided nationally, it often changes in the process of its implementation (Lipsky 1979). So although this chapter is concerned predominantly with evidence-based policy, it will inevitably also relate to policy-making at the meso level (for example, organisational decision-making) and even touch on the frontline evidence-based practice issues.

Finally, we use the phrase *evidence-based policy* throughout this chapter even though, as we argue later, we see the role of evidence as informing policy rather than driving it. In many ways we would be happier with the phrase 'evidence-informed' or even 'evidence-influenced policy', but because 'evidence-based policy' is now part of the accepted lexicon, we continue to use it in this chapter.

The historical context of evidence-based policy

The provision of analysis for policy has been described as old as the state itself (Parsons 1995). However, in the case of the United Kingdom at least, the specific character of the relationship between research and social policy was shaped during the expansion of both activities in the 19th and 20th centuries (Abrams 1968; Bulmer 1986; Finch 1986). In particular, university social science departments flourished and a range of other organisations (such as think tanks and research foundations) emerged after World War II to feed an increased appetite for social knowledge. The conviction was that research could and should be of direct use to government in determining and achieving its social policy objectives, establishing what has been called a *social engineering* role for research (Janowitz 1972). However, this early enthusiasm was followed by increasing disillusionment during the 1970s and 1980s about the ability of research and analysis to provide answers to complex social problems, bringing into question the whole enterprise of creating social knowledge for direct use by governments (Finch 1986).

Renewed enthusiasm for the insights offered by research emerged in the 1990s and this was epitomised in the United Kingdom by the rhetoric of Tony Blair's Labour government when it won the 1997 general election. Its slogan – 'what matters is what works' – was intended to signal an end to ideologically based decision-making in favour of evidence-based thinking. The present-day concept of evidence-based policy flourished during this period as the Labour government articulated its expectations about 'modernised government' and 'modernised policy-making':

> This government expects more of policy makers. More new ideas, more willingness to question inherited ways of doing things, the use of evidence and research in policy-making and better focus on policies that will deliver long-term goals [Cm 4310 1999, para 6].

Although the intensity of interest in evidence-based policy in the United Kingdom may be unique, discussion of these issues is certainly not just a British affair. There are similar debates in Australia, Canada, New Zealand, the United States, and in many other European countries (CfEBP 2001; Head 2008; Latham 2001; Marston & Watts 2003; Morton & Nutley 2007; SPEaR 2001; WT Grant Foundation 2008; Zussman 2003).

Finally, as noted in the introduction, interest in evidence-based policy has been paralleled and to some extent preceded by a related debate about evidence use in practice – that is, in frontline service delivery. This is seen most vividly in the healthcare sector but is also evident in other public services such as social care, education and criminal justice services.

Interest in evidence-based practice can be partly explained by increased distrust of the professions charged with delivering public services, coupled with the growth of an increasingly educated, informed and questioning public (Davies, Nutley & Smith 2000). Evidence-based practice is one way of addressing these concerns by seeking to ensure that what is being done is worthwhile and that it is being done in the best possible way, even though it might not always meet this objective.

Defining evidence-based policy

Definitions of evidence-based policy (and practice) range from rather narrow interpretations of its meaning to broader, all-encompassing views about what it represents. A fairly common narrow definition sees it as a movement that promotes a particular methodology for producing a specific form of evidence: systematic reviews and meta-analyses of robust (often experimental) research studies aimed at assessing the effectiveness of health and social policy interventions. Such a 'movement' is also sometimes seen as primarily about promoting the translation of systematic review evidence into guidelines for practice that may ultimately be transformed into centrally imposed, evidence-based programs of intervention.

At the broader end of the spectrum, evidence-based policy (and practice) has been defined as an approach that 'helps people make well-informed decisions about policies, programmes and projects by putting the best available evidence from research at the heart of policy development and implementation' (Davies 2004, p 3). Under this broader view, which we would endorse and ultimately broaden further, what counts as evidence is more wide-ranging than just research from evaluations of 'what works'. It encompasses a more diverse array of research methods exploring a wider variety of research questions – not just what works, but also what is the nature of the problem, why does it occur, and how might it be addressed. This wider range of questions brings the possibility of research having an indirect (conceptual) impact on policy choices, by reshaping the ways people think about policy issues, as well as directly impacting on instrumental choices. Under this broad view of evidence, 'fitness for purpose' acts as the main criterion for determining what counts as good evidence. Thus evidence from a range of research and evaluation studies sits alongside routine monitoring data, expert knowledge and information from stakeholder consultations. And its role is to inform policy rather than to drive it.

A further element of a broad definition of evidence-based policy is the need to consider the role played by evidence (particularly research evidence) in relation to policy. While research can play an important and positive role in informing or even supporting policy decisions, this is not always the case. Research can also seek to critique and challenge established policy frameworks. Box 1.1 defines some potential roles for researchers in influencing public policy, and demonstrates the wide scope for research use beyond the instrumentalist 'evidence-based' agenda. Research can have an important role to play in *shaping values*, and it should not therefore be relegated to a purely

Box 1.1 Public policy and the researcher's stance

It is possible to identify three key stances for researchers to adopt in relation to influencing public policy:

1. *The consensual approach.* The consensual approach refers to situations where there is broad agreement among policy-makers and researchers about the main issues of concern and the ways in which these should be addressed. Researchers then work within the existing paradigm, aiming to provide policy-makers, practitioners and other stakeholders with knowledge about how best to improve service delivery and service outcomes. Their focus is on improving the efficacy of decision-making and the outcomes of service activities. Such an approach is the mainstay of the evidence-based policy and practice agenda.

2. *The contentious approach.* In the contentious approach, researchers place themselves more on the sidelines of public policy. They may not always contribute to policy development directly, but maintain a critical stance in relation to government, society and its institutions. The role of researchers in this approach is to act as 'moral critic'. Examples abound of researchers pursuing such an agenda, not just through academic journals but also through articles and letters in the general media. For example, there is a long tradition of critique, commentary and analysis of governments' performance measurement and management approaches and the development of a target culture (Smith 1995; Mannion, Davies & Marshal 2005; Bevan & Hood 2006).

3. *The paradigm-challenging approach.* More radically, researchers might take a stance outside the prevailing paradigm, using their work to problematise established frameworks and ways of thinking. They may, for example, propose new principles for action for which they hope political support will follow. One example is the body of work on 'positive psychology' (Seligman 2005), which seeks to redirect the agenda for mental health away from one focused on ill health and dysfunction to one focused on wellness, wellbeing, and happiness (see for example, <www.ppc.sas.upenn.edu>). Another is the work of the New Economics Foundation, which seeks to 'improve quality of life by promoting innovative solutions that challenge mainstream thinking on economic, environment and social issues' (<www.neweconomics.org>).

Source: Adapted and augmented from Rein (1976) and Weiss (1995). Reproduced from Nutley, Walter & Davies (2007, pp 11–12), with permission.

technical role of helping decide between competing options that seek to operationalise fixed and pre-existing values. The more challenging and contentious stances of research play an important role in promoting the democratic and intellectual health of society, but they are somewhat sidelined in more traditional definitions of the evidence-based policy agenda.

Critiques of the evidence-based policy agenda

Concerns have been expressed at the 'inherently conservative' nature of evidence-based policy (perhaps leading to the perpetual delay of reform until sufficient evidence is gathered; Davey Smith, Ebrahim & Frankel 2001). More usually, though, critics have focused on the inappropriate idealism of evidence-based policy – the so-called *dual follies* that underpin the very idea of policy being evidence-based (Clarence 2002).

The first of these 'follies' is the assumption that evidence, including research evidence, can provide objective answers to inherently political policy questions. Evidence, it is said, can never be objective as all knowledge is ultimately socially constructed.

The second alleged 'folly' concerns the assumption that policy-making can or indeed should become a more rational decision-making process, one that is influenced primarily by the weight of evidence. Politics and the art of muddling through, it is argued, overwhelm and undermine attempts to introduce these more deliberative processes (Clarence 2002; Parsons 2002; Leicester 1999).

The response from the proponents of evidence-based policy to the first issue has been to acknowledge that research and evaluation rarely provide definitive answers, especially when questions relate to what works in what circumstances in tackling complex social problems (Sanderson 2002). There is also ready recognition from many proponents that what counts as evidence is inextricably bound by our ways of thinking about the social world (Mulgan 2003). The conclusion drawn is that expectations of what research and other forms of evidence can tell us need to be managed carefully, with all knowledge being treated as provisional, but this does not mean that research has nothing of importance to say.

The response to the second charge, that it is politics and not evidence that drives policy processes, has been to emphasise that evidence is only one of the many factors that influence the policy process (Davies 2004; Mulgan 2003; Nutley & Webb 2000). Terms such as evidence-informed, evidence-influenced and evidence-inspired can be seen as reflecting this rebalancing. The aim of an evidence-informed process is to try to increase the relative prominence given to evidence during the policy process, with due acknowledgment that other factors, such as ideology, professional norms, expert views, personal experience, media interest and politics, will all remain influential.

Studies of the extent to which policy processes are in fact influenced by evidence have provided some limited support for the idea of evidence-informed policy in the United Kingdom (Coote, Allen & Woodhead 2004; Fear & Roberts 2004) and in the United States (Auspos & Kubisch 2004), but they have also shown the many ways in which research and other evidence is used selectively to support an ideological argument or promote pre-existing plans. Moreover, there is often a gap between the rhetoric of evidence-based policy and what happens on the ground. Thus despite official assertions to the contrary, social programs tend to be designed 'on the basis of informed guesswork and expert hunches, enriched by some evidence and driven by political and other imperatives' (Coote, Allen & Woodhead 2004, p xi). That this is the case partly reflects the nature of the policy process but it is also due in many instances to the lack of appropriate evidence on which to base the detailed planning and commissioning of social programs. It is also compounded by widely differing views about what constitutes 'evidence' (Coote, Allen & Woodhead 2004).

We note that the extent and precise nature of research use in policy is often the subject of competing opinions and claims, but that the dispute is often not so much about *whether* research has been used, but more about *how* it has been used. Thus despite the sustained critique of evidence-based policy, it seems reasonable to conclude that evidence will continue to feature in the knowledge-swirl that underpins policy thinking, policy choices and program implementation. This is a vision of the policy process where research is 'on tap' and not 'on top' (Etzioni 1968).

An additional concern that is worthy of specific attention is the potential for the evidence-based policy agenda to result in the politicisation of research. There has long been an argument about the need to ensure the separation of research and policy in order to protect the independence of research and its ability to speak truth to power and play a role in holding governments to account (for example, Campbell 1969; Rein 1976).

The evidence-based policy (and practice) movement is sometimes seen as a threat to this independence. Hope (2004) has argued that as political life becomes 'scientised' through systematic evidence playing a greater role in shaping and governing social life, so the structures of authority in both policy and research settings lose their autonomy. Not only is science seen as a legitimate guide to politics, but politics also has a say in science – what research is endorsed and supported and how it is conducted: 'The value of science ceases to be derived from its methodology alone and is now also to be derived from its promises of applicability and utility' (Hope 2004, p 291).

The desirability of developing more focused and applied research strategies has also been questioned due to the uncertainties about whether applied research has more impact than basic research. Wilensky (1997) argues that we should resist the temptation to oversell the practical value of applied research:

> The idea that applied research in the social sciences (as opposed to basic research) is more relevant to the public agenda and public policy is a mistake; it tends to divert money, talent, and attention away from the job of developing cumulative knowledge about culture, social structure, and politics ... good basic research deals with persistent problems of the human condition and is therefore public policy research in the broadest sense [Wilensky 1997, p 1242].

There is little doubt that the evidence-based policy agenda has focused government attention on research and development strategies and, within this, processes for commissioning research. As a result, government more directly influences not only *what* gets studied but *how* as well, including what counts as good-quality research. In addition, as we discuss later, the evidence-based policy agenda has also opened up a more interactive relationship between research and policy, for example by inviting independent researchers into policy deliberations. Questions arise about whether researchers can maintain independence in this process, and the extent to which they may suffer from policy 'capture'.

Promoting evidence-based policy

Good empirical evidence about what works to improve evidence use in policy contexts is relatively thin on the ground, so this section not only draws on documented and evaluated studies of evidence use, but also seeks to capture experiential knowledge about what has been tried and what seems to be effective.

Discussion of the evidence-based policy agenda is often underpinned by an implicit assumption that it is the consensus-based use of evidence that needs to be improved (see Box 1.1). Here researchers and other analysts work within the existing paradigm around the main issues of concern and how these should be addressed. In doing so, they provide policy-makers with knowledge about how best to improve public service delivery and service outcomes. Thus attention is focused on improving the instrumental uses of evidence (to inform policy directions and policy choices), although due acknowledgment is sometimes made of the broader and longer-term conceptual impacts of evidence, particularly research evidence, on policy. In such a consensus-based view, an under-use of evidence is generally presumed, and there is also concern that when evidence is used, it is sometimes used as political ammunition, which tends to be construed as a form of misuse.

In outlining key initiatives to enhance the use of evidence in policy-making, we examine the ways in which these initiatives tend to be based on a 'supply and demand' framing of the problem. Thus they focus on how to improve research supply, how to increase policy demand for that research, and how to increase the interplay between supply and demand. We go on to outline strategies for improving evidence use that draw on a broader framing of this issue by acknowledging the many diverse routes through which research influences policy.

Supply-side initiatives

An emphasis on supply-side issues locates the 'problem' of evidence use in the lack of an appropriate flow of evidence into the policy process. We illustrate this perspective and some associated initiatives by focusing on the supply of research evidence. Initiatives to address the supply of research have sought to build research capacity and have also targeted the way in which research is commissioned by, and communicated to, those in policy roles.

There has been significant government investment in the research infrastructure in many countries over the past decade, much of which has been focused on higher education institutions. For example, the UK government via the Economic and Social Research Council (ESRC) has ploughed significant funds into developing research methods and the capabilities of social scientists, particularly to address the perceived lack of expertise in quantitative research methods. The ESRC has worked with the government to fund specific research programs in areas of need, such as the teaching and learning research program. It has also sought to fund the development of multidisciplinary centres of expertise in areas such as social inequalities in health and the social implications of new technologies. The rationale underpinning this activity is that research use is hampered by a lack of good applied research that addresses key policy questions.

A further set of initiatives has sought to improve the quality of the research and evaluation studies commissioned by government departments. In the United Kingdom, these initiatives resulted in a series of Cabinet Office reports, for example: *Adding It Up*, an overview of analysis in government (Cabinet

Office 2000); *The Magenta Book*, which provides guidance on policy evaluation and analysis (Cabinet Office 2003a); a set of guidelines on assessing qualitative research (Spencer et al 2003); and *Trying It Out*, on the role and process of pilots in policy-making (Cabinet Office 2003b). The *Adding It Up* report provided the foundation on which the others were built and it included the general advice that government departments should submit their internal research and analysis to external peer review in order to improve its robustness. In Australia, the Australian Bureau of Statistics (ABS) has done some similar things in recent years to improve the quality of research and data analysis, including providing free access to all ABS data.

Emphasis has also been placed on making the evidence base of existing research and evaluative studies more accessible. Online databases of studies have been developed around a wide range of policy and practice issues, such as Social Care Online (<www.socialcareonline.org.uk>).

Beyond improving the nature, quality and accessibility of individual research projects and programs, supply-side approaches have also sought to address the way in which a range of research is synthesised for policy users. The international Cochrane collaboration (<www.cochrane.org>) and Campbell collaboration (<www.campbellcollaboration.org>) have invested considerable energy in promoting and improving the methods of systematic review. The rationale for this is that policy-makers need to consider where the balance of evidence lies on a particular issue, such as the effectiveness of screening technologies in healthcare, or the impacts of rehabilitation programs for young offenders. It is known that the results of single studies can be misleading, and there is a limit to the extent to which policy-makers can be expected to develop their own overviews of the evidence on a particular issue. Furthermore, idiosyncratic research reviews may be as misleading as single studies (Sheldon 2005). Systematic review methodologies therefore aim to address these issues by ensuring that search strategies are comprehensive, fully documented and replicable, and that study selection and synthesis methods are robust and justifiable. A central preoccupation of supply-side initiatives is thus the development of these rigorous methods of research synthesis and communication.

Many see systematic review work as a breakthrough in moving towards a robust, cumulative and synthesised knowledge base that can better inform policy and practice. However, there is little evidence to suggest, particularly outside of health care, that systematic review findings are used more than the findings of other forms of review activity or indeed the findings of single studies. It seems that the consumers of policy research have often not found the outputs of systematic reviews sufficiently relevant or useful (Sheldon 2005; Lavis et al 2005). Within the constraints of a supply and demand view of research use, this is often ascribed to the disappointing nature of the findings of many systematic reviews. Too often, it seems, expensive reviews conclude that there are very few robust studies relevant to the issue under consideration and that it is not possible to draw firm conclusions of the kind that policy-makers demand (Young et al 2002).

There are hopes that this is a temporary problem that will improve as the number of robust primary research studies increases. Systematic review methodologies are also developing to enable synthesis of a broader range of study findings, so that they can address a wider range of policy and practice questions (Mays, Pope & Popay 2005). For example, realist approaches to review activity hold out the hope of producing syntheses of research which directly address the key concerns of those in policy roles: not just whether a study found an intervention to have a certain effect, but also why and how this might vary between settings (Pawson et al 2005). Interviews with policy-makers suggest that they would benefit from research reviews that provided further information relevant for their decision-making, for example the context and factors that affect a review's local applicability and information about benefits, harms/risks and the costs of interventions (Lavis et al 2005).

Finally, in addition to capacity building, research commissioning and systematic review activity, supply-side approaches to improving research use have focused on research communication activities, particularly the ways in which research findings are presented and translated for policy audiences. Much of the activity here has concentrated on identifying the ways in which researchers can improve how they communicate (disseminate) their findings in policy contexts and good practice guidelines abound (see Box 1.2). Yet despite the strong focus on supply-side initiatives for improving the research–policy relationship, an issue that has not really been tackled is that of incentives for researchers to carry out such dissemination activities. As the Commission on the Social Sciences (2003) noted, researchers must be given inducements to engage in the 'sometimes fraught and time-consuming business of communication'. In fact, in most academic systems there are few incentives for academics to spend time on wider dissemination and communication activities (Davies, Nutley & Walter 2007).

Box 1.2 Improving dissemination: key recommendations

For research commissioners:
- Time research to deliver solutions at the right time to answer specific questions facing practitioners and policy-makers.
- Ensure relevance to current policy agenda.
- Allocate dedicated dissemination and development resources within resource funding.
- Include a clear dissemination strategy at the outset.
- Involve professional researchers in the commissioning process.
- Involve service users in the research process.
- Commission research reviews to synthesise and evaluate research.

For researchers:
- Provide accessible summaries of research.
- Keep the research report brief and concise.
- Publish in journals or publications that are user-friendly.
- Use language and styles of presentation that engage interest.
- Target material to the needs of the audience.
- Extract the policy and practice implications of research.
- Tailor dissemination events to the target audience and evaluate them.
- Use a combination of dissemination methods.
- Use the media.
- Be proactive and contact relevant policy and delivery agencies.
- Understand the external factors that are likely to affect the uptake of research.

Source: Adapted from JRF 2000. Reproduced from Nutley, Walter & Davies (2007, p 239), with permission.

Overall, supply-side initiatives seek to enhance the relevance, availability, credibility and user-friendliness of research that is produced for policy consumption. Such initiatives may thereby increase the chances that such research gets seen, and even acted upon, by policy-makers, but there is as yet little robust evaluation work to confirm this.

However, supply-side approaches tend to assume a one-way flow of research into the policy community, and a relatively passive role for policy-makers in the research use process. The rational, linear, 'producer-push' model that underpins these kinds of approach has been subject to sustained critique because it rarely reflects the way in which research actually gets used in policy contexts (Huberman 1994; Cousins & Simon 1996). Supply-side initiatives are, however, rarely implemented in isolation. They are often coupled with a range of complementary activities aimed at the demand side of the equation, and it is to these issues that we now turn.

Demand-side initiatives

The call for more evidence-based policy processes in the late 1990s has focused attention on the demand for evidence as well as its supply. In doing so, the emphasis has been on reforming policy processes in order to inculcate more evidence-informed deliberations. In the United Kingdom, government reports have outlined a number of initiatives and recommendations for increasing the demand for evidence, including: requiring evidence-based spending bids; making a commitment to publish the rationale and evidence for policy decisions; training policy staff in evidence use; and expecting greater use to be made of pilot projects.

Whether such initiatives have had the desired effect is debatable. Although a UK government review, *Better Policy Making* (Bullock, Mountford & Stanley 2001), provides 130 examples of good practice from a diverse range of departments, initiatives and policy areas, these are not necessarily representative or evaluated. Such examples begin to show what might be possible, but cannot really be seen as firm evidence of any sustained ramping-up of evidence use in policy-making.

The aim of the policy reforms and associated initiatives has been to change the culture of policy-making, including policy-makers' attitudes to and understanding of evidence. By and large this has meant introducing greater instrumental rationality into the policy process. While government documents note that policy-making does not consist of a neat set of stages, which are negotiated solely on the basis of rational argument, they nevertheless recommend a somewhat rational–linear model as something to aspire to (Reid 2003).

A good example of where this appears to have materialised is in the introduction of arrangements to institutionalise and systematise health technology assessment (HTA). The broad aim of HTA is to provide policy-makers and clinicians with reliable and robust evidence on the clinical and cost effectiveness of particular drugs, medical appliances or therapies (Sackett et al 1996). In the United Kingdom, the National Institute for Health and Clinical Excellence (NICE) was established by the government in 1999 to decide whether selected health technologies should be made available throughout the National Health Service in England and Wales. Since its establishment, NICE has assessed a wide range of health technologies and its decisions about many of these have received widespread attention – for example the media interest in the debate surrounding the availability of Herceptin (a treatment drug for use in early stage breast cancer). Given the political sensitivity of many such decisions it would hardly be surprising if the decisions of NICE were shaped more by lobbying than by evidence and rational argument. However, a study of decision-making in NICE found that while the appraisal process was not immune to lobbying, arguments based on quantitatively oriented, experimentally derived data held sway (Milewa & Barry 2005). These data also took precedence over more subjective, experientially based perspectives. It is important to bear in mind, however, that this may in part reflect the fact that clinical rather than social evidence is to the fore in such decision-making processes. In other contexts – such as social care or education – where the nature of evidence is more contested, and there is less agreement about basing decisions primarily on empirical data, more 'rational' modes of argument may be harder to sustain.

In sum then, there has been a significant level of activity devoted to improving evidence use in policy settings by addressing both evidence supply and policy-based demand. Such initiatives have focused on coupling dissemination activities on the supply side with more facilitative and incentive-based approaches to enhance the demand for evidence. We have noted that the impact of the supply-side activities does seem to have been somewhat limited to date, but demand-side initiatives may have gone some way to engendering a more evidence-aware culture in policy-making.

Between supply and demand

The language of supply and demand is suggestive of a market for evidence. If there were a well-functioning market in this area there would be little need to talk about initiatives to improve the linkages between supply and demand, as they would come together in a marketplace where the discipline of competition would ensure a balanced interaction between supply and demand. However, the research–policy 'market' exhibits many imperfections and seems prone to market failure. Indeed, the analogy of a market may not be the best way of reflecting the diversity of means by which research flows into (and out of) the policy world. It is not surprising then that some research uptake initiatives in policy settings have sought to improve the linkages between research and policy using network-based rather than market-based approaches. This is partly fuelled by an alternative framing of the research use 'problem': that it does not relate primarily to supply or demand issues, but to the lack of connection between the two. In response, two forms of activity seem to be prevalent:

activities to integrate researchers within the policy process; and initiatives to establish intermediary organisations and institutions to act as brokers between research supply and policy demand.

Many of the initiatives aimed at improving the connection between research and policy have focused on the location of researchers and their involvement in the policy process – be they internal (government) researchers or external researchers based in universities and other research organisations. Taking internal researchers first, in the United Kingdom there has been a good deal of discussion in recent years about the capacity and location of government researchers and their integration into the policy process. In general, these researchers are viewed as key enablers of improved research use, through their role in commissioning and managing research and evaluation projects and ensuring that the findings from these are summarised for and communicated to policy staff within government. In effect, government researchers are seen as internal brokers or, as one report phrased it, 'system-aware brokercrats' (Clark & Kelly 2005). In recognition of this wider role, the number of researchers employed by the UK government has more than doubled since 1997, and new research units have been established in departments that had no previous history of research (Government Social Research 2002).

Significant emphasis has been placed on ensuring that government researchers are involved in the policy process from the earliest phases of problem identification right through to policy implementation and evaluation. One way of achieving this is to co-locate these researchers alongside their policy colleagues, but there is as yet only limited evidence about the effectiveness of such initiatives (Nutley, Bland & Walter 2002). Informal discussions with insiders do, however, suggest that government researchers are now more likely to be consulted earlier in the policy process than hitherto, especially when there is a clear decision to review and develop policy in a specific area. However, practice varies across departments and policy areas (Bullock, Mountford & Stanley 2001) and it is not clear that early involvement necessarily leads to sustained interaction.

Turning to external researchers, there has been a range of initiatives targeted on the involvement of these researchers in the policy process. In general terms this has involved secondments of academic researchers into government to work in policy advisory roles. Researchers have also become involved in the policy process through their ad hoc participation in advisory and consultation groups, and in certain areas in the United Kingdom, through their membership of Policy Action Teams. In terms of specific research projects, the way in which research is commissioned from external researchers has in some circumstances changed from a client–contractor relationship to one where external researchers and their policy clients work more as partners, with interaction encouraged throughout the research project. Evaluations of the effectiveness of these approaches for involving external researchers are thin on the ground, but there is some evidence from both policy and practice settings about the benefits of developing sustained interaction between researchers and policy-makers (Walter, Nutley & Davies 2003).

The second major approach to bridging research supply and demand involves initiatives to establish intermediary organisations and individuals to act as brokers between research and policy communities. In policy settings, knowledge brokers – whether individuals or agencies – are an important route through which research reaches those who might use it. We have already mentioned the role played by internal government researchers as knowledge brokers. In addition there is a wide range of other broker agencies, including specific government agencies, charitable foundations, think tanks and professional organisations.

The linkage activities of these intermediaries amount to a potentially more iterative and dynamic research use process than the more conventional linear–rational models of this process. They begin to acknowledge the complexity of the research–policy relationship, particularly its multi-streamed nature, and focus on interactions between policy-makers and researchers as key to getting research used. As such, the linkage activities recognise that research evidence may not arrive as uncomplicated 'facts' to be weighed up in making policy decisions, but may be translated and reconstructed through ongoing dialogue with research producers.

Such relationships may in turn better support a more conceptual and perhaps even contentious role for research in the policy process than conventional supply and demand initiatives. The extent to which the influence of research can indeed move beyond a consensus-based role will however likely depend on the degree of independence researchers can secure and maintain in relation to the policy process (an issue addressed earlier).

With this broader role for research in mind, we now consider initiatives that potentially challenge as well as support the status quo, and are aimed at stimulating research use in wider public debates about policy, encompassing a broader range of actors than just researchers and policy-makers.

Improving evidence use by drawing on broader models of policy influence

Research evidence may influence policy indirectly as well as directly, through many non-official routes – such as policy, issue or advocacy networks – that effectively limit the potential for government control of evidence, its interpretation and its use. Such routes may offer opportunities for research to influence policy in more challenging ways: ways that go beyond a limited consensus-based and instrumental role for research.

Beyond the institutions of government there is a wide array of formal and informal relationships (policy networks across many organisational actors) shaping policy agendas and decision-making. Around many major issues, organisations and networks have emerged that have long-term interests and knowledge in shaping policy (see, for example, Jung & Nutley 2008). Some of these are charitable agencies with a strong research function and a clear advocacy remit; others are led by academics and researchers.

Think tanks and charities can have significant influence, although they vary widely in their roles, staffing and funding, and in their relationships with both research and policy. Think tanks and charities may draw on existing research to develop policy analyses, or they may carry out their own in-house research or commission others to do so. They tend to be more flexible and innovative than other research commissioners, often seeking to bring research producers and research users together as part of the process. They are also very likely to make significant use of service users, clients or carers to ensure that these perspectives are reflected in campaigning activities, alongside those of professionals and other 'experts'. Typically charities and think tanks use a wide range of routes for influence, including publications, conferences, policy briefings and other forms of dissemination, public meetings and lobbying (Commission on the Social Sciences 2003). Thus one of the main ways by which research evidence becomes known and discussed within policy networks is through the process of advocacy by think tanks, charities and other interest groups (Sabatier & Jenkins-Smith 1993). These interest groups are important purveyors of data and analysis: 'it is not done in the interests of knowledge, but as a side effect of advocacy' (Weiss 1987, p 278). Although research evidence used in this way can tend to be used for tactical advantage rather than for illumination, 'when research is available to all participants in the policy process, research as political ammunition can be a worthy model of utilisation' (Weiss 1979, p 429).

Agencies involved in research advocacy (such as think tanks, charities, research intermediaries and campaigning organisations) may devote considerable resources to exploiting and developing the evidence base, and they can be seen to deploy a number of strategies to increase the impact that their evidence-informed advocacy may have on policy. Informal analysis suggests at least three key areas of activity in getting the evidence heard. First, such agencies rarely take the policy context as a given, but instead seek actively to reshape that context. Publicity campaigns with persuasive, professionally-produced material, often utilising the mainstream media, can begin to shape public opinion and change the climate within which policies are being made. More direct contact with ministers and policy-makers is sought through specialist advisors and lobbying. In comparison to academic researchers, such activities are often pursued with great vigour, stamina and creativity by 'policy entrepreneurs'. Such activists also often demonstrate considerable savvy about the political process, fine-tuning their activities to exploit windows of opportunity brought about by political cycles or propitious circumstance.

Second, independent evidence advocates often build alliances or networks with others of similar view, seeking synergies that are sometimes wide but relatively shallow (for example, marshalling the broadest array of support to campaign on a single common issue) and sometimes relatively narrow but deeper, more strategic and sustained. Third, some of these agencies have the resources to develop demonstration projects showing 'evidence in action'. Such working projects provide concrete exemplars that can be used to help persuade those engaged in the wider policy process. Demonstration projects can help allay fears about 'implementation failure' and can provide valuable knowledge about implementation processes that work. These strategies together hint at the possible development of more substantial 'knowledge-purveying infrastructure' that goes far deeper and broader than individual researcher-led advocacy.

Focusing on agencies engaged in research advocacy, and their embedding in policy networks and policy communities, highlights the potential for a different vision of how the policy process might be improved to encourage greater research use. This shifts away from ideas of 'modernising' policy processes, with an emphasis on central control and rationality, to ideas of opening up or 'democratising' that process, so that a greater diversity of voices and views can be heard (Parsons 2002; Sanderson 2006). Indeed, political science has long been concerned to see how the institutions and mechanisms of government might be changed to facilitate more participative, deliberative and bottom-up approaches to policy analysis, and the growing interest in evidence advocacy is a part of that concern. Such reforms will likely involve shifts in power and authority as well as the design of new institutions; Bell (2004) suggests that this might happen more easily locally and regionally, rather than nationally. The promise of 'opening up' policy processes to greater network and community engagement has been described as 'ideally about inductive reasoning and learning. It is slower and more cumbersome than more centrist and deductive modes of knowledge for governance, but it does promise better knowledge and probably better legitimacy' (Bell 2004, p 28).

Many of the initiatives highlighted earlier, around establishing knowledge-brokering bodies, facilitating service-user consultations and making research summaries more readily available, may facilitate just such an opening up of evidence-informed policy debates. Initiatives such as the Policy Action Teams and policy advocacy networks have also served to widen the range of people involved in policy development. If policy processes *are* democratised, then policy discussions are likely to contain a greater variety of voices: researchers of various hues; practitioners from sundry work backgrounds; and clients/users in all their diversity. But this approach is not without its challenges and will involve acknowledging that the use of research in such pluralistic discussions is an inherently political process. Evidence from research is contested, not fixed, and, like the policy process itself, is deeply infused with values. Albaek (1995) has argued that policy-making and research (and, we would add, practice) involve values, choices and assumptions, and that such views and interests need to be engaged as part of the policy process, with interaction and learning among different stakeholders and fluid boundaries between scientific and political argumentation: 'research contributes to the public reflection which grows up during a decision-making process in which opposing interests scrutinize the pros and cons of options and objectives' (Albaek 1995, p 95).

It is important to note from this therefore that there may be significant tensions between instrumentalist evidence-based approaches to policy development and more inclusive and participative approaches (for example, see Quinn 2002). Not least of the challenges is that the scope of what counts as evidence may be greatly enlarged and the primacy of research as privileged evidence is likely to face significant dissent.

Broader models of policy-making open up more radical opportunities for research and other forms of evidence to have an influence, moving beyond expectations that it will simply support or refine current policy preoccupations to a hope that it will challenge those preoccupations or even stimulate paradigmatic shifts in thinking. In undertaking such a role it is to be expected that the sources and nature of evidence will be more inclusive and eclectic. This may pose problems for those who espouse a narrower, more restrictive definition of evidence as that based on rigorous – often academic – research. It will also pose significant new challenges as values, preferences, experience and tacit knowledge enter the dialogical mix, more often and more openly.

Possible futures for evidence-based policy

There are questions about whether enthusiasm for evidence-based policy is now beginning to fade. There is no doubt that 'what works' and 'evidence-based policy' have been useful rhetorical devices for governments wishing to signal an end to ideologically led decision-making, but over time this rhetorical power has diminished. Enthusiasm for evidence-based policy has also suffered as a result of disappointments in the early outcomes of several high profile evidence-based policy programs. For example, in April 1999, the UK government launched the Crime Reduction Programme (CRP), a three-year £400 million cross-government commitment to achieving a sustained reduction in crime. At the time it was described as 'the biggest single investment in an evidence-based approach to crime reduction which has ever taken place in any country' (Home Office 1999, p 3). A review of the implementation of the CRP (Homel et al 2004) documented many problems and a failure of the program to achieve a number of its overt goals. Several commentators have dubbed it an overall failure (Maguire 2004; Hope 2004; Tilley 2004) and the fact that it was not extended to run for ten years, as was originally intended, may be a signal of its failure in political terms.

Disillusionment also arises from the sometimes unrealistic expectations about what research and other forms of evidence can tell us. Despite a lot of valuable effort to improve research and evaluation methods, research rarely provides definitive answers, particularly in the field of health and social problems and the social programs designed to combat these. However, with large increases in funding for research come increased expectations about the contributions that such research should make to the success of policy interventions and day-to-day practice (Commission on the Social Sciences 2003). Some of these expectations are likely to prove unrealistic and to result in disappointment.

A more positive diagnosis is that evidence-based policy has entered the 'mature phase of its policy life cycle' (Ferlie 2005, p 193). It may have a lower political and rhetorical profile in the United Kingdom than in the late 1990s, but there has been an institutionalisation of evidence-based approaches through the establishment of organisations such as NICE – with guidance emanating from these organisations increasingly being seen as having some directive force. In addition, the revised registration requirements of many public service professions have also served to institutionalise the expectation that these professionals will operate in an evidence-informed way. Regulatory and oversight agencies too now place greater store on assessments against defined evidence-informed standards. Thus in both policy and practice arenas, evidence has achieved a prominence and an embedding that is unlikely to diminish greatly in the immediate future.

What does this imply for future initiatives to improve the use of evidence in policy-making? Activities in this area seemed set to continue for the foreseeable future, and it is likely that these activities will continue to be framed in terms of increasing supply and demand. This is not necessarily a bad thing, but there may be more that can be done to promote evidence uptake and impact. A consistent theme from those who have examined how research evidence actually gets used is that it is an interactive and social process of learning that is strongly influenced by the contexts of that use: situated interaction and intermediation seem to be key.

Interaction and intermediation – particularly the drawing in of a multiplicity of voices and agencies into policy deliberations – offer many more opportunities for research to become part of the policy discourse. However, the result is likely to be a far cry from a rational and linear process of instrumental research use. The degree of contestation and debate that inevitably arises is likely to encourage more challenging roles for research: roles that go beyond simply supporting developments within current policy and service paradigms, to questioning and challenging these paradigms. While clearly demanding in many ways, such open, pluralistic, interactive and informed policy communities have exciting possibilities and democratising potential.

This is a vision for vibrant and inclusive policy processes: processes involving active policy networks, covering a wide variety of agencies and intermediaries, and drawing on diverse sources of knowledge, only one of which is research evidence. It is a vision that is most challenging for those who would like to see a centrally managed set of strategies for developing evidence-informed policy, as it will involve a good deal of 'letting go' of policy debates and the evidence that shapes them.

From the government side, there will need to be a willingness to actively engage with a wider range of actors – for all the difficulties, tensions and delays that might ensue. Outside government, there is already a growing awareness of what might be achieved with evidence through being policy savvy, media aware and advocacy oriented. Some advocacy-oriented agencies in the United Kingdom (as diverse as the Joseph Rowntree Foundation, the World Wildlife Fund, The Health Foundation and Barnardos) are already showing the way with creative mixed strategies involving vigorous attempts to shape the policy context, the creation of active alliances around key issues, and the development of demonstration projects that signal what can be done on the ground.

A key message then is that orderly and controlled evidence supply and policy processes – though not without some value – are likely to be insufficient to promote a genuinely rich and inclusive policy dialogue where research infuses and informs all aspects of debate. Instead there is much more that governmental and non-governmental agencies can do to help to shape an environment in which productive evidence-informed interactions are more likely than unproductive evidence-oblivious clashes.

Concluding remarks

We have argued that evidence-based policy is sometimes defined narrowly as the use of particular forms of systematic review evidence to make more rational decisions about policy choices. However, our conclusion is that such a definition underplays and potentially undermines the broader role that can be played by a wide range of evidence in more open and interactive policy processes. Evidence-based policy initiatives based on this broader view are more likely to move research and other evidence beyond a simplistic rational and consensus-based role in the policy process, to one which also questions and challenges. This is not to deny that promoting a rational ideal for the evidence–policy interface can be of some value, but to suggest that a better balance needs to be struck between these kinds of initiatives and those that allow a more open and interactive process for using evidence in policy.

PART A
Frameworks for using evidence

2 Evaluation principles and practice

Ralph Hall

The field of evaluation has developed relatively recently, as governments and charitable organisations funding human services programs have sought evidence of the effectiveness of these programs.

In the latter part of the twentieth century governments spent increasing proportions of their budgets on programs in education, health, housing and welfare to address problems of poverty, unemployment and disadvantage. This resulted in an increased taxation burden on the community to pay for these programs, which in turn placed pressure on governments to account for this expenditure by providing evidence that these programs were working. Evaluation became an important component of government accountability for expenditure on these programs. In 1993, for example, the US government passed the *Government Performance Results Act* requiring federal government agencies to evaluate their performance. The demand for competent evaluators grew as a consequence. The profession of evaluation grew to fulfil this role and led to the formation of professional evaluation associations to foster the development of evaluation expertise. The American Evaluation Association was established in 1985 and has over 5000 members. Other evaluation bodies have been set up throughout the world: the Australasian Evaluation Society is the professional organisation for Australia and New Zealand.

This chapter outlines the main features of program evaluation design, along with the related topics of needs assessment and evaluability assessment.

Characterising the program

A human services program is an intervention designed to improve some aspect of quality of life for the participants. It can be a training program designed to improve job-seeking skills for the long-term unemployed, an exercise and dietary program for obese participants, or a shelter for the homeless. These human services programs differ in a number of ways that are relevant to evaluation. The following are some of these key features:

- *Stage of program development.* Programs may be new, developing or mature. This is an important feature of a program for evaluation purposes, since a new program is unlikely to have developed sufficient outcomes to warrant an outcome evaluation whereas a mature program should have developed outcomes.
- *Goals of the program.* Program goals are a key feature relevant to evaluation. Goals need to be clearly formulated and realistic. It may not be feasible to evaluate a program that does not have well-defined goals.
- *Conceptual structure of the program.* This refers to the plan of operation and underlying logic of the program. It is the theory underlying its operation.
- *Organisational structure of the program.* The organisational structure refers to the way in which the program is delivered: that is, whether it is delivered in one site or multiple sites; whether it is a national or regional program; and whether it has one component or many components.
- *Program outcomes.* Have the outcomes of the program been identified and are they measurable?

Identifying program outcomes

Calls for demonstrations of the effectiveness of social programs have led to the need to identify program outcomes. As a consequence, governments have required information on the overall effects of their policies. Have government interventions in social conditions improved quality of life? In this section we will look at the way in which *performance measures* have been developed and used in evaluating programs.

The term *performance measurement* refers to measures designed to assess the performance of organisations or programs. Such measures, when they are cast in a form that enables comparisons from one organisation or time period to another, are often referred to as *performance indicators*. When standards for assessing performance are obtained by establishing *best practice* among competitors, then the process is referred to as *benchmarking* (Hall 2001).

Martin and Kettner (1996) have developed a systems model for organisational performance that characterises efficiency, quality and effectiveness of performance, as shown in Figure 2.1.

Figure 2.1 A systems model for performance measures

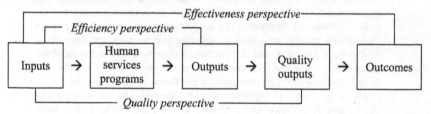

In this model:

- *inputs* are the resources that go into a human services program, such as staff, clients, buildings and equipment;
- *process* refers to the actual treatment or service delivery (that is, the human services program) during which inputs are translated into outputs;
- *outputs* are the immediate products of the program, such as clients completing training;
- *quality outputs* are those outputs that meet a specified quality standard; and
- *outcomes* are the results, impacts and accomplishments of the human services programs.

This model can be used to give more precise definitions of efficiency, productivity and effectiveness. *Efficiency* is defined as minimising the inputs for a given level of outputs, whereas *productivity* is defined is maximising outputs for a given level of inputs. *Effectiveness* refers to the impact of the program, that is, the extent to which the program achieves socially useful outcomes.

Human services programs are designed to address social problems or to fulfil social needs. Education and health services fall into the latter category, whereas drug rehabilitation and homelessness programs fall into the former.

Box 2.1 gives examples of performance measures for three different programs.

Box 2.1 Examples of performance measures

1. *Homelessness.* Martin and Kettner (1996) describe a program addressing the problem of homelessness. The program provides long-term shelter and a comprehensive program of services including basic education, job training, money and debt management, and drug abuse counselling. The assumption here is that homelessness results from chronic problems that require prolonged treatment. The output measures for such a program include the number of clients completing job training, the number of shelter days provided, and the number of clients completing drug abuse counselling. Outcome measures focus on the proportion of clients who have found long-term accommodation and are no longer homeless.

2. *Higher education teaching.* Graduates of universities in Australia are sent the Course Experience Questionnaire to complete. This questionnaire asks graduates to rate various aspects of their experience of the course they have completed, including assessment of teaching quality. The ratings are used by the Australian government as a measure of the quality of the educational experience provided.

3. *Equity in higher education.* Martin (1994) developed performance indicators for participation by disadvantaged groups in higher education in Australia. Since disadvantaged groups are spread unevenly across Australia, Martin devised an indicator that compared the proportion of each disadvantaged group enrolled in a university with the proportion of that group in the population of the state in which the university was located. The indicator was the ratio of the two proportions. The target indicator value was 1, since the ratio of the disadvantaged group in the population to the proportion of the disadvantaged group in the relevant population will be equal if the group is represented in the student body in the same proportion as it exists in the population. The indicator will be greater than 1 if the disadvantaged group is over-represented and less than 1 if it is under-represented. In a trial applying this performance indicator to six universities, Martin found indicator values of 0.95 to 1.98 for students from non-English speaking backgrounds.

Problems in implementing performance measures

Performance measures are designed to provide evidence about the success or otherwise of programs and policies. Their capacity to do this effectively has been questioned by Perrin (1998) who has listed a number of criticisms of performance measurement. McDavid and Hawthorn (2006) have likewise outlined a number of problems with performance measures. Some of these are:

- *Lack of fit between organisational capacity and performance measures.* McDavid and Hawthorn (2006) point out that outcome performance measures may well be beyond the capacity of the organisation to deliver, resulting in what appears to be poor performance. In such situations there is pressure to manipulate the performance measures to make the program appear to be operating more efficiently. McDavid and Hawthorn give an example of health providers placing patients on a 'consultative review' list, instead of a waiting list for surgery, to make the performance indicator look better than in actually was.
- *Ambiguity of terms and concepts.* Terms can be interpreted differently. Perrin (1998) reports a number of cases where there is very little consistency in the way terms are defined, making the resulting performance indicators meaningless (see, for example, Box 2.2).
- *Goal displacement.* Goal displacement occurs when organisations focus on indicators rather than on real outcomes. Perrin argues that goal displacement diverts attention away from, rather than towards, the real goals of the organisation. If, for example, performance of a psychiatric rehabilitation centre is judged by the extent to which clients are not readmitted to hospital, then strategies to minimise readmission are likely to predominate over other means of rehabilitating clients. This may not be in the long-term interest of client wellbeing, as recognition of symptoms and the need for readmission is one factor contributing to the rehabilitation of many seriously mentally ill clients.
- *Meaningless and irrelevant measures.* Perrin points out that much of the data collected from frontline workers can be unreliable, due to the workload of the worker and the nature of the data required. He reports that many frontline workers simply put down what looks to be a reasonable figure instead of reporting accurately.

Even where reporting is accurate, performance indicators may still be misleading. Any attempt to reduce complex phenomena to a few quantitative measures runs the risk of distorting the program effects. That is, complexity of organisational outcomes cannot always be measured.

Box 2.2 What counts as a disability?

> Canadian legislation governing federally regulated industries requires organisations to develop and implement plans to improve employment opportunities for disadvantaged groups. People with disabilities formed one of these groups. One bank showed substantial improvement in its performance indicator in this category. A legal centre representing people with disabilities became suspicious and investigated the claim. They found that the bank had included in its definition of people with disabilities people who wore glasses, thereby dramatically increasing the numbers in this category (Perrin 1998, p 371).

Strategies for improving performance measures

The criticisms made by Perrin (1998) have in turn been criticised by Bernstein (1999) and Winston (1999), who argue that they can be overcome by careful design. Perrin himself suggested a range of strategies for improving performance measures so as to overcome the problems identified above. The following is a list of some strategies for improving performance measures.

- *Develop performance measures carefully*. Bernstein (1999) argued that performance measures could be improved by recognising the variation in types of performance measures, by pre-testing them appropriately, and by exercising care in their definition.
- *Identify activities appropriate for measurement*. Not all activities of organisations can be captured by performance measures. Identification of those activities that can be measured will aid the use and interpretation of these measures.
- *Involve stakeholders*. Performance measures are likely to be more widely understood and accepted if a range of stakeholders, including staff, clients or consumers, are involved in their construction and review.
- *Use multiple indicators*. A range of indicators is more likely to provide valid performance measurement for complex organisational activities. These indicators can relate to all aspects of the organisation, rather than focusing on single outputs or outcomes.

Performance measures can be useful in program evaluation, provided care is taken in their construction to ensure they are measuring the appropriate variables. Evaluators need to avoid the trap of using such measures because they are easy to obtain rather than because they measure variables of interest.

Despite the difficulties in devising valid performance measures, governments and other organisations funding evaluations require feedback on whether a program is producing socially useful outcomes, so the pressure to identify and measure these outcomes is increasing.

Where adequate outcomes have not been defined, an evaluator needs to consider whether an evaluation is appropriate and what alternatives are available under such circumstances.

Assessing program need

Before a program is devised there must be some evidence of need. Human services programs are designed to meet the needs of groups of people within a community. Ascertaining need is clearly an important part of program planning. Without a proper understanding of the needs a program is designed to satisfy it is unlikely that the program will be effective.

Inadequate assessment of need is a common cause of program failure. Posavac and Carey (2007) have identified four ways in which failure to determine need results in programs being unsuccessful.

1. A program is based on assumed need rather than actual need.
2. A program takes inadequate account of the context for delivery.
3. A program designed to satisfy unmet needs is poorly implemented.
4. Potential participants in a program do not realise that they need the services (for example, see Box 2.3).

Care therefore needs to be taken in identifying needs to form the basis for program planning. McKillip (1998) has identified five types of needs, data on which are obtained from different sources.

1. *Normative need.* Established by obtaining expert opinions about what services ought to be provided.
2. *Felt need.* Expressed preference for services in the target group, usually obtained through surveys or community consultations.
3. *Expressed need.* Established by determining actual usage of services by a target group.
4. *Comparative need.* Established by collecting information on service use by groups similar to the target group.
5. *Maintenance need.* A need that is only uncovered when a service is withdrawn.

Box 2.3 Failure to recognise need

> Interventions aimed at addressing obesity in children by providing opportunities for participation in physical activities such as organised sport, physical education programs in schools and in after-school centres encounter the problem that neither the parents of obese children nor the children themselves recognise that there is a problem. Behaviour and dietary patterns leading to obesity have been established over a long time and are resistant to change.

Identifying these needs involves the use of different methods of data collection. For example, interviews with experts and service providers can provide information on normative need, while analysis of existing statistics and records can provide information on expressed need and comparative need.

The nature of program evaluation

Having decided that a program is needed and one has been devised and implemented, then at some stage an evaluation of it will be appropriate. We are now in a position to look at the main approaches to the evaluation of policy programs.

Program evaluation has been defined by Scriven (1993, p 9) as the determination of the merit or worth of a program. This definition has attracted some controversy as some evaluators believe that evaluation should contribute to the improvement of a program rather than make judgments about its worth (see Weiss 1998, p 4).

Scriven recognised these different purposes of evaluation by distinguishing between formative and summative evaluation. A *summative evaluation* is one that is designed to provide information on the impact of the program. This information may be used to decide whether the program has been effective, whether it should be continued, or, if it has been concluded, whether it has been successful.

A *formative evaluation* is one that is designed to provide information on how the program might be developed or improved. Formative evaluations are more likely to be conducted during the early stages of implementation of a program, when alternative approaches to delivering the program are being considered.

Process and outcome evaluations

While formative and summative evaluations focus on how the evaluation information is to be used, some approaches focus on what it is that is being evaluated. This has led to the distinction between process and outcome evaluations. A *process evaluation* focuses on how the program is being delivered, whether it is being delivered according to its charter, what kinds of services participants are being given, and what facilities are available to the program. An *outcome evaluation* focuses on the impacts or effects of the program. These effects or outcomes may be either short-term or long-term effects.

The distinctions between these types of evaluation are summarised in Table 2.1.

Table 2.1 Types of evaluation

Evaluation questions	Evaluation focus	
	Formative	Summative
Process	How is the program being delivered and can delivery be improved?	Is the program being delivered in accordance with its design?
Outcome	How can the program be improved to achieve better outcomes?	Is this program achieving outcomes to warrant its continuation?

This classification of evaluation types shows that evaluation is a complex process, requiring detailed knowledge of the program to be evaluated as well as the context in which the evaluation is to be conducted.

The main influence on the type of evaluation to be conducted is not so much the content of the program but how the program is being delivered and the purpose of the evaluation. Some examples of program evaluations illustrate these differences:

1. *Service integration for older people with complex health needs.* Bird, Kurowski and Dickman (2005) reported an evaluation of a 'patients first' model of service integration for older people with multiple chronic conditions and complex healthcare needs in Melbourne, Australia. This model combined services from a number of areas of expertise into a

single team to coordinate services for the participants. The evaluators used a combination of quantitative and qualitative methods to conduct the evaluation. The quantitative data included records from care facilitators and questionnaires completed by clients. Qualitative methods included focus groups with the care facilitators and the project management team. Challenges confronting the evaluation included a high non-response rate from the clients, typical of aged care participants, and an initial resistance to the evaluation by the program staff. An action research approach gained support from the staff and overcame the latter problem. The evaluators concluded that the program had a beneficial impact on the health and wellbeing of the participants and facilitated a coherent team approach by the project staff. Since this evaluation focused on improvements to the delivery of the services it can be seen as a formative–outcome evaluation.

2. *Peer-led sex education in England.* Oakley et al (2004) reported a process evaluation of a peer-led sex education program involving 27 coeducational comprehensive schools in England. Year 12 student volunteers were trained as peer educators to provide classroom sessions to year 9 students, focusing on relationships, sexually transmitted infections and contraception. The process evaluation focused on documenting how the program was delivered in practice, to compare the processes involved in peer-led sex education with teacher-led sex education, and to describe the experiences of the peer educators. It is an example of a summative–process evaluation.

3. *Evaluation of the Australian Supported Accommodation Assistance Program.* Wyatt, Carbines and Robb (2005) reported an evaluation of the fourth quadrennium of the Supported Accommodation Assistance Program (SAAP IV). The program is an Australia-wide initiative involving the federal government, state governments and more than 1200 non-government organisations in the delivery of services to the homeless. The evaluators adopted a 'utilisation-focused' approach (see later in this chapter) designed to maximise use of the evaluation findings. This approach involves consultation with key stakeholders with a capacity for implementing recommendations arising from the evaluation. Because of the size of the program and its diversity the evaluation took the form of a strategic review, focusing on outcomes and future directions. The complete evaluation report can be found at

<www.facs.gov.au>. The evaluation can be classified as a summative–outcome evaluation, since the program had been in existence for a number of years and had developed readily identified outcomes.

4. *Homeless Families Program.* The Homeless Families Program was developed in the United States in 1990 to address the problem of family homelessness. It was implemented in nine cities, with the goal of improving family residential stability and promoting self-sufficiency among homeless families. Each family was assigned a case manager who assisted the families in accessing services such as mental health and employment services. The program was evaluated by Rog (1994) and was chosen as an exemplary evaluation by the *American Journal of Evaluation* (Rog 1999; Fitzpatrick 1999). This evaluation fits into the category of a formative–outcome evaluation.

These four examples illustrate the wide variety of programs that evaluators can be called upon to evaluate. There are of course many other areas in which programs are delivered and evaluated.

Assessing program evaluability

Not all programs are in a condition where they can be meaningfully evaluated. This may be due to one or more of the following factors:

- the program does not have a clear set of goals;
- no adequate data are available on program performance;
- there are no clear guidelines on how the program should be delivered;
- there is disagreement among program stakeholders about the nature of the program; or
- there is no need for the program.

Wholey (1987) has developed a method to determine the extent to which programs can be evaluated. He called this evaluability assessment. Evaluability assessment requires an intensive analysis of the program by the evaluators, working in association and consultation with program stakeholders. This usually involves: reviewing program documents (policy statements, funding proposals, meeting minutes and so on); conducting site visits to view the program in operation; interviewing program clients, implementers and managers; and holding discussions with key stakeholders.

The evaluability assessment determines whether the program meets the following criteria:

- program goals and objectives are well defined and plausible;
- performance data on program outcomes are available and adequate; and
- intended users of the program agree on how the evaluation information will be used.

The program is ready for a formal evaluation if these criteria are satisfied.

Conducting evaluations

Once it has been established that there is a need for the program and that the program is evaluable, the evaluator must decide on the approach to be taken. The evaluator will need to consider what evaluation methodology to use, and how program goals, stakeholder consultation and program theory will be addressed.

Evaluation methodology

The evaluation methodology refers to the methods used by the evaluator to collect necessary information about the program. These methods draw on the wide range of available social research methods, particularly case studies, surveys and experiments. They are described in detail in social research methods texts (for example, Bickman & Rog 1998; Neuman 2003), as well as in evaluation texts (for example, McDavid & Hawthorn 2006; Rossi, Lipsey & Freeman 2004; Weiss 1998), so will not be outlined here.

In choosing the evaluation methodology to be used, the evaluator will be guided not only by the characteristics of the program and the purposes of the evaluation, but also by their own approach to evaluation.

Differences in approaches to evaluation have led to frequent debates about how evaluations should be conducted (Alkin 2003). The most widely debated issue concerning the appropriateness of methodological approaches is that of experimental versus non-experimental methods (see Donaldson & Christie 2005; Mohr 1999).

Advocates of the experimental approach argue that program outcomes can only be determined by a properly designed randomised controlled trial (RCT). In its simplest form, a randomised controlled trial entails allocating potential recipients of the program randomly into two groups: a treatment group to which the program is administered, and a control group receiving existing services. Outcome measures are then taken at an appropriate time after the program is delivered and the two groups are compared. The program is deemed to be effective if the outcomes for the treatment group are significantly better than those for the control group. The structure of this experiment is represented in Table 2.2.

Table 2.2 Simple randomised controlled trial

Group	Condition	Outcome measure
Treatment group	Program administered	O_T
Control group	No program administered	O_C

As Mohr (1999) points out, this approach is based on a counterfactual logic. That is, it compares the outcome with the intervention with the outcome if there is no intervention. It does not provide any information on how the program achieves the outcomes, if any. It treats the program as a 'black box', an intervention having unknown content.

Critics of this approach seize on this black box analogy to argue that an analysis of program content is an integral component in an evaluation. They argue that many program outcomes are either not measurable or are inappropriately measured in the simple terms required by the logic of the randomised controlled trial.

They further argue that randomised controlled trial methodology is flawed. Events impact on participants in unpredictable ways and these can affect program outcomes; it is not possible to control all variables that might influence the findings of the trial. These critics (see Mohr 1999) argue that qualitative methods using a case study methodology are more likely to take into account the complexities of program operation and provide better evidence on which to base an evaluation.

This and other debates over the appropriateness of research methods in evaluation mean there is no consensus over which methods to use. This situation is further complicated by differences among evaluators over the role of program goals, program stakeholders and program theory in the evaluation process. These will be discussed in the following sections.

Program goals

The existence of clearly defined program goals and objectives is not only an important criterion in the evaluability of a program, but also a sign that the program has been adequately conceptualised.

A program goal is defined by McDavid and Hawthorn (2006, p 440) as 'a broad statement of intended outcomes'. These broad statements are translated into more specific objectives.

There is some controversy over whether program goals should be the focus of an evaluation. That is, should an evaluation seek to determine whether program goals have been achieved?

Scriven (1993) has argued that focusing on program goals can bias the evaluation against unanticipated effects of the program. These effects, which he calls side effects, may be overlooked in an evaluation that just determines whether the program goals have been achieved. He advocates the use of *goal-free evaluation*. This approach takes no account of program goals but focuses on program effects or impacts.

It is not necessarily the case, however, that taking program goals into account means that side effects will be overlooked. An evaluator may make a point of looking for unintended consequences of a program as well as ascertaining whether goals have been achieved. The two activities are not mutually exclusive as Scriven seems to imply.

The role of stakeholders

Consultation with stakeholders is an important component in all forms of social research, but it takes on a greater role in evaluation research. Stakeholders, particularly those closely associated with a program, have a vested interest in the outcome of an evaluation, needs analysis or efficiency analysis, more so than in other forms of social research. Program delivery staff may think that their jobs are at stake if the program is deemed not to be effective or to be inefficient. Program participants may fear that discontinuation of the program will leave them with no alternative services; and the body funding the evaluation may well want to have a say in how the evaluation is conducted.

There is substantial disagreement among evaluators about the extent and nature of stakeholder involvement in an evaluation. This issue is probably the one that most divides evaluators. Scriven's goal-free evaluation approach involves minimal consultation with stakeholders, whereas Fetterman's *empowerment evaluation* approach seeks to empower stakeholders to conduct the evaluation themselves (Fetterman 2000).

Even among those evaluators who include stakeholders, there are differences in the nature and extent of this involvement. Cousins and Whitmore (1998) have identified two streams of participatory evaluation, which they call practical participatory evaluation (PPE) and transformative participatory evaluation (TPE). The former involves stakeholders with the main purpose of maximising use of evaluation findings, whereas the latter sees stakeholder involvement as a means to promoting democratic social change.

A brief description of some of these different approaches will be given here to illustrate the ways in which stakeholders are involved. More extensive descriptions can be found in Fitzpatrick, Sanders and Worthen (2004), Rossi, Lipsey and Freeman (2004), or in many of the other reference works on program evaluation.

- *Utilisation-focused evaluation.* Utilisation-focused evaluation has been developed by Patton (see Patton 1997). It is based on the premise that the purpose of an evaluation is its use. To facilitate use of evaluation findings, Patton advocates identifying what he calls 'intended users' and involving them in all stages of the evaluation. By involving these key stakeholders, Patton argues that the findings from the evaluation have a much greater chance of being implemented.
- *Empowerment evaluation.* Fetterman and his colleagues (Fetterman 2000; Fetterman, Kaftarian & Wandersman 1996) have developed an approach they call *empowerment evaluation,* which seeks to empower stakeholders to conduct their own evaluations. The external evaluator acts as a facilitator, whose role is to assist the stakeholders by providing professional advice in the evaluation process. Proponents of empowerment evaluation argue that participants gain expertise in ongoing evaluation of the program, are effective in using the results of the evaluation, and develop skills in advocacy and implementing program changes.
- *Inclusive evaluation.* Mertens (1999; 2003) has developed an approach to evaluation that involves including the least powerful and most marginalised stakeholders in the evaluation process so as to ensure that their interests and viewpoints are represented. The aim of an inclusive

evaluation is to facilitate social change so as to promote social equality. The evaluator is a change agent, actively involved in improving the situation of marginalised groups.

Theory-driven evaluation

Program theory is a general term used to describe the development of theories about the operation of human services programs. The program theory seeks to ascertain *how* the program produces the desired outcomes. Program theory is defined by Weiss (1998, p 57) as 'the mechanisms that *mediate* between the delivery (and receipt) of the program and the emergence of the outcomes of interest'.

The mediating mechanisms referred to by Weiss are assumed to operate in a causal way to bring about program outcomes. They are usually diagrammed as a flow chart or causal chain, as in Figure 2.2 (adapted from Rossi, Lipsey & Freeman 2004, p 143).

Figure 2.2 Program theory for a job-training program

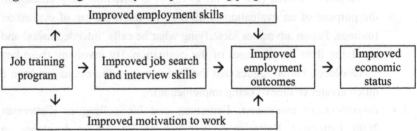

Program theories can form the basis for an evaluation of the program. This approach, referred to as *theory-driven evaluation*, represents one of many alternative approaches to the evaluation of programs. Theory-driven evaluation has been advocated by Chen (1990) and Donaldson (2003), among others.

The political context of evaluation

In evaluating a human services program, conducting a needs analysis or conducting an evaluability assessment, evaluative decisions are involved. This is what makes research on these topics different from other forms of applied research.

Although evaluative research shares research methods, data collection and analysis procedures with all forms of applied social research, the researcher does either make evaluative recommendations about need, efficiency or effectiveness, or provide information to stakeholders to make such evaluative decisions.

This means that there is a much greater political component in evaluative research than in most other applied research topics. If findings do not support the prejudices of influential stakeholders then the researcher runs the risk of having the research criticised or discredited.

Stakeholder involvement is one way of minimising the chances of this happening, although it does not remove the risk altogether. Researchers need to resist pressure from influential stakeholders to compromise research integrity in order to produce outcomes favourable to those stakeholders.

The use of findings is a major concern of most evaluative researchers. The focus of evaluative research is to determine whether an intervention is needed (needs analysis), whether a program is evaluable (evaluability assessment) or is achieving useful outcomes (program evaluation). So there is little point to conducting such research if the findings are ignored. Most evaluators therefore take steps to increase the likelihood that their findings will be acted upon. They do this by communicating their findings widely, enlisting the co-operation of key stakeholders and producing reports with clearly identifiable findings and recommendations where appropriate.

Conclusions

Evaluation methods and performance measures have been developed to assist governments, non-profit organizations and other agencies delivering human service programs in deciding whether these programs are achieving useful outcomes. This task has turned out to be more complex than early evaluators had imagined. Determining what a program has achieved is fraught with political, theoretical and methodological difficulties.

This chapter has sought to capture the extent of these difficulties by discussing key debates that have taken place over the nature of evaluation and outlining major theoretical approaches to conducting evaluations.

Although there are still many areas of disagreement among evaluators there is agreement that the field of evaluation is a specialised area of study requiring training and a professional focus.

To enhance the status of evaluation as a profession, associations have been established throughout the world. *The American Evaluation Association* is the largest and most influential of these associations, having around 5000 members drawn from all states in the USA and from over 60 other countries. Its mission is to improve evaluation practices, promote evaluation use and as a profession and to contribute to knowledge about effective human action.

This, along with similar organisations in other countries, has served to promote the development of evaluation as a profession and to provide a forum for evaluators to discuss and debate approaches and methodologies, thereby ensuring the continuing development and improvement of evaluation as a valuable tool in improving social conditions.

3 A practical guide to cost–benefit analysis

Leo Dobes

Versatile and comprehensive, cost–benefit analysis (CBA) can be applied to any number of policy issues.

Construction of a dam or a road are relatively straightforward candidates for cost–benefit analysis and are often used as examples in textbooks. But cost–benefit analysis has also been used to assess the net social benefits of an almost endless range of regulatory and policy issues. A small, illustrative selection could include: the benefits of health warnings on cigarette packets (Abelson 2003a), the social cost of compulsive gambling (Productivity Commission 1999), provision of government services in Rural Transaction Centres (Dobes 2007), the economic costs of regulating optometry services in the United States (Haas-Wilson 1986), climate change (Nordhaus 1991), and a switch to insensitive munitions in defence (White & Parker 1999).

Although the term cost–benefit analysis is increasingly used by financial analysts to refer to the (solely financial) implications of a project or activity, its more accurate meaning is in its use by governments. Government projects and policies often have no market equivalent, or are intended to rectify some form of market failure – ultimately the justification for the government's intervention in the area – so cost–benefit analysis is used to assess the value of a project or policy to society as a whole.

When economists refer to cost–benefit analysis, they mean *social* cost–benefit analysis: reflecting the fact that the analysis is not limited to the standpoint of a government budget, a firm's profits, or an individual's interests. This has important methodological implications. A social perspective will encompass more than purely financial considerations, and the often-conflicting interests of many individuals will need to be taken into account.

Cost–benefit analysis in practice

One of the major difficulties faced by those wishing to apply cost–benefit analysis is that the techniques involved presuppose a reasonable knowledge of micro-economic concepts, as well as practical estimation techniques. Often, a degree of ingenuity or lateral thinking is required as well. Unfortunately, there is no mechanistic, 'cookbook' approach that can be applied across the board.

One way of examining a policy issue is to undertake a purely qualitative analysis, listing the pros (benefits) and cons (costs). Advice to ministers by public servants often takes this approach. However, some quantification is usually preferable, if only because it better indicates the relative magnitude of each benefit and cost being considered. The disadvantage is that quantification usually requires significant amounts of data and time, so the cost of commissioning a major cost–benefit analysis can be prohibitive. Quantification can also result in rubbery figures that do not inspire confidence in policy-makers: cost–benefit analysis is by no means a perfect analytical tool.

In practice, an analytical checklist or sequence of steps can be used to facilitate a cost–benefit analysis, or to help assess the credibility of a study that is already completed:

1. Identify and specify objectives and policy alternatives.
2. Determine 'standing'.
3. Identify and catalogue the impacts of the project or policy, and those of its alternatives.
4. Predict impacts of policy alternatives over the project life cycle.
5. Estimate the economic value of the costs and benefits.

6. Estimate the net present value of the costs and benefits.
7. Allow for uncertainty.
8. Conduct sensitivity analysis.
9. Undertake distributional analysis to assist decision-makers.
10. Make a recommendation.

The remainder of this chapter explains each step in more detail, and illustrates the process of cost–benefit analysis using a hypothetical policy example: introducing a tax to reduce the number of four-wheel-drive vehicles on the roads.

More detail on cost–benefit analysis is available in readable texts such as Abelson (2003b), Boardman et al (2006), Department of Finance and Administration (2006), Gramlich (1981), Luskin & Dobes (1999), Mishan (1988), Musgrave & Musgrave (1976, chs 7–8) and Sugden & Williams (1978).

Prime minister versus petrol heads

Former Australian prime minister Paul Keating is famously supposed to have once deprecated the growing number of four-wheel-drive (4WD) vehicles, calling them a 'pox ... of significant proportions' and wishing that he could 'tax them off the roads'. An approach to undertaking a cost–benefit analysis of this proposition is outlined below.

1. Identify and specify objectives and policy alternatives

As with any analytical problem, an essential first step is to gain a comprehensive understanding of the issue or problem to be analysed. Why, for example, are 4WDs perceived to be undesirable? Is it purely an aesthetic issue, or do they create more tangible problems? If they are a problem just in urban areas, are they also a problem elsewhere? What is the evidence to support any specific views?

A clear understanding of the expected outcome of specific measures is also a key piece of information. Will reduced use of relatively heavy 4WDs reduce wear and tear on urban or rural roads? If the aim is to reduce noxious and greenhouse emissions, do 4WDs really have higher per-kilometre fuel usage than other vehicles or transport modes? If the objective is related to congestion and safety (because the greater height of 4WDs means other drivers cannot see past them and therefore need to leave larger gaps in traffic), will the effect be significant if their numbers are reduced? Will safety improve, given the apparently higher propensity of 4WDs to roll over, or because of fewer injuries caused to other vehicles in a crash situation?

An alert analyst will also identify any pragmatic constraints at an early stage of the analysis. For example, if 4WD usage is reduced suddenly, can public transport systems cope with the consequential increase in demand for alternative transport services? In other words, how realistic would it be to ban 4WDs outright, or to impose a prohibitive tax on them? Consulting a wide range of stakeholders is always a good idea in identifying relevant issues and constraints.

A good example of a pragmatic constraint involved the proposal to build an inland rail line between Melbourne and Brisbane. The proponents argued that a railway would expand agricultural development in cotton-growing and horticultural areas. However, following advice from agricultural specialists, the cost–benefit analyst took into account the fact that, in reality, additional production would be limited by the availability of water (Luskin & Dobes 1999, p 148).

Finally, a key feature of cost–benefit analysis is that it compares a proposed project or policy to alternative courses of action. Often, one alternative is the status quo: the future effects of 'doing nothing' define a base case against which alternative policies or projects are compared. Delaying the introduction of a policy or commencement of a project is an alternative that should also be considered.

In the case of the 4WD example, alternative measures include: to ban the use of such vehicles outright; to allow their use only on odd or even days of the month; to allow their use only in non-metropolitan areas as off-road vehicles; to impose specific taxes on 4WDs to reflect the additional costs of emissions or congestion that they create; to subsidise public transport to encourage 4WD users to switch away from their vehicles, and so on. For the purposes of this example, the proposed mechanism to reduce the use of 4WDs is increased annual registration fees – effectively a tax (price) instrument.

However, cost–benefit analysis itself uses resources and can be expensive to undertake. It is therefore desirable to strike a balance between analysing a large number of alternative policies or measures, and the cost of doing so. Boardman et al (2006, p 7) recommend considering only four to seven alternatives, because decision-makers and analysts find it cognitively difficult to handle comparisons between more options than this.

2. Determine 'standing'

Settling the issue of 'standing' – whose benefits and costs should be counted in a cost–benefit analysis – is an important, if occasionally controversial, consideration.

Most cost–benefit studies take a national perspective. This makes sense for a geographically isolated country such as Australia, because it has a relatively homogenous population that shares a common way of life. And given that 4WDs are used in both rural and urban areas, and for travel between the two areas, it is at least arguable that the interests of everyone in society should be taken into account. Even if the government were to decide to target only the use of 4WDs in capital cities, it would still be important to consider effects in non-metropolitan areas. A broader, socially inclusive approach also has the advantage of eliminating the need to make special allowance (and hence undertake calculations) for people who cross seemingly clear boundaries: for example commuters from Bendigo to Melbourne, or Wollongong to Sydney. A resident of Gulargambone who visits Sydney only once a year is a marginal case, but the analyst would need to exercise some judgment (possibly in consultation with the person who has commissioned the study) about the materiality of the case.

Non-nationals usually require even more judgment. For example, the construction of a potentially polluting nuclear power plant in Darwin raises the question of whether the costs and benefits accruing to residents of Indonesia should be included. It is at least arguable that they should not; but that any negative or retaliatory foreign policy outcomes, as well as the willingness of Australian residents to pay for avoidance of pollution of Indonesia, should be included. Similarly, the benefits of travel-time savings to foreign tourists of an upgraded road in Victoria would not normally be counted; but any additional income (minus additional costs) accruing to local businesses due to a directly attributable increase in tourism would be included.

A supra-national perspective may also be valid. A World Bank study into poverty reduction measures, for example, may include all the costs and benefits accruing to the global population. Climate change is also a supra-national issue. However, its analysis poses a methodological challenge because the costs of reducing greenhouse gas emissions are borne by individual countries, while all countries will reap the benefits.

At the sub-national level, on the other hand, a cost–benefit analysis may be conducted from the perspective of a state or local community. But caution is required, because project benefits that are directly attributable to a local population are generally much smaller than those potentially available at a national level. For example, the direct benefit to tourists from New South Wales visiting Melbourne would not normally be counted in a project to expand Melbourne's Arts Centre.

At the individual level, the cost–benefit analyst (possibly in consultation with the decision-maker) may need to resolve issues such as whether to include incarcerated criminals, or illegal immigrants, or the Australian-born children of illegal immigrants. Zerbe (1991) argues that such issues can be resolved on the basis of existing legal rights: for example, the pleasure gained by a thug who bashes someone should not be counted because assault is illegal. However, Boardman et al (2006, p 38) rightly point out the limitations to this narrowly legal approach, using examples such as the legal status of slaves in the antebellum United States, Jews in Nazi Germany, and non-whites under apartheid in South Africa.

A more fundamental dilemma is posed in regard to the treatment of projects and policies that extend beyond a single generation. The question of intergenerational equity has become interwoven with the vexed issue of the most appropriate discount rate (see section 7 below) to be used in cost–benefit analysis. However, it is also an issue from the perspective of 'standing', because it is often asserted that the current generation must, for reasons of ethics, take into account the interests of future generations. Only humans have standing, however; animals and the environment do not; an issue discussed in Box 3.1.

Box 3.1 Two legs good, four legs bad?

> Cost–benefit analysis generally adopts an anthropocentric approach. Animals do not have separate 'standing': their value to society is determined by the willingness of humans to pay. The same is true of the environment, and of institutions such as schools: they themselves do not have standing, only the humans affected by policies relating to the environment or institutions.
>
> It is not clear whether this approach is tenable in the longer term as social attitudes to so-called 'charismatic megafauna' change. For example, *The Economist* (17 June 2006, pp 13–14) reports discussion of possible changes to the law in Spain to recognise as a separate class the great apes (chimpanzees, gorillas and orangutans), which appear to share with humans the mental faculties of self-awareness and consciousness.

3. Identify and catalogue impacts of the project or policy, and its alternatives

Having determined the objectives of the study, identified any constraints, and specified the standing of those affected by the proposed policy or project, the next step is to determine all the costs and benefits involved. To do this, it is important to distinguish the following:

- real resources versus pecuniary effects;
- direct and indirect costs and benefits.

A popular view of economics is that the value of everything is counted in dollar terms. True; but only to the extent that the use of dollars provides a handy numeraire to express value in a common unit that allows aggregation. Value could just as easily be expressed in the numbers of seashells or kitchen tables that could be exchanged for the good or service being valued.

In fact, economists generally think in terms of *real resources* when assessing the potential impact of proposed policies or projects. A reduction in the use of 4WDs may, for example, reduce the amount of petrol and engine oil consumed (assuming that the average fuel consumption of the 4WD 'fleet' is greater than other forms of transport, including other types of passenger vehicles that would be used as substitutes by those who reduce their use of 4WD vehicles). If 1 million litres of petrol are saved each year, they can only be aggregated with the, say, 10,000 litres of engine oil saved per annum if both are expressed in a common monetary unit. Adding physical units would be conceptually as problematic as adding kilograms of apples and oranges.

The savings of 1 million litres of petrol and 10,000 litres of engine oil per annum represent benefits to the community because these resources are not used in operating 4WDs. That is, the engine oil and petrol can be used for other purposes (running more cars, or running buses) at no extra fuel cost to the community. Alternatively, the value they represent in dollars can be spent on an equal value of other goods and services, such as more schools or hospitals.

Care is required to distinguish benefits or costs composed of real resources from mere changes in prices (*pecuniary effects*). For example, if most 4WD users switch to trains for transport, the price of train tickets may well increase due to the additional demand for train trips. (For the purposes of this example, assume a private train operator whose trains run on electricity generated from nuclear energy). The increased price of train tickets is neither a loss nor a gain to the community: train users lose, but their loss is offset by the gain reaped by the train operator. Since both the train operator and the train user are part of Australian society as a whole, the gains and losses cancel out from a national perspective.

Although there is no precise or rigorous distinguishing rule, *direct costs and benefits* (often called primary) are those that are closely related to the objective of the project or policy. *Indirect costs and benefits* (often called secondary) have more of an incidental nature, like by-products.

For example, a reduction in use of 4WDs may increase the use of buses and trains. If the additional use of trains results in the coincidental discovery and development of improved computer software that permits the running of more trains per hour on each line, the increased efficiency of train operation would be considered to be a benefit in a secondary market.

Similarly, a project to improve irrigation may be intended primarily to increase production of grapes. Spin-off or secondary benefits of a dam to store the water may include better flood control, or recreational waterskiing. The development of teflon-coated frying pans is an oft-quoted example of a widely recognised indirect benefit of technology developed with the primary objective of landing a man on the moon.

Both direct (primary) and indirect (secondary) costs and benefits should in principle be included in an assessment of a policy or project. However, Boardman et al (2006, ch 4) consider that it is usually sufficient to include only effects that occur in primary markets. Caution is also required when dealing with secondary markets to avoid possible double counting. An example is presented in Box 3.2.

A useful means of checking that all relevant costs and benefits have been considered is to use the tabular format presented by Musgrave & Musgrave (1976, p 160), even if not all the effects can be quantified. Table 3.1, for example, lists some examples of costs and benefits that might be attributed to reducing the number of 4WD vehicles using roads. (In this case, as an example only, the reduction is assumed to be affected by substantially higher annual registration charges). Note that the list should not reflect the prejudices of the analyst – it should contain as many effects as can be identified by members of the relevant community. A number of the items in Table 3.1 were in fact gleaned from comments about 4WDs on Internet blogs.

Table 3.1 includes both tangible and intangible costs and benefits. However, there is no conceptual reason for distinguishing them in this way. Rather, the purpose is to separate them into those that can usually be estimated fairly

readily – like the tangible benefit of reduced petrol usage – and the more ethereal effects where creativity and special techniques are required to estimate values (like the loss to the community of reduced 4WD driving skills).

Box 3.2 The trap of double counting

Real benefits are the benefits derived by the final consumers of a project or policy. It is therefore important to count benefits only once.

Reduced use of 4WDs in congested urban areas may reduce the extent of congestion: all users of roads in such areas benefit from a saving in the real resource of time spent travelling. Similarly, if reduced use of 4WD vehicles results in fewer roll-over accidents the community as a whole will save on resources that might otherwise have been devoted to hospital care of the injured (doctors, nurses, bandages and so on).

If a large number of 4WD owners in a previously congested area of a city (such as Toorak or Sydney's North Shore) switch to train travel so that traffic congestion in that area falls, the benefit to all remaining road users can be measured in terms of saving in time. Because reduced congestion in that area of the city makes living there more attractive, the value of land and houses is likely to rise, with the result that owners of houses and land increase their wealth.

Caution is required, however, to avoid counting the same benefit twice. The benefit gained in our example is the saving in travel time. It is *because* of this benefit that house and land prices in the area rise. To count both the saving in travel time *and* the increased value of houses and land would therefore mean counting the same benefit twice. It is for this reason that only the saving in the cost of travel time would be counted as a benefit in this example.

As a separate point, it would also be wrong to include as a benefit any increase in value of land and houses in the area of (now) lower congestion because the increase in prices will be due to increased demand from people wanting to move there. The areas from which these people would move are likely to see falls in house prices (or flat rentals and hence prices) as demand falls there. The rises and falls in house and land prices in the those areas would tend to cancel out, so that the community as a whole would be neither better nor worse off in terms of wealth. There is no saving in real resources, merely a set of pecuniary effects.

These points may be confusing to those who are aware that economists do sometimes use changes in house values to estimate benefits. In fact, there is no problem with using house prices to estimate benefits. For example, a government may decide to improve access to jobs for residents of western Sydney by building a new railway line. Other things being equal, an increase in house and land prices will reflect the benefit gained by people already living in the area as well as those who now wish to move there. Having estimated the benefit in this way, it would now be incorrect to *also* count as a benefit any savings in travel time for those who previously used a car but now catch the train.

Table 3.1 Costs and benefits of reduced 4WD usage through increased annual registration fees

Category	Benefit	Cost
Real direct (primary)		
Tangible	• lower use of petrol and oil • travel time savings from reduced congestion • fewer injuries to 4WD occupants from roll-over accidents • fewer serious injuries to non-4WD victims of crashes involving a 4WD • reduced road repair costs, especially dirt roads in rural areas • reduced health effects from noxious emissions	• administrative resources used to formulate policy • additional administrative resources to collect higher fees each year • resource cost of increasing operational capacity of public transport
Intangible	• reduced emissions of greenhouse gases • possible reduced road rage among non-4WD drivers	• loss of pleasure of driving or owning a 4WD (additional deadweight loss by buyers and sellers due to higher registration fees) • increased insecurity of 4WD owners who switch to smaller vehicles
Real indirect (secondary)		
Tangible	• discovery and development of improved train control technology	• previous 4WD owners possibly subject to assaults late at night, like other train users
Intangible	• Australia admired for reducing greenhouse emissions	• reduced pool of trained 4WD drivers in community: society loses skills
Pecuniary effects and transfer payments		
	• increased house and land prices in areas where traffic congestion has decreased • increased or decreased annual registration fee collections for 4WD vehicles is a transfer payment if used for general budgetary purposes of government (that is, consolidated revenue item)	

In general, values of tangible goods can be determined from markets (or shadow pricing where markets are distorted), and intangibles tend to be goods and services associated with externalities (spill-over effects). In Table 3.1, an example of an intangible secondary benefit is the increased admiration internationally for Australia for decreasing greenhouse gas emissions by reducing use of 4WD vehicles.

4. Predict impacts of policy alternatives over the project life cycle

Benefits and costs usually accrue over time. It is therefore useful to sketch the project in the form of a timeline like the one in Figure 3.1 (arrows showing costs and benefits can be labeled with dollar amounts, where known).

Figure 3.1 Illustrative timeline of hypothetical costs and benefits over four periods of increased annual registration fees for 4WDs

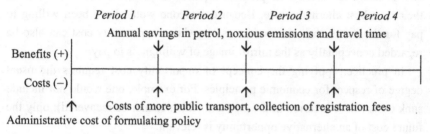

One advantage of a diagrammatic presentation is that it can confirm the analyst's understanding of the overall project, including when different costs and benefits may be realised. A timeline can also be used to check that the project will not face cash flow problems: if high financial costs are incurred at an early stage and are not matched by cash receipts, for example, planned government expenditures may need to be brought forward to cover any shortfall.

The costs and benefits shown in Figure 3.1 are illustrative only. They are a selection of the items identified in Table 3.1. Note that the timeline shown in Figure 3.1 presupposes certainty in the value and timing of costs and benefits. In situations where it is not clear what outcomes may occur, a dendrogram (tree diagram) can be drawn, as in Figure 3.4 below, which illustrates cost–benefit analysis in situations of uncertainty.

5. Estimate the economic value of the costs and benefits

Rather ironically, there may be a smidgen of truth in the hoary chestnut that economists 'know the cost of everything, but the value of nothing'. In many projects it is reasonably easy to determine the opportunity cost of resources used. However, benefits are often more difficult to evaluate, because they require knowledge of society's willingness to pay for specific goods and services.

Because resources (be they iron ore, people, buildings, clean air, roads, time, land, machines, and so on) are scarce, if society chooses to use a resource for a specific purpose, that resource will be unavailable for use in alternative activities. That is, there is an *opportunity cost* to society in using a resource, which is the lost opportunity of using the same resource for another purpose.

If society chooses to employ resources on a particular project, it will therefore need to forgo the benefit of an alternative project. The net opportunity cost of using resources to implement a policy or project is their net value in their next best alternative use. Because someone would have been willing to pay for the use of the same resources elsewhere, opportunity cost can also be regarded conceptually as the mirror image of willingness to pay.

In practice, applying the concept of opportunity cost requires the usual degree of respect for economic principles. For example, one would not include sunk costs (those incurred in the past and which cannot be recovered): only the future cost of an alternative opportunity is relevant.

Practical valuation of opportunity costs depends on the type of market. In a reasonably competitive market such as that for steel, for example, the market price and quantity used (total expenditure) will generally provide a good estimate of the opportunity cost of using steel in a project. But if the government purchases a large quantity of concrete to build a dam, the price of the concrete may rise as increasingly costly sources (for example, imports compared to local sources) are drawn on for the supply of concrete. The analyst consequently needs to decide which price to use: the one before the project began, or the higher price established in the market as a result of the government's purchases of concrete. One rule of thumb is to simply take the average of the higher and lower prices.

Determining the opportunity cost of labour is a problem where market distortions such as legally imposed minimum wages create unemployment. One approach is to assume the opportunity cost of unemployed labour to be zero. However, this ignores the opportunity cost of the leisure time that would be forgone by an unemployed person who accepts a job: time that may have been spent growing vegetables in the garden, minding children, or just relaxing; all of which have an economic value. Boardman et al (2006, ch 4) provide a very useful exposition of alternative approaches to valuing the opportunity cost of unemployed labour.

The main costs identified for the policy of reducing 4WD use by increasing annual registration fees are the administrative costs of formulating the policy and collecting higher fees, and the costs of increasing the capacity of the public transport system to carry those who stop using their 4WD vehicles.

The administrative costs of formulating and implementing the policy could include time spent by public servants drafting policy submissions, preparing a cost–benefit analysis, and in discussions with technical experts, lawyers and the minister. Administrative costs might also include time spent by members of the legislature in passing any requisite legislation, promulgation of the legislation, and necessary changes to computer programs in the collection agency to reflect higher fee levels. If 4WD owners are already charged an annual registration fee, the ongoing additional cost of an increased fee would probably be close to zero once computer software had been adjusted. Most of these costs could be estimated on the basis of relevant market prices, including the salaries of parliamentarians, public servants, information technology programmers, consultants preparing a cost–benefit analysis, and so on.

The additional annual cost of public transport services would include any major purchases of rolling stock in the first year, and any additional fuel, maintenance, staff (ticket sales, cleaning carriages, station security, and so on) required in each year to carry extra passengers. Irrespective of any accounting practices by the train operator, depreciation would not be included as a cost because that would involve double-counting resources used by the project once the capital cost of the rolling stock had been included in the first year. Nor would any additional insurance premiums paid by the train operator for carrying additional passengers be included: insurance payments are essentially a financial transfer, rather than representing a use of real resources by society.

When it comes to valuing benefits, the most fundamental concepts used in social cost–benefit analysis are *consumer surplus* and its counterpart, *producer surplus*. Consumer surplus measures the net benefit to an individual of a good or service, and producer surplus measures the net benefit to a producer of producing a good or service. The sum of producer and consumer surplus is termed *social surplus* because it is a measure of the net benefit to society as a whole. These concepts are explained in detail in most modern textbooks on microeconomics.

The concept of consumer surplus is illustrated in Figure 3.2 as the triangular area ABC. It is the difference, for all potential consumers of 4WDs in the community, between the amount that individuals are willing to pay (the demand curve) and the amount that they actually have to pay (the horizontal line AB, which represents the market price of $50,000 for each 4WD vehicle).

Figure 3.2 Willingness to pay, price, and consumer surplus

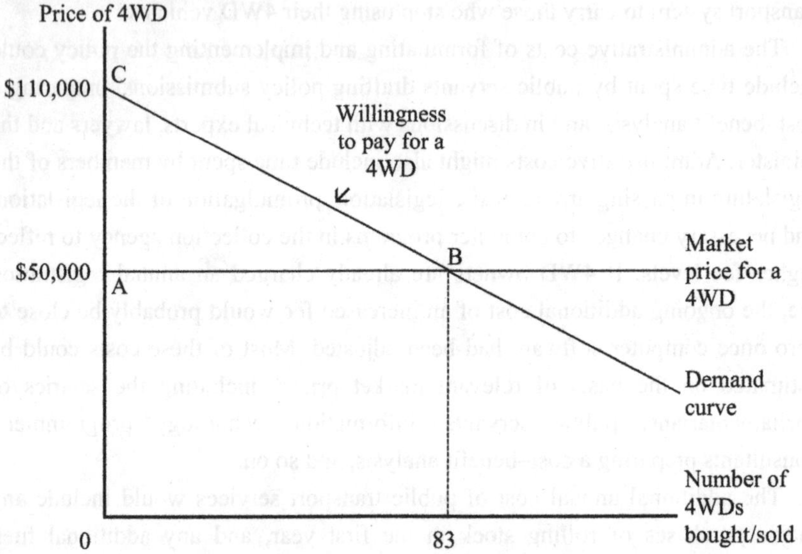

Price of 4WD

$110,000 C

Willingness
to pay for a
4WD

$50,000   B   Market
        A   price for a
                         4WD

                         Demand
                         curve

                         Number of
                         4WDs
0   83   bought/sold

The demand curve – drawn here as a straight line for convenience – reveals that at least one potential buyer in the community is willing to pay $110,000 for a 4WD because of the pleasure or utility that they would get from owning it. If someone in our fictional community had been willing to pay $250,000 for the 4WD, then the demand curve would have intersected the price axis much higher up, at $250,000.

Other potential consumers will not be willing to pay a price as high as $110,000. But they may be willing to pay a range of prices less than this: say $99,000 or $67,500. Some will be willing to pay only the market price of $50,000, and not a cent more. The downward slope of the demand curve illustrates this, because it orders potential buyers along the horizontal axis from the first buyer (who is willing to pay $110,000) to the eighty-third buyer (who is willing to pay $50,000).

In Figure 3.2, 83 people are willing to pay *at least* $50,000 for a 4WD. A salesperson looking at the demand curve would realise that he or she could sell 84 vehicles, but the person buying the eighty-fourth vehicle would only be willing to pay less than the $50,000 market price; as would the buyers of the eighty-fifth, eighty-sixth, and so on. Because our salesperson has a heavy mortgage and four hungry children we will assume that he or she will not sell below the market price, and only 83 vehicles will be sold.

The person who buys the eighty-third vehicle is willing to pay $50,000 for it, and that is what they are actually asked to pay. Their level of happiness or satisfaction at owning the vehicle is exactly offset by the $50,000 that they give up in exchange for a 4WD: that is, $50,000 in happiness or satisfaction from alternatives such as restaurant meals, holidays, donations to charity, and so on. This eighty-third buyer therefore gains no surplus happiness. Their consumer surplus is zero because their willingness to pay for the vehicle is exactly offset by what they must pay.

On the other hand, the person who is willing to pay $110,000 for their 4WD but only needs to give up $50,000 (the market price) in alternative enjoyments, is left with a consumer surplus of $110,000 – $50,000 = $60,000: shown as the distance AC in Figure 3.2. This $60,000 in consumer surplus is a psychic gain only. It can't be used to buy other goods or services, but is a measure of the complementary happiness or satisfaction to the consumer who obtains a 4WD.

Similarly, all the other 81 buyers of a 4WD between points C and B will also experience some amount of consumer surplus. The total consumer surplus gained in the community is the amount accrued by the 83 buyers, and can be readily calculated as the area of the triangle ABC:

$$\text{Consumer surplus} = (0.5 \text{ s } 83)(\$110,000 - \$50,000)$$

$$= \$2.49 \text{ million}$$

There are several important points to note:

- Although consumer surplus has been measured in dollar units, it represents the additional utility or happiness of people, not their expenditure on goods or services. This underscores the focus of cost–benefit analysis on the *value* that society places on goods or services, not on their price. Detractors often fail to appreciate this distinction between price and value.
- Economists seek to avoid ascribing arbitrary values to social benefits. In the case of the 4WDs in our example, the consumer surplus is estimated using observed behaviour or information based on past experience.
- Even if we did not know the exact shape (equation) of the demand curve in Figure 3.2, a rough estimate could be obtained by interviewing a random sample of the community and asking individuals about their maximum willingness to pay for a 4WD vehicle (yielding an estimate of

point C) and identifying individuals willing to pay $50,000 or more (point B). Alternatively, data already available about sales of 4WDs in other cities could be used if the analyst felt confident about their applicability to the community under study.

- In some cases – for example, in estimating the value to society of preserving the Namadgi National Park – it is not possible to observe the willingness to pay of individuals. In such cases, contingent valuation methods are often used (these are explained below). Despite suffering from the usual drawbacks of any survey, they offer some insight into the order of magnitude of the value that a community may place on an environmental or other non-marketed good.

- If the government were to impose higher registration fees on 4WD vehicles in order to discourage their use, it would effectively raise the cost to people wishing to buy them. As can be seen from Figure 3.2, if the price line AB were moved upwards to represent this higher cost to the buyer, the amount of consumer surplus would be reduced. (The extent of the loss to society would actually be measured by the smaller quantity of 'deadweight loss' experienced by only those consumers who no longer bought the vehicles: for detail see the texts recommended in the section above, 'Cost–benefit analysis in practice'.) In other words, while the community may gain some environmental advantages by reducing the number of 4WDs on the roads, part of the community (especially those who would have liked to own a 4WD but are not willing to pay the higher cost) loses consumer surplus or happiness due to the government's imposition of higher registration charges.

An analogous concept – producer surplus – applies to the sellers of the 4WD vehicles. Producer surplus – akin to a profit – is the difference between the price received for a vehicle and the opportunity cost of selling it (shown as the triangle ABD in Figure 3.3). Note that an increase in registration fees would not constitute a price increase for the seller (because the fee is appropriated by the government) so producer surplus would not increase due to the increase in fees. Indeed, producer surplus would fall as the number of 4WD vehicles sold was reduced (due to higher costs faced by buyers), with producers also suffering a 'deadweight' loss (see texts recommended above in the section on 'Cost–benefit analysis in practice' for an explanation of 'deadweight loss' to producers).

Figure 3.3 Opportunity cost, price, and producer surplus

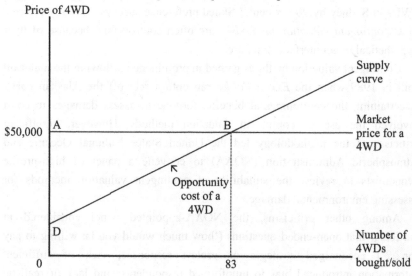

As can be seen from Table 3.1, the loss of consumer and producer surplus from the imposition of higher registration fees on 4WD vehicles is only one part of a large number of costs and benefits that need to be calculated. Much of the effort involved in cost–benefit analysis is due to the collection of the information required to carry out the calculations.

Estimating peoples' *willingness to pay* for project or policy outcomes is often problematic. Environmental effects in particular are often intangible and therefore difficult to value. The two major approaches used to estimate willingness to pay are *revealed preference* and *stated preference*.

As the name suggests, revealed preference methods rely on observed behaviour to infer willingness to pay. For example, the value of time saved travelling on less congested roads could be inferred from the value attached by car users to their work time (after-tax wage rates are often used) or to their leisure time, depending on which is lost when travelling. If the analyst wishes to estimate the additional value of houses in areas where congestion is reduced, so-called hedonic pricing methods can be used to compare the difference in value commanded by a house in a less congested neighbourhood and a similar one close to a busy road.

Where it is not possible to compare a specific effect to similar effects in a market elsewhere, the main recourse is to asking people directly what their willingness to pay would be. In its crudest form, such a question might be framed as 'how much would you be willing to pay to reduce the number of 4WDs in Sydney by 90 per cent?' Stated preference surveys – usually referred to as *contingent valuation methods* – are often controversial because of their hypothetical or counterfactual nature.

Contingent valuation methods gained in prominence following the major oil spill in 1989 when the *Exxon Valdez* ran onto a reef off the Alaskan coast. Ascertaining the environmental benefits forgone to assess damages in court involved the use of contingent valuation methods. However, significant criticism of the methodology led the United States National Oceanic and Atmospheric Administration (NOAA) to convene a panel of high-profile economists to review the suitability of contingent valuation methods for assessing environmental damage.

Among other criticisms, the NOAA-appointed panel considered in particular that open-ended questions ('how much would you be willing to pay for…?') encouraged strategic or protest responses; lack of sufficient information introduced bias to uninformed respondents; and lack of realistic budget constraints meant that respondents might state a willingness to pay that was beyond their means in real life. The panel accepted much of the criticism levelled at the manner in which contingent valuation surveys were conducted at that time, but was nevertheless 'unpersuaded' by more extreme arguments that the method provides no useful information (Arrow et al 1993, p 42). Boardman et al (2006, ch 14) provide a good review of some of the methodological innovations since the report of the NOAA panel.

Like all social survey techniques, contingent valuation methods suffer from various drawbacks. Some of these can be overcome through the use of protocols designed to reduce response bias, and others through more sophisticated methods such as discrete choice (conjoint analysis) models. Ultimately, judgment is required by the cost–benefit analyst regarding the validity of empirical results and the relative importance of any uncertainty in the overall results obtained. A particularly contentious area of valuation is the value that society places on a statistical life, often referred to imprecisely as 'the value of life' (see box 3.3).

Analysts occasionally seek to include taxation revenue as a benefit – for example, in taxing petrol, alcohol or tobacco to reduce consumption. In general, however, taxes are simply a *transfer payment* and should not be counted as a benefit or a cost in a cost–benefit analysis undertaken from a national perspective.

Box 3.3 The meaning of life

Economists do not presume to value life itself. What economists mean by 'the value of life' is the value placed by society on a statistical life. Value is estimated by the willingness to pay to avoid changes in risk: for example, the amount drivers are willing to pay for seatbelts in order to avoid a given risk of death in a crash. Other methods used to estimate the value of life or limb include jury awards for damages, insurance premiums, danger money paid in some occupations, and the sale of organs.

The value of statistical life is sometimes estimated using the 'human capital' approach. In essence, statistical life is valued on the basis of potential earnings over a remaining lifetime for various age groups. However, this approach is not consistent with the principle of measuring benefits on the basis of willingness to pay, and it produces biased results because it ignores the value of retirees, the long-term unemployed, and other non-wage-earners.

Because governments spend tax revenue on general community needs, the taxes paid by one section of the community (drivers, drinkers, smokers or wage-earners) are gained by other parts of society. Society as a whole neither gains nor loses, even though individuals may do so. However, a tax may also reduce the general size of the market for the good on which it is levied, resulting in a 'deadweight loss' that should arguably be included as a cost to society in a cost–benefit analysis.

Even where the costs and benefits of a particular policy or project are known with sufficient certainty, care is required in estimating their level, particularly where estimates are made over long periods. Sensitivity analysis (described in section 8 below) can assist in checking the effect of such estimates on the overall results of the analysis.

Boardman et al (2006, pp 18–22) discuss the importance of being aware of bureaucratic and political bias. Central agencies such as departments of finance (the 'guardians') tend to regard revenues accruing to government as good, and expenditure as bad: they generally oppose spending, and apply higher discount rates to estimate present values. 'Spenders', on the other hand, apply low discount rates and emphasise perceived benefits over costs. For example, underestimation of costs, and an apparent expectation by the Queensland Department of Main Roads that the Commonwealth would cover any cost overruns on the Ipswich and Logan motorways, led the then Federal Minister for Transport and Regional Services to announce that the Commonwealth would in future cap funding for each road project, as well as insist that state and territory governments contribute to road construction costs (Vaile 2007).

Bias in estimates of future costs and benefits is not limited to the protagonists in bureaucratic processes. Flyvbjerg, Skamris Holm and Buhl (2005) reviewed over 200 public works projects in 14 countries, finding that road traffic forecasts were not generally overestimated but were often very inaccurate, while forecasts of rail patronage tended to be seriously overstated. On the other hand, Harrington, Morgenstern and Nelson (2000) found that, in 14 cases out of a sample of 28, ex-ante estimates of the cost of compliance with environmental regulations were higher than actual values. An unanticipated use of new technology to reduce emissions in response to the regulations was seen as a contributory factor in the underestimations.

6. Estimate the net present value of the costs and benefits

Costs and benefits attributable to a project or policy typically occur at different points in time. For this reason, *discounting* is a critical issue in cost–benefit analysis. Detailed examples of the practical arithmetic of discounting can be found in texts such as Brealey and Myers (1991). The focus of this section is on the conceptual issues involved.

The first of these issues is the concept of individual time preference and the return on investment. People generally prefer to put off paying bills as long as possible, but to obtain goods and services (benefits) as early as possible: hire-purchase arrangements are an example. Benefits received (and costs met) in the future are perceived to be worth less than the same benefits received (and costs paid) today.

Economists recognise this phenomenon as *time preference*: the preference of consumers for earlier rather than later enjoyment. People with a low rate of time preference are more patient: they are happier to postpone consumption of benefits to the future through saving. Conversely, a high rate of time preference is associated with greater consumption earlier rather than later.

Time preference can also manifest itself from the producer's perspective as the return expected from an investment. A gardener may forego the consumption of a sack of potatoes today and plant them, producing two sacks at the end of the season. Given the gardener's expectation of two sacks for one, his or her time preference in this activity is 100 per cent: a doubling in value of the one-sack investment over the growing season.

On a practical level, discounting is the obverse to compound interest, which measures how much a present-day investment will be worth in the future. Discounting measures how much future benefits or costs are worth today. For example, if the rate of interest (termed a 'discount rate' when used in reverse to compound interest) is 10 per cent, a project that is expected to yield a one-off gain in a year's time of $220,000 would be worth only $200,000 today ($220,000/1.1). If the discount rate were 5 per cent, the same sum would be worth $209,524 today ($220,000/1.05).

Arithmetically, costs and benefits are divided by a number larger than one, so that the absolute value of the cost or benefit is reduced in size. In effect, discounting applies 'time-weights' to policy impacts that occur in different years. Because the discounting factor increases exponentially as one goes further into the future (just like compound interest), the effect of future policy impacts is assigned a correspondingly diminishing amount of importance.

An example of calculating the present value (*PV*) of a benefit of $100 received at the end of each year over a five-year period, at a 10 per cent per annum discount factor, is as follows (note: all benefits are discounted back to the beginning of year 1):

$$PV = \frac{\$100}{(1.1)^1} + \frac{\$100}{(1.1)^2} + \frac{\$100}{(1.1)^3} + \frac{\$100}{(1.1)^4} + \frac{\$100}{(1.1)^5}$$

$$= \$100(0.91) + \$100(0.83) + \$100(0.75) + \$100(0.68) + \$100(0.62)$$

$$= \$379$$

The sum of the discounted benefits is referred to as the *present value* of the series of annual benefits. A similar exercise can be conducted for any associated costs. The difference between the present values of the costs and the present values of the benefits yields the *net present value*.

Alternative approaches to evaluating the costs and benefits of projects and policies over time include the 'payback period', calculation of an 'internal rate of return', and benefit–cost ratios. Each of these is problematic, so economists, and probably an increasing number of investment evaluators, favour the use of net present values.

Because future costs and benefits are valued less than equivalent costs and benefits that occur closer to the present, a valid comparison of all the costs and benefits over the life of a project or policy requires that they be valued from a common perspective: that is, as if they were realised at the same point in time. *Discount rates* effectively act as relative prices, which permit conceptually valid comparisons of future and present goods and services.

Most studies discount all costs and benefits back to the year zero (by convention, the beginning of the project or policy). However, it would be just as valid to compound them all forward to the end of the project, or even to choose some point in between.

A common misconception is that discounting is carried out to allow for inflation. Cost–benefit studies can use either inflation-adjusted or non-adjusted figures; in either case discounting is still required to ensure comparability because of the phenomenon of time preference. Provided that the analysis is consistent in using either inflation-adjusted ('real') or non-adjusted ('nominal') values, the answer in net present value terms is identical. We need to be consistent when valuing costs and benefits; but even with real values we need to adjust for inflation.

As the discount rate increases, fewer projects are likely to be found feasible, especially where costs are incurred early in the project but benefits accrue only much later. It is not surprising, then, that the choice of discount rate is one of the most contentious areas of cost–benefit analysis (see Zhuang et al 2007 for a discussion of the debate). Its importance is seen above, where the differential effect of 5 and 10 per cent discount rates results in different present values.

Proponents of spending programs like health or roads, or those who attach more importance to longer-term environmental benefits or intergenerational issues, tend to favour low, so-called *social rates of return*. The guardians of the public purse, and those who attach greater importance to economic efficiency in decision-making, often tend to favour higher rates: particularly rates that are set in the markets, because they are readily observable, and guard against 'crowding out' private investment projects.

There are good arguments in favour of both the market-based approach and the 'social rate' model, so this important issue is unlikely to be resolved soon. Unfortunately, this only helps to reinforce the tendency by government agencies to resort to their various 'preferred' rates, often without even knowing why a particular rate was chosen in the first place.

Australian road projects, for example, have traditionally been evaluated using a 7 per cent discount rate, while 4 per cent has been used for rail projects, but the reasons are lost in the mists of time. The Commonwealth Department of Finance has recommended for almost two decades that government agencies use rates from 8 per cent upwards. The UK Treasury (2003, annex 6), on the other hand, recommends a social rate of time preference of 3.5 per cent, with progressively declining rates for periods beyond 30 years.

A pragmatic compromise is the BTRE (2005, p 46) approach of using the long-term government bond rate following adjustment of all costs and benefits for risk (see section 7 below). But even this approach suffers from the problem of long-term bond rates varying over time: Australian rates were in the region of 4 per cent in the 1930s, rising steadily to between 10 and 14 per cent in the 1980s and falling to longer-term levels of 5 per cent or so this century.

7. Allow for uncertainty

Cost–benefit analysis normally requires some estimate of future levels of costs and benefits. However, estimates entail varying degrees of uncertainty, so some adjustment may be required to ensure comparability, just as discounting was used to adjust the values of benefits and costs realised in different time periods. Such adjustments recognise the fact that 'a safe dollar is worth more than a risky one', or more colloquially, 'a bird in the hand is worth two in the bush'.

In the past it has sometimes been the practice to take into account the (usually unspecified) risk of a project by increasing the discount rate. This practice – sometimes referred to as a 'fudge factor' – is now generally considered inappropriate, except possibly under very restrictive conditions. Quiggin (2005) explores some of the implications.

In our example of increased registration fees for 4WD vehicles, the government might expect that a 60 per cent increase in annual fees will reduce the number of kilometres travelled – and hence petrol consumed – by 4WDs by, say, 90 per cent. On this basis, the analyst would include a 90 per cent saving in petrol for each year of the project.

However, a more sophisticated approach would be to allow for the inherent uncertainty in any estimate of the extent by which petrol usage will fall. Drawing on expert opinion or on relevant information in previous studies, the analyst may conclude that there is an 80 per cent chance that consumption will fall by 90 per cent, and a 20 per cent chance that it will fall by only 70 per cent. The expected value (EV) of the reduction in consumption is then estimated as an average of the two possibilities:

$$EV = 0.9(0.8) + 0.7(0.2)$$

$$= 0.86$$

Figure 3.4 uses a decision tree to illustrate the example of courtship and marriage.

Figure 3.4 Decision-tree analysis: marriage example

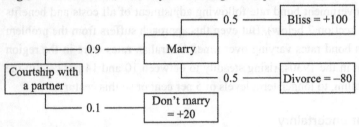

Notes: (1) Risk-free discount rate to be applied to NPV. (2) Deferred option of longer courtship not considered. (3) Artificial units, not dollars.

The (hypothetical) values attached to each of the possibilities (+100 for marital bliss, –80 for divorce and +20 for non-marriage) are adjusted by their probability of occurrence and aggregated to produce an *expected value (EV)*.

$$EV \text{ of courtship} = 0.9(EV \text{ of marry}) + 0.1(EV \text{ of don't marry})$$
$$= 0.9(0.5(100) + 0.5(-80)) + 0.1(20)$$
$$= 11$$

Had the data been discounted to take into account different time periods, the result would have yielded an expected net present value.

8. Conduct sensitivity analysis

Sensitivity analysis is a bit like a sanity check. Estimates of costs and benefits are likely to be influenced significantly by some of the assumptions made or by values used for variables. It is therefore sensible to try out different values or to vary assumptions made, in order to see how sensitive the results are to changes in key assumptions or variables.

For example, if we expect a large drop in petrol usage due to increased registration fees for 4WDs, and if that component of the analysis has a large bearing on the final result, then suitable qualifications and warnings to decision-makers would be desirable. A study will be more informative to decision-makers if it reveals the extent to which the results are influenced by particular assumptions made or data used.

Common practice is to use a range of discount rates to test the sensitivity of the result to discounting. However, other factors should also be considered, particularly the degree of optimism or pessimism that may have influenced projections of costs and benefits. Varying the timing of a project – for example, by deferring it by a few years – may also provide insights into optimal timing of an investment.

9. Undertake distributional analysis to assist decision-makers

There is no reason why the results of a cost–benefit analysis should not be presented in a way that shows how various stakeholders are likely to be affected by a government project or policy. Indeed, information on who gains and who loses, and by how much, would undoubtedly be of interest to decision-makers.

Alexander (1978) presented the results of a study of five development options for the Blue Mountains in the form of a planning balance sheet, which identified all producer and consumer stakeholders. More recently, Krutilla (2005) has developed a similar tableau format that shows the distributional consequences for stakeholders of various project alternatives.

10. Make a recommendation

The primary objective of cost–benefit analysis is to determine whether the overall wellbeing (termed 'welfare' by economists) of society is likely to increase or decrease as a result of implementing a specific policy.

As long as a project or policy has a positive net benefit (social benefits greater than social costs), society as a whole can expect to benefit from its implementation. For this reason, the decision rule that is applied in cost–benefit analysis – when all policies and projects are independent of each other (there are no synergies or other interactions) – is simply that all policies and projects with positive net present values should be adopted.

Implementing only those projects and policies that contribute more to society's welfare than they cost results in the best (that is, the most efficient, welfare-maximising) allocation of society's scarce resources, such as people, buildings, machines, land, water, clean air, roads, iron ore, and so on. Economists refer to such outcomes as promoting *allocative efficiency*.

In analysing the effect of a policy or project on society as a whole, allocative efficiency is therefore assessed against the so-called *Pareto principle*. An allocation of goods is Pareto efficient if there is no alternative allocation that can make at least one person better off without making anyone else worse off.

In practice it would be administratively impossible, or extremely costly, to arrange for those gaining from a project to compensate the losers. For this reason, cost–benefit analysis relies on a weaker form of the Pareto principle – known as the Kaldor–Hicks criterion – which maintains the decision rule of adopting all projects and policies that yield net positive benefits, because the losers can be *potentially* compensated by the rest of society.

In the real world, not all policies or projects are subjected to cost–benefit analysis. Those that are may be approved even when the net social benefit is negative, or they may be rejected even if net benefits are positive. Elected politicians, as the ultimate decision-makers, take into account a broader set of criteria than economic efficiency. Income distribution, electoral considerations, employment levels, or the provision of so-called 'merit goods' such as education, for example, may be pertinent at the political level.

A benefit to decision-makers of having available a rigorous cost–benefit study is that they are able to weigh up the potential loss of net social benefits against broader social or political considerations on the basis of knowledge rather than mere speculation. Indeed, in the author's experience, ministers have at times expressed frustration at public servants who do not provide them with sufficient analytical information, or simply seek to second-guess the minister's presumed favoured political outcome.

The thorny issue of equity in cost–benefit analysis

No analytical tool – including multi-criteria analysis (see chapter 4) – is capable of providing an objectively determined outcome that is 'equitable'. Subjective value judgments are inevitably required if one section of society (such as the poor) is to be favoured over others in the name of equity.

One means of incorporating subjective values into cost–benefit analysis is to attach 'distributional' weights to benefits and costs. For example, benefits that accrue to lower-income groups can be doubled or tripled (or multiplied by some other factor) in order to make the project more viable. This approach is far from perfect, but the following safeguards can improve its credibility:

- distributional weights should be determined by elected representatives rather than by bureaucrats or analysts;
- weights should be determined before the cost–benefit analysis begins, to ensure that weights are not used to 'correct' the analysis in some desired direction if initial results appear undesirable;

- two versions of the cost–benefit analysis should be produced – one with weights, and one without – to make transparent the magnitude of the effect of attaching distributional weights;
- alternative policies should be explored (for example, it may be more efficient to use income tax to redistribute wealth directly, leaving government projects such as building dams to proceed on their own merits); and
- the two versions of the cost–benefit analysis should be published to allow for critique of methodology and public discussion.

Nevertheless, it needs to be constantly kept in mind that decisions based on distributional weights are unlikely to produce allocatively efficient outcomes. If inefficiency retards general economic growth, it is possible that the objective of assisting the poor, for instance, will be self-defeating. In other words, the future costs, as well as the benefits, of an 'equitable' approach need to be taken into account.

4 Multi-criteria analysis
Wendy Proctor

Decision-making can involve issues that are extremely complex and there may be many critical trade-offs involved. More than one decision-maker often makes these complex decisions, and different decision-makers may have different views on what is important and what is not. In the case of decisions involving public goods and public policy, the decision-making process may also require participation and acceptance by stakeholders. Given these complexities and requirements, decision-aiding techniques have been developed in recent years to assist in imposing structure and transparency on the decision-making process.

Multi-criteria analysis (MCA) is a means of simplifying complex decision-making tasks that may involve many stakeholders, a diversity of possible outcomes and many and sometimes intangible criteria by which to assess the outcomes. In many public decision problems, such as those involved with environmental policy, the objectives of the decision may conflict with each other, and the criteria used to assess the effectiveness of different policy options may vary in importance. Multi-criteria analysis is an effective technique for identifying trade-offs in the decision-making process, *with the ultimate goal of achieving the most favoured outcome for the stakeholders involved.* Its origins lie in the fields of mathematics and operations research, and it has had a great deal of practical use by public planners in areas such as the siting of health facilities, motorways and nuclear reactors (Massam 1988). In recent years it has gained popularity as a tool for making decisions involving complex environmental, economic and social issues (for example, Resource Assessment Commission 1992; Fernandez 1996: Joubert et al 1997).

This chapter outlines multi-criteria analysis as a decision-aiding process and gives an overview on how this technique can be used effectively in difficult decision problems. Some disadvantages of multi-criteria analysis are also outlined, and a variation of the process known as deliberative multi-criteria evaluation, which overcomes these disadvantages, is described.

Definitions

Multi-criteria analysis (MCA) refers to the class of decision-aiding techniques that:

- help in identifying key issues or problems;
- decide between a finite number of options to address these issues;
- use a set of criteria to judge the options;
- assign weights to each objective/criterion; and
- use a method by which the options are ranked, based on how well they satisfy each of the criteria.

The terminology used in many multi-criteria analysis studies differs: practitioners should therefore define the terms they use to avoid confusion. For example, the term *option* is used here and is synonymous with terms such as 'alternative', 'scenario', 'plan', 'policy', 'action' and 'candidate' used in other studies. 'Options' are those decision outcomes or policy alternatives among which a decision has to be made. Ultimately, the chosen option will be the one that best satisfies most of the objectives or an overall objective.

Similarly, the term *criteria* is used here but is often synonymous with the terms 'goals' and 'attributes' found in other studies (Yoon & Hwang 1995). Criteria are those aspects of each option by which we assess how each option contributes to the desired objective.

Multi-criteria analysis is one specific type of decision-aiding process among a broader group of processes called multi-criteria decision-making (MCDM) methods. All multi-criteria decision-making methods are techniques to aid the decision-maker(s) choose between options or alternatives, which often have multiple or conflicting objectives and criteria for evaluation.

The whole group of multi-criteria decision-making methods is divided into two sub-groups. The first group, including multi-criteria analysis (the focus of this chapter) refers to techniques that facilitate a decision between discrete *pre-defined* options. The second group, classed as multi-objective decision-making (MODM) methods, refers to techniques that *design* the options using continuous data and mathematical optimising or linear programming methods (see Resource Assessment Commission 1992; Kazana 1999; and Yoon & Hwang 1995, for more detailed discussion of the range of multi-criteria decision-making methods).

All multi-criteria decision-making methods attempt to find a solution that is as close as possible to ideal or optimal by choosing among conflicting objectives. In multi-criteria analysis problems, this solution is *subjective* on the part of the decision-maker (depending largely on the weight assigned to each criterion or sub-criterion by each stakeholder). In decision theory terms this solution is known as a non-dominated solution. In economics it is referred to as a Pareto-optimal solution, as follows:

> A feasible solution in MCDM is non-dominated if there exists no other feasible solution that will yield an improvement in one objective/attribute without causing a degradation in at least one other objective/attribute (Hwang & Yoon 1981, p 23).

Under the multi-criteria analysis group of techniques a further distinction can be made based on the nature of the criteria. Both qualitative, ordinally measured criteria and quantitative, cardinally measured criteria can be used.

The historical development of multi-criteria analysis

Multi-criteria analysis has been developed and refined within many different disciplines. Its origins as a structured decision-making aid began in the late 1950s in the area of operations research. Hwang and Yoon (1981, p 5) cite Churchman, Ackoff and Arnoff (1957) as being the first to use a formal multi-criteria analysis. During the late 1960s, multiple criteria methods became popular and emerged as a distinct class of decision-making techniques, especially in France with the origin of the concordance methods (Nijkamp, Rietveld & Voogd 1990). In 1968, MacCrimmon provided the first survey of multi-criteria analysis techniques (Hwang & Yoon 1981, p 5). The development of linear programming methods after World War II also led to a movement away from the optimisation of single argument objective functions to that of multiple argument objective functions (Nijkamp, Rietveld & Voogd 1990). Since this time, many different disciplines have refined and applied multi-criteria analysis to many different decision-making problems including operations research, decision theory, management science, regional planning, economics, policy analysis, psychology and marketing research. During the 1970s there was a huge growth in the number of works in both the theory and application of multiple criteria methods (Rietveld 1980; Nijkamp, Rietveld & Voogd 1990). The first international conference on the whole set of multi-criteria decision-making processes was held in 1972, and by 1976, Zeleny was able to provide a large bibliography of almost 400 published works directly related to multi-criteria decision-making (Zeleny 1976). The rapid growth during the 1970s in techniques that addressed problems involving multiple goals and multiple decision-makers has been put down to several factors:

> In the 1970s this situation has changed for several reasons, particularly because of the increasing awareness of negative external effects of economic growth and the emergence of distributional issues in (regional) economic development. These developments led to a need for more appropriate analytical tools for analysing conflicts between policy objectives (Nijkamp, Rietveld & Voogd 1990).

In Australia, the use of multi-criteria analysis has been growing, with an early trial application to forest policy by the Resource Assessment Commission (1992) and some applications to water catchment issues (Llewellyn 1985; Assim, Bari & Hill 1997) and natural resource planning (Proctor 2001; Qureshi & Harrison 2001; Hajkowicz 2000; Gomez 2000; Robinson 1998).

Various developments have been made in multi-criteria analysis to take into account feedback between different decision-making criteria (in a method called the 'analytic network process', described by Saaty 1996), to incorporate the results into geographical information systems and also to take account of risk and uncertainty in the analysis (Lai & Hwang 1996; Munda, Nijkamp & Rietveld 1994).

Including the public in public policy decision-making

Public goods (as opposed to private goods) are defined as those goods that can be used or consumed by an individual without affecting the amount left for other individuals, and which no one can be excluded from consuming (this defines them as having the properties of being 'non-rival' and 'non-excludable'). A popular example is the air that we breathe. Public policy-making often involves making decisions about public goods (for example, environmental management decisions) and typically, good public policy-making will require public involvement in the decision-making process.

This leads into one of the most important aspects of public policy-making in a democratic society: the question of 'who decides?' In recent years, increasing attention has been given in the literature to incorporating public participation into public policy formulation, particularly in natural resource policy (Buchy, Ross & Proctor 2000; Buchy & Hoverman 2000; Race & Buchy 1998; Bass 1995; Slocum 1995; Cassels & Valentine 1988; Fagence 1977). The advantages of allowing public involvement in public policy-making have been well documented and such participation often strives for wider community understanding and therefore sanctioning of the policies concerned (Hoverman 1997). Decisions are more likely to command assent and therefore lead to the desired outcomes if they have been formulated with public support.

The need for some sort of participatory framework to policy formulation has therefore emerged out of a growing interest by individuals in public good issues, a grassroots desire by individuals to become involved in the policy-making process, and also recognition by governments that involving the general community early in the process can avoid disagreements and conflict in later stages.

Policy-makers may also have recognised that including the community in the policy process brings other advantages. Howlett and Ramesh, for example, have observed that 'one of the most important resources of interest groups is knowledge: specifically, information that may be unavailable or less available to others. The members of such a group often know the most about their area of concern' (1995, p 57). Bass goes further in analysing public participation in natural resource policies by concluding that 'successful strategies appear to be participatory but those with little participation have poor take-up' (1995, p 22). Although commenting mainly on the situation in developing countries, Bass summarises the benefits of public participation in policy development as:

- more involvement of community and private sector than in government-only processes;
- greater public debate and understanding of issues;
- increased benefits from more group dynamics;
- discovery of relevant local information;
- a broader basis of skills, ideas and inputs;
- a tendency for external inputs to be less dominant;
- a better consensus on trade-offs;
- more practical objectives;
- a policy/strategy result that does not surprise stakeholders;
- improved accountability and political credibility;
- stronger partnerships and commitment to implementation; and
- the possibility of long-run cost savings from greater resource mobilisation.

Multi-criteria analysis includes the public as stakeholders in the decision-making process, allowing ownership and ratification of the decisions so that the above benefits can be achieved.

Structuring the decision-making process

Multi-criteria analysis provides a means for expressing and exploring a logical process, often implicitly carried out by an individual when coming to a decision. In complex decision-making tasks, which sometimes involve many alternatives and many criteria for assessment, a structured process can be lost in the complexity of the issues. In general, a multi-criteria analysis seeks to:

- identify issues, concerns and the decision problem;
- identify alternatives or options to be considered in making a decision;
- identify a set of criteria and stakeholder preferences for the criteria; and
- provide a method by which the alternatives are to be ranked and preferences aggregated.

Finally, a sensitivity analysis is carried out to examine which parameter is critical in determining the ranking of the options. In many types of multi-criteria analysis, the ultimate outcome is a preferred option or set of options that is based upon a rigorous definition of priorities and preferences decided upon by the decision-maker. Multi-criteria analysis should be primarily regarded as an aid in the process of decision-making and not necessarily as a means of coming to a singular optimal solution. As such, the process is valued for the enlightenment and unravelling of issues that it can provide. The process adds to the knowledge of the decision-maker and is greatly aided by including the decision-maker in each step of the analysis. This is one reason why some forms of multi-criteria analysis are regarded as superior to other decision-aiding techniques (for example, mathematical programming methods and cost–benefit analysis) that more closely resemble 'black box' approaches. Such techniques are designed to provide an 'optimal' result at the end of the analysis, and so do not necessarily increase the understanding of important elements of the process, especially to those who are not familiar with such mathematical models.

Other techniques (such as cost–benefit analysis) are not designed to unravel the decision-making problem, or to provide a process that will enlighten the decision-maker and add to the decision-maker's knowledge of the problem. The non-transparency and singular solution nature of such techniques may only result in increased mistrust in the process by those who are not familiar with how a decision was finally made (Prato 1999).

Steps in multi-criteria analysis

A series of steps should be closely followed in order to conduct the multi-criteria analysis effectively. In the first step, the feasible options or potential outcomes are identified by the analyst to clarify the decision problem. The stakeholders/decision-makers are then chosen. Next, the decision-makers seek to identify the overall objective that is to be achieved in the process, agree on which of the suggested options are to be analysed, and then identify the criteria by which to judge the selected options. An important part of the process is then to apply weights to each of the criteria. These reflect the particular preferences of the decision-makers in how important each criterion is in relation to the overall objective. The analyst then chooses an appropriate form of multi-criteria analysis with which to analyse the data and aggregate the preferences. The next step is to assess each of the options. This is done by examining how each option performs under the different criteria and the weightings. The sensitivity of the ranking of options can then be estimated with respect to the chosen weights and method of aggregation. The whole process may be repeated with 'finetuning' by the decision-makers to aspects related to their inputs. This part also allows for any trade-offs to be identified in the overall decision process.

The following sections provide a detailed description of, and guidelines for, each of these major steps in turn.

Choosing the stakeholders

There are many different methods for choosing the stakeholders who will take part in the decision-making process. For example, stakeholders could be chosen by election from interest groups, or by inviting people to volunteer to participate (self-selection).

The most common, and probably simplest, method in stakeholder choice is that of *stratified sampling,* where quotas are stratified by social and demographic categories such as gender, age, social class and locality. A sample is chosen to represent these categories, in order to get a broad cross-section of the demographic make-up of the population that will be affected by the decision outcome.

Another common method employed to choose stakeholders is that of *stakeholder analysis.* Stakeholder analysis is a means of identifying the principle stakeholders in a process (which can be at various spatial levels, for example, local, regional and national) by investigating their roles, interests, relative power and capacity to participate in the process. The extent of co-operation or conflict in the relationship between stakeholders can also be identified and the findings of the analysis can then be interpreted and how these findings should be incorporated into project design can then be defined. Stakeholder analysis typically uses social surveys and institutional analysis to derive these answers.

In recent years there has been increasing debate about which method for choosing stakeholders should be used. In particular, opinions vary as to whether the method should select a wide range of stakeholders according to demographic characteristics, or a wide range of interests and arguments.

An alternative to stratified sampling and stakeholder analysis is known as *Q Methodology.* This method chooses stakeholders with a wide range of views on the key issues involved in the process, and ensures adequate representation of these issues in coming up with a decision (Brown 1980). Q Methodology aims to understand the subjective viewpoints of individuals; a small number of participants are subjected to attitudinal assessment to determine what they define as important. The process therefore uncovers issues that individuals themselves (and not the researchers) find important. The Q Methodology process starts with a task known as 'concourse definition', where the full breadth of social discussions and discourses surrounding the particular problem are collected from newspaper articles, radio broadcasts, political speeches, neighbourhood discussions and so on. A 'Q set' selection then occurs, with the narrowing down of statements into key issues for stakeholders to rank. This usually involves no more than 60 statements in total. A 'P sample' selection stage is then carried out, where the participants represent a wide variety of the viewpoints collected. 'Q sorting' then occurs, where participants rank the statements in the Q set based on how strongly they agree or disagree with them. A factor analysis of Q sorts then identifies clusters or groups of people with similar viewpoints, and a choice of participants with wide-ranging views can then be selected as the stakeholders (see <www.qmethod.org> for more explanation of the process).

How the public is practically and effectively involved is guided by a set of 'principles of good practice' developed by Buchy, Ross and Proctor (2000). They consider that 'the appropriateness of a particular strategy will depend more on the way techniques are implemented than on a specific choice of technique; regardless of what form of participation is followed, certain general principles of good practice have to be observed.

The first principle involves ensuring *commitment and clarity*. This can be achieved by all members of the process undertaking a *disclosure of interests*, having *agreed objectives and expectations* for the process, and ensuring *transparency* of the process. The second principle involves aspects of *time and group dynamics*. This involves paying attention to the design of the process and having particular concern for the time allowed, to ensure *continuity* of the process and *follow-up* of important issues. This emphasises the importance of the process to those involved, and allows the recommendations arising from public involvement to be carried out.

Another important principle involves *issues of representation*, including catering for cultural differences by being sensitive to the needs and customs of different cultural groups (for example, indigenous groups) and different organisations (for example, voluntary groups), and ensuring *representation and equity* for all stakeholders.

The final principle involves measures that will allow for *enhancing the skills and personal growth* of all those involved. This empowers the community through the *provision of information* and enhances their knowledge so that they will be in a better position to make decisions. Ensuring adequate resources and quality information are essential in this pursuit.

These principles, therefore, not only refer to the way stakeholders should be chosen but also to how the process should allow for appropriate representation and input from each of them. For example, the workshop process itself should be effectively facilitated so that each individual is allowed to have their say in the process and raise issues of importance to them.

Table 4.1 gives an example of stakeholder representatives for a forest management problem; the process seeks to identify an appropriate level of forest resources dedicated to logging and recreational activities.

Table 4.1 Stakeholders for a forest management problem

Stakeholder	Issues relating to tenure	Issues relating to management
Conservationists	Tenure allowing conservation	Ecologically sustainable forest management, biodiversity, water and heritage preservation
Forest industry representatives	Regulation determining access and use	Jobs, regulation, resource security, flexibility
Indigenous people	Recognition of custodianship, access and intellectual property rights	Co-management, cultural and economic resource preservation
Bushwalkers	Tenure that allows conservation	Facilities, conservation
Private landholders of forested land	Land ownership, regulation, for example, clearing	Appropriate fire, pest and weed management, industry demand for their products
Graziers	Consent to wilderness assessment	Appropriate fire, pest and weed management
Minerals representatives, apiarists and other product representatives	Access	Resource security
Tourist industry representatives	Access, regulation of various activities	Conservation, resource security, facilities and amenities
State Forests	Control over management, land ownership	Productivity and long-term resource security
National Parks and Wildlife Service	Control of management, land ownership	Funding, conservation, tourism
Federal government departments	Power of management	Management according to different values, funding
Local government	Cultural uses	Jobs, regional security and growth, community and cultural heritage, ability to adapt

Choosing the options and the objectives

The choice of options, and of the overall objective or objectives, are important and closely related steps in any decision-making process. Although the objectives and options are chosen by the decision-makers, input from other sources, such as expert advice, can occur. The options may even be based on output from computer simulation models. Often, the options and objectives that are to be decided upon are already given, for example, by the political process. The objective can be as broad as necessary, but overall agreement should be reached by the decision-makers.

Examples of possible objectives for the forest management problem are as follows:

- protect conservation values;
- ensure the long-term ecologically sustainable management of forests;
- develop an internationally competitive forest products industry; and
- effectively use other regional economic and social resources.

The options could reflect each of the preferred scenarios of the decision-makers or could be based on an amalgamation of plans of the decision-makers. Massam (1988, p 36) suggests a benchmarking approach as a framework for the options, which should include:

- the status quo;
- an ideal best plan;
- an hypothetical worst plan; and
- a plan of minimum satisfaction.

The options should be sufficient in number to represent a realistic selection for the decision-makers, but should not be so numerous as to make the analysis unwieldy or unnecessarily complex. Often, certain options can be rejected on the basis of budgetary or other constraints.

For the forest management problem, the options can include:

- current area available for logging;
- reduced areas available for logging;
- no logging in any area; and
- increased areas available for logging.

Selecting the criteria

The decision-makers select the criteria, but criteria can be suggested by the analyst so that the decision-makers are not starting from scratch. The criteria are designed to compare and assess each of the options and therefore must relate to the overall objective of the decision-making task. Initially, criteria can be very broad and then broken down into components or sub-criteria, and even lower-level sub-criteria. Ideally, the lowest level of the structure contains sub-criteria that are measurable (quantitatively or qualitatively), called *indicators*.

In general, the criteria should be *complete and exhaustive* in that they cover all possible aspects of the decision-making problem or process. The criteria should also contain *mutually exclusive* (non-redundant) items so as to prevent 'double-counting' and to better allow 'trade-offs' to take place. The criteria should be *clearly defined* and directly relevant to the defined problem. Because it is often necessary to break criteria down into sub-criteria in order to make meaningful measurements, they should be *decomposable* into smaller measurable units. For example, a criterion such as 'quality of life' may be measured as an index based on the sub-criteria of level of income, access to health care and level of education. This relates to the next attribute, which is that the criteria should be *minimal* so that no other smaller set of criteria can be measured. Finally, the number of criteria should ideally be *restricted* so that weighting the criteria does not become unmanageable.

Advice on the number of criteria or sub-criteria in any group varies, but most practitioners regard seven to 12 criteria as the maximum (Yoon & Hwang 1995, p 8; Resource Assessment Commission 1992, p 17). However, the analytic hierarchy process (Saaty 1982) manages large numbers of criteria. Under this technique, when the number of objectives or criteria becomes large, then a hierarchical structure of objectives and/or criteria is imposed. Nijkamp, Rietveld & Voogd (1990) regard one important advantage of this approach to be that it avoids a subconscious bias towards data-rich criteria and indicators.

For the forest management example, criteria selected can include:

- area of native habitat retained;
- quality of water;
- change in wage levels;
- change in tourism revenue;
- change in jobs; and
- access to bushwalking.

Weighting the criteria

In multi-criteria analysis, the preferences of the decision-maker are accounted for by the weighting or scoring placed on each of the criteria and sub-criteria. For example, all criteria may be weighted equally, or may be ranked from most to least important, or different weightings applied to the criteria. The weights may be qualitatively expressed, quantitatively expressed or a mixture of both. In analyses that involve many different decision-makers, weightings can be the most important and informative part of the whole process. It allows stakeholders to express differing views explicitly, and it helps identify those areas which are of most importance to them and which warrant careful investigation. The weightings make explicit those areas that may ultimately require possible trade-off solutions, and thus they provide points of focus for a complex decision problem.

Different multi-criteria techniques employ different methods for extracting weightings from the decision-makers. Weighting techniques can be divided into direct and indirect estimation methods. *Direct estimation* includes those methods that ask the decision-maker to explicitly weight the items, either as an ordinal ranking of priorities or as some cardinal measure of each criterion against the other. This is designed to give the exact worth of each item compared to another item. Examples of direct estimation methods include the rating method, the ranking method and paired comparisons. *Indirect estimation* techniques may include, for example, information on weights used in past studies, information on a ranking of similar options, and rankings that are elicited in an iterative and interactive way (see, for example, Nijkamp, Rietveld & Voogd 1990, p 49).

A simple weighting example is to ask each stakeholder to distribute 100 units across the various criteria, giving more units to criteria deemed to be more important than those with fewer units. This method means that the weightings are already 'normalised' (that is, that they all sum to 100). For those methods that derive weights by other means, such as rankings or pairwise comparisons, weightings will need to be normalised for them to be incorporated into the mathematical aggregation method. The 100-unit method also lends itself to other methods such as visual weightings, where 100 small objects (for example, haricot beans) are given to each stakeholder and they are asked to place their weights (reflected in the number of beans) onto a marked area representing and describing each of the criteria.

It is important that the particular weighting or prioritising method chosen should take into consideration the cultural and other aspects of the stakeholders. Some stakeholders may be more comfortable with mathematical weighting methods, while others may prefer a simpler ranking or visual weighting method.

Evaluating the options

The options are assessed in two stages: first, by how important each of the criteria and sub-criteria are to the decision-maker (the weightings), and second, by how well each option rates in terms of each of the criteria and sub-criteria of assessment.

The second stage is displayed by means of an impact matrix, where each of the components represents the impact of each option according to each of the criteria (Table 4.2).

Table 4.2 Example of an impact matrix for a forest management problem

Criteria	Options			
	1 No logging in any area	2 Reduced areas available for logging	3 Current area available for logging	4 Increased areas available for logging
Area of native habitat retained (%)	100	86	65	42
Quality of water (index)	95	77	68	60
Change in wage levels ($)	-234,000	-45,000	0	137,000
Change in tourism revenue ($m)	37	15	0	-10
Change in jobs (number)	-34	-6	0	7
Access to bushwalking (ha)	124,000	67,000	54,000	23,000

The final ranking of each of the options is then calculated by a mathematical operation using the impact matrix and the criteria/sub-criteria weights. The form of this mathematical operation (often referred to as the 'aggregation procedure'; Munda, Nijkamp & Rictveld 1994) often describes the particular type of multi-criteria analysis employed. Several studies report that there is a lack of information regarding the relative merit of using one approach against another, or regarding which particular circumstances would favour the use of a particular multi-criteria technique (see, for example, Resource Assessment Commission 1992, p 23; Millet 1997, p 41). In fact, evidence suggests that the large bulk of research on multi-criteria analysis and related techniques has been directed at theoretical issues, with less regard to issues concerned with the practical use of these techniques (Millet 1997).

The simplest aggregation method is the average weighted method, which sums the weighted impacts for each of the options. A simplified example is the impact matrix shown in Table 4.3. This table uses three criteria: the environmental criterion, measured by a water quality index; the social criterion, measured but the number of hectares available for recreation purposes; and the economic criterion, measured by the average income per year under each different option.

Table 4.3 Impact matrix for a lake management process

Criteria	Option *a* Business as usual	Option *b* Open access	Option *c* Restrict access
Environmental (water quality index)	30	10	60
Social (recreation access - ha.)	10,000	20,000	5,000
Economic (income levels - $/year)	30,000	20,000	12,000

The values in this impact matrix need to be converted to proportions to 'wash away' the effect of units of measurement. Unless this is done, criteria measured with units in thousands will have a disproportionate effect on the final result. Thus option *a* under the environmental criterion has a standardised value of:

$$30 \div (30 + 10 + 60) = 0.30$$

Similarly, option *a* will have a standardised value for the social and economic criteria respectively of:

$$10000 \div (10000 + 20000 + 5000) = 0.29$$

$$30000 \div (30000 + 20000 + 12000) = 0.48$$

We then need to apply weightings to these values that reflect the relative importance of the criteria. The weightings given to the different criteria are given in Table 4.4:

Table 4.4 Priority weighting by criteria

Criteria	Priority weighting
Environmental	0.65
Social	0.22
Economic	0.13

To obtain an overall ranking of the options under all of the criteria combined, a weighted sum of each option's performance under each of the criteria is calculated. Thus option a scores on the environmental, social and economic criteria respectively:

$$0.30 \times 0.65 = 0.1950$$

$$0.29 \times 0.22 = 0.0638$$

$$0.48 \times 0.13 = 0.0624$$

If we calculate these scores for each option and sum them we find that option c is the highest performing option (Table 4.5).

Table 4.5 Calculations for overall priority

Criteria	Option a Business as usual	Option b Open access	Option c Restrict access
Environmental	0.1950	0.0650	0.3900
Social	0.0638	0.1254	0.0308
Economic	0.0624	0.0416	0.0247
Overall priority	0.3212	0.2310	0.4455

Sensitivity analysis

Although not always undertaken in multi-criteria approaches, sensitivity analysis of the results is an extremely important part of the multi-criteria analysis process. For example, a sensitivity analysis of the results may be carried out in order to take into account the uncertainty in estimating some of the figures involved. Different decision-makers will likely have different weightings, each of which can be analysed. Similarly, the impacts of the various options under different criteria may fall within a statistically estimated range that can be incorporated into the analysis. Sensitivity analysis can also consider the effects of different techniques used in the weighting procedure.

It is of great importance that the sensitivity of outcomes can be tested for different values of the most crucial and contentious criteria and impacts. For example, in a group decision-making situation, if it were found that there was a great disparity in preferences for a certain criterion then it may be enlightening to find out how the overall results change with the changes in preference levels for this criterion. If the results are not greatly affected, then the criterion can take less importance in the overall process and the decision-makers can concentrate on other criteria and trade-offs. If the results are extremely sensitive to this criterion, then closer scrutiny should be given to it by confirming values and measurements.

Sensitivity analysis is given a dominant role in a technique incorporating multiple decision-makers and risk analysis, called multi-criteria mapping (Stirling & Mayer 1999). 'Mapping' refers to that part of the analysis where the results are expressed in terms of various, systematically applied sensitivities, with '... prescriptive conclusions being drawn only conditionally, by reference to the clearly defined perspectives taken by different participants' (Stirling & Mayer 1999, p 69). Another example of sensitivity analyses accounting for risk and uncertainty involved with the data uses Monte Carlo simulation to estimate probability distributions for the underlying data sets, so that the estimated means and variances of the data can be incorporated to assess outcomes (Van Delft & Nijkamp 1977).

Interacting and iterating

The analyst can achieve greater understanding of the decision-making problem by interacting with the decision-makers. This will allow further iterations in the analysis if necessary, and also identify where trade-offs can be made. In group decision-making situations, this step can be crucial if the ultimate aim of the analysis is to reach some compromise or agreement on the outcome. Often, interaction and further iterations can be facilitated by the use of computer software models that allow for faster manipulation of the data. For spatial data, the incorporation of geographical information systems into the multi-criteria analysis (Janssen & Rietveld 1990) is a very effective way of interacting with stakeholders. For example, for a decision concerning different areas of land being put to different purposes, it could be possible to link the outcomes of a multi-criteria analysis to a graphical interface depicting these different land-use options.

Advantages and disadvantages of multi-criteria analysis

Multi-criteria analysis has the great advantage of providing a framework or approach to complex decision-making problems. It allows the problem to be broken down into workable units and structured in such a way that enables some exploration of the complexities of the problem. This is done essentially through the process of identifying objectives, criteria and indicators. Applying multi-criteria analysis in a heuristic way enables the process to aid learning about complex issues. Multi-criteria analysis, however, is not good at addressing the issue of interactions between the analyst and decision-makers in eliciting and revising preferences as part of the iterative process. In particular, the multi-criteria analysis is typically a process to be carried out by a single decision-maker. When multiple decision-makers are involved (as is the case with natural resource management decisions), with different priorities and therefore different weightings for the decision criteria, the multi-criteria analysis process usually addresses this by taking some sort of average of these weights. A lot of valuable information in critical trade-offs and outliers may be lost by this simple averaging procedure. When the analysis concerns only one decision-maker, the mathematical incorporation of the preference weights into the decision-making problem is relatively straightforward. When it concerns more than one decision-maker, the process becomes more complex and controversial because a matrix of different preference weights for different decision-makers has to be reduced to a single vector in order for a single optimal solution to be found. Such a reduction may be performed by taking a simple average, a modal or even a median figure over the range of the weights, but such reductions may lose important trade-off information related to the outcomes of the analysis under extreme weightings. There is no clear consensus in the literature on how to reduce many different preference weightings for the criteria.

A variation on multi-criteria analysis: Deliberative multi-criteria evaluation

A process that has been developed to effectively incorporate multiple decision-makers' perspectives into a multi-criteria analysis process is known as deliberative multi-criteria evaluation (DMCE) (Proctor & Drechsler 2006).

Deliberative multi-criteria analysis is a technique combining multi-criteria analysis with a deliberative procedure – the citizens' jury. The multi-criteria analysis structures the decision-making process, while the citizens' jury allows effective interaction and deliberation between multiple decision-makers.

The citizens' jury has its origins in Germany in the late 1960s with the *plannungszelle* (planning cell) technique (Dienel 1988). The first citizens' jury was conducted in the United States in 1971 (Crosby 1999). This approach has had widespread use, particularly in deciding health issues in Europe (Lenaghan 1999) and in deciding environmental issues in Europe (O'Connor 2000) and the United States (Crosby 1999). It has had growing use in Australia (James & Blamey 1999; Robinson, Clouston & Suh 2002; Niemeyer & Blamey 2003; Western Australian Department of Infrastructure and Planning 2005).

The citizens' jury is based on the judicial model for assessing the guilt of people charged with a criminal offence. For juries concerned with a public decision-making process (such as the allocation of health funds or the identification of protected areas), the typical jury size has ranged from ten to around 20 participants. The jury is given a specific charge that is well worded, clear and direct. Ideally the process uses a facilitator and the jury is given sufficient time to deliberate, ask questions and call witnesses. This may take several days. Decision problems that are highly complex or contentious, and that require many witnesses, may take much longer. Witnesses are chosen based on their expert knowledge and can and should be selected to represent differing viewpoints. The jury should be comfortable that adequate time has been given to all viewpoints. The final outcome is usually a consensus position reached by the jury, often documented in a report to the agency that has established the jury.

The steps in the citizens' jury process are as follow (adapted from Jefferson Center 2004):

1. *Jury selection.* This is done after a random selection of potential participants, usually via a telephone survey to ascertain their willingness to participate. The jury is then selected based on demographic and attitudinal characteristics to best reflect a sub-sample of the relevant stakeholders.
2. *Witness selection.* Experts are selected to represent all issues and perspectives of the argument. Experts are to give information to the jurors so that they can make fully informed decisions.

3. *Charge*. The charge is what the jury has to decide upon; it should not be too broad or too narrow. Unlike a criminal charge, it does not usually demand a 'yes' or 'no' answer, but takes the form of a series of questions to be addressed. The charge provides focus for the jury.

4. *Hearings*. The hearings represent the meetings attended by the jurors and are presided over by an independent facilitator (judge), with the expert witnesses providing information and answering questions as necessary. The rules of procedure are clearly established at the beginning of the process, and time is given to allow the jurors to get to know each other and take part in discussions and deliberations. This process may take several days or one meeting or separate meetings.

5. *Recommendations*. At the end of the process the jury must provide agreed recommendations and reasons for these recommendations.

Citizens' juries are effective for allowing interaction between decision-makers and analyst and for conducting an iterative process. In general, however, citizens' juries do not provide a means of structuring the decision-making problem. A logical way of overcoming both these problems and increasing the advantages of both is to combine the citizens' jury and multi-criteria analysis approaches (Figure 4.1).

Figure 4.1 Deliberative multi-criteria evaluation

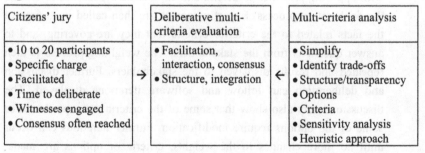

Citizens' jury		Deliberative multi-criteria evaluation		Multi-criteria analysis
• 10 to 20 participants • Specific charge • Facilitated • Time to deliberate • Witnesses engaged • Consensus often reached	→	• Facilitation, interaction, consensus • Structure, integration	←	• Simplify • Identify trade-offs • Structure/transparency • Options • Criteria • Sensitivity analysis • Heuristic approach

Deliberative multi-criteria evaluation combines the facilitating qualities of the citizens' jury process with the analytical and integrating qualities of the multi-criteria analysis technique by giving the jury the charge of coming to agreement on the weightings for the decision criteria. As the weightings typically vary for different jurors, the deliberative process and discussions are prompted by those with wide disparities in their weights arguing their case.

Where big disagreements on weightings exist, expert witnesses can be called in to give more information. The multi-criteria analysis software can then be displayed iteratively as the jurors agree to change their weightings, and iterative sensitivity analysis can also be conducted to determine if the variation in the weightings makes any difference to the overall ranking of the different options.

The steps in the deliberative multi-criteria evaluation process are:

1. Choose the stakeholders (jurors) as outlined in the previous section, 'Choosing the stakeholders'.
2. Meeting 1: Stakeholders develop and agree on objectives, options for evaluation and criteria to measure options; and stakeholders individually and independently weight the criteria.
3. The impact matrix is developed to show options, criteria, indicators and impacts.
4. Weightings are analysed to assess where the big discrepancies in stakeholder preferences are, so that experts can be called in to the next meeting to discuss and explain those criteria.
5. Meeting 2: A facilitated process starts, with weightings identified for each stakeholder displayed to all the participants so that each can see the initial priorities of every individual. The outcomes of the multi-criteria analysis software results are also displayed. The facilitator calls on those with opposing priorities to defend and explain their positions to initiate the deliberation process. Expert witnesses are then called in to present the facts related to the criterion/criteria that they are covering, and to answer questions from the stakeholders. The weighting process is then repeated and results displayed to the stakeholders. Further discussion and deliberation can follow and software iterations displayed. The discussions may also show that some of the criteria are superfluous or some of the options require modification. Further iterations can occur until no more changes to the weights, criteria or options are made. Before a final outcome is reached it may be necessary to carry out more research or investigation if the criteria and/or options have been modified as part of the process.

Deliberative multi-criteria evaluation has been used extensively in complex and sometimes difficult decision problems involving multiple stakeholders with diverse interests (see, for example, Proctor, McQuade & Dekker 2006; Cook & Proctor 2007).

Conclusions

In this chapter, a structured decision-aiding process, suited to public policy decisions such as those involving natural resource management, has been outlined. The multi-criteria analysis process has been designed to aid in decisions characterised by great complexity and many trade-offs. A variation on this process, deliberative multi-criteria evaluation, has also been developed and explained here to better take into account multiple decision-makers with varying and opposing preferences and priorities. In recent years, the greater movement towards the incorporation of stakeholder involvement in decisions that will affect them has meant an increase in the demand for such structured and facilitated decision-aiding methods.

5 Economic modelling and forecasting

Peter Abelson

This chapter provides an introduction to economic modelling and forecasting. An economic model is a simplified representation of economic phenomena. Some of the concepts and issues discussed in this chapter are also covered in chapter 12, and it may help to read these two chapters in conjunction with each other. Some of the main forms of economic models are:

- simple statistical models;
- market-specific models;
- macroeconomic models;
- input–output models; and
- computable general equilibrium models.

This chapter draws on a 2006 report entitled *Audit of Economic Models for Aviation, Tourism and the Australian Economy* prepared by Applied Economics P/L in association with the Sustainable Tourism Collaborative Research Centre for Tourism Economics and Policy Research for the then Australian Department of Industry Tourism and Resources. The authors of this consultancy report were Philippa Dee, Larry Dwyer, Peter Forsyth, Roselyne Joyeux and Glenn Withers as well as the present author.

We will see that these models are not mutually exclusive and can often be used in combination to assess the impact of proposed changes or actions. We will illustrate the general concepts involved in economic modelling and forecasting with reference to a 'live' policy issue, namely modelling the impact of liberalising aviation policies on the Australian economy, and particularly on the tourism sector.

Modelling requirements

Economists use economic models to explain and predict different types of economic outcomes. These outcomes include quantities and prices of goods, revenues and costs, wages, the rate of interest, exchange rates and trade outcomes, to name but a few. These outcomes may be modelled at the level of the firm, industry or market. They can also be modelled at the level of a region or the economy as a whole. To understand the alternative economic models that can be used to inform decision-making, we need to be clear about the outcomes we require the model to produce.

It is important to note that different stakeholders will often be interested in different types of outcomes. Thus the outputs required of a model of the impacts of liberalising aviation by the Australian and state governments and by industry may well differ. The Australian government is likely to be most interested in national outcomes, though not exclusively so. Industries are likely to have a more sectoral and geographic perspective, though again not exclusively so.

National effects

There are two main kinds of output that affect the nation as a whole and which may be the desired outcome of an economic model: national economic activity as measured by changes in gross domestic production (GDP); and the national welfare effect. As will be seen, national economic activity and welfare are related, but they differ in significant ways.

GDP equals the sum of gross value added (GVA) in each of 17 major industry sectors (plus the value of ownership of dwellings) plus indirect taxes. The value added in any sector equals the gross expenditure (or gross output) in the sector less the value of goods and services purchased for, or used up in, the process of production in that sector.

On the other hand, the national welfare effect is the sum of benefits (or surpluses) to Australian producers, consumers, governments and third parties that arise from a particular change. Benefit is defined here, as is usual in measures of economic welfare, as the value of the activity to consumers or producers over the (opportunity) cost to consumers or producers of acquiring that benefit. The opportunity cost of something is its highest value in alternative use; the cost of not using some other way. All inputs to production are likely to have an opportunity cost. The larger the sum of the net benefits, the greater is the gain in economic welfare, which is also described as national net social benefit.

The concept of net social benefit or welfare is broader than production or income as measured by GDP. The following examples from airline deregulation and the tourism industry illustrate how welfare effects are not necessarily reflected in, or measured by, change in GDP.

- The benefits to Australians currently travelling overseas who pay lower prices to foreign airlines and who purchase goods and services while overseas do not show up in GDP figures. This is an example of a 'terms of trade' effect.

- GDP does not measure consumer surpluses associated with increased overseas trips. Suppose that an Australian consumer is faced initially with a $2500 airfare from a foreign airline and chooses to purchase an imported television for $2000. Now the airfare falls to $2000, and the consumer purchases the airfare instead of the television. The consumer is better off because she is making a preferred purchase, but there is no change in Australian GDP.

- If the tourism sector expands by employing previously unemployed labour and leisure has a value (work has an opportunity cost), GDP increases by more than net welfare.

- Suppose that a worker is indifferent between working for $60,000 in a coal mine in the Hunter region or for $40,000 in tourism employment in Port Macquarie on the New South Wales coast. Currently he works in the mine because there is no tourism job available. With a fall in airfares as s result of deregulation and an increase in tourism, he takes a new job for $45,000 in Port Macquarie. There is a welfare gain of $5000 (in welfare terms the worker is $5000 better off), but GDP has fallen by $15,000.

- GDP does not include non-market effects, notably environmental effects such as aircraft noise or emissions of greenhouse gases.
- Some income from GDP may accrue to foreigners.

For most policy purposes, the welfare effect is more important than the output effect. Economic activity is a major component of welfare but not the whole of welfare. Sometimes an economic activity measure can be used as a proxy for economic welfare, but this should be done cautiously.

Regional effects

Typically state and local governments are most interested in economic effects at the state, regional or local level. The economic effects here are usually regional output and employment. Industry also has an interest in regional impacts because these can strongly influence local planning decisions and other industry facilitation processes.

It should be noted that the regional economic impact could exceed the national impact. For example, tourism expansion in one region might draw on resources from other regions (Forsyth 2005a). An increase in output in one area is then partly offset by lower output in another area, so that the total national effect can be significantly different from the regional outcome.

Changes in regional output effects may also exceed the regional net welfare benefits when:

- previously unemployed local resources are brought into production and these resources have a leisure opportunity cost; and
- labour or other factors of production move into the region in response to increased demand.

Furthermore, studies that focus exclusively on the production side of economic activity may overlook effects for consumers and third parties.

A change in gross expenditure is sometimes assumed to be synonymous with a change in gross output and regarded accordingly as an important output of an economic model. However, changes in total output depend on the availability of resources and can be estimated only after allowing for the opportunity cost of production (losses in other sectors). Forecasts of gross expenditure are an important input to estimates of changes in regional output, but expenditure itself is often a misleading indicator of regional output effects.

Industry effects

The purpose of economic modelling can be to assess the impact of possible changes on a specific industry or industries alone. There is a great variety of market data that can be relevant to such an assessment. Such data are often commodity or service specific and area specific. For example, the core data needs of the aviation and tourism industries include:

- gross national expenditure on aviation and tourism, including (i) numbers of tourists by type and origin and (ii) expenditure per tourist by type and origin;
- numbers employed nationally in the aviation and tourism industries;
- gross expenditure and/or employment in major industry sub-sectors (such as airports, airlines, domestic transportation, accommodation, food and drink, recreational services, and other retail);
- models of impacts of specific kinds of tourism expenditure, such as expenditure on major events, arts, culture and entertainment, tourism retailing, and educational tourism;
- gross expenditures and/or employment by industry by region; and
- gross value added in aviation and tourism industries.

Table 5.1 provides a summary of the major economic outputs that may be required by the main stakeholders in aviation and tourism and the national economy. The output(s) and level(s) of analysis desired by decision-makers then frames the choice of economic models, and the various choices are discussed in the following sections.

Table 5.1 Major outputs required for aviation and tourism analysis

Level of analysis	Output required
National impacts	Gross domestic output and employment
	Gross value added in aviation and tourism sectors
	National welfare (net social benefit) effects
Regional impacts	Regional output and employment
	Regional welfare (net social benefit) effects
Industry impacts	Gross expenditure in aviation and tourism
	Number of tourists and expenditure per tourist
	Gross expenditure on industry sub-sectors
	Gross expenditure by region

Basic statistical models

Basic statistical models draw on generic statistical methods (discussed in chapter 12) to describe economic phenomena. There are three types of basic statistical models:

- univariate time series;
- multivariate time series; and
- multivariate structural estimation models.

Univariate time series models

A univariate time series model can provide forecasts without requiring knowledge of, and forecasts for, any other explanatory variables. Such a model is a sophisticated form of extrapolation that takes the systematic components of past behaviour and projects them into the future.

Univariate time series models depend upon sets of time series data. The pattern of movement of this series of data is broken down into various components. The variable, as recorded over many observations through time, is decomposed into the trend, cycle and seasonality elements.

An example is airline passenger numbers over a given route. We can make a forecast of passenger numbers for this route for the next year by looking at monthly data collected for the past ten years. This data series is broken down into the long-term trend of passenger numbers, cyclical ups and down around this trend over shorter periods such as 3–5 year intervals, and seasonal variation such as summer highs and winter lows.

Univariate time series modelling is useful where knowledge of the determinants of the primary variable is limited, or data for other explanatory variables are difficult to obtain, but good historical data on the primary variable are available. However, such time series models are not designed to forecast over long horizons. In our example, a forecast of passenger numbers in ten years time, based on the behaviour of passenger numbers over the previous ten years, is a risky business; predicting what these numbers will be over the next year is less so.

Where longer-term forecasts are needed or where interest also lies in multi-variate understanding of causation and behavioural relationships, for either industry or government purposes, univariate time-series analysis can be used as a check on the effectiveness of more elaborate methodologies, which are based on data for additional variables.

Multivariate time series models

Multivariate time series models are more complex than univariate models in that the forecast values of the variable of interest (such as passenger numbers) are explained not just by the past values of the variable of interest, but also by the past values of other variables in the model. In this way, multivariate time series modelling can be used to test which variables help to explain the past history of another variable. The model is thereby 'built up' from the statistical analysis (rather than from economic theory, as is the case with multivariate structural estimation models, discussed below). This statistical testing of which variables are related to the primary variable of interest can verify the existence of a causal relationship and its strength, and can be important where data for full structural estimation are not available. Analysis of dependent variables can still proceed without problems of bias due to omitted independent variables affecting the results.

Multivariate structural estimation models

Structural estimation models, unlike time series models, take their lead from economic theory, which specifies in general terms how a variable of interest (the dependent variable) is influenced by other explanatory variables (independent variables). For example, consumer theory tells us that the number of airline passenger flights undertaken is a function of the price of such flights, the price of complements and substitutes (for example, rail or car travel), income levels, and a range of possible other variables relating to the characteristics of the flights and the surrounding environment. Data are thereby obtained (if possible) for the variables that the theory puts forward as important.

The relationships indicated from the process of theorising can be expressed in a single equation, where a set of independent variables determines the value of a dependent variable such as passenger numbers. Alternatively, the relationship may be more complex and be expressed in a system of interlocked equations. Thus, for a region, tourism spending may be a function of, among other things, the level of unemployment. But the unemployment level in a tourism-oriented local economy may itself be a function of tourism spending.

Empirical estimates are commonly achieved by using regression methods (discussed in chapter 12) to estimate the magnitudes of the relationships – that is, the degree to which variation in one variable affects another variable of interest. The results of this quantitative analysis can be used to inform other types of economic modelling. These other forms of modelling, into which the results of basic statistical models can feed, are the subjects of the following sections.

Market-specific models

Market-specific models are concerned with outcomes in specific markets. They are sometimes described as partial equilibrium models because they tend to focus on particular markets and to ignore flow-on effects of changes in these markets on other parts of the economy. However, this is an over-simplification because, as described below, studies of markets can examine and model the effects in related markets for substitute or complementary goods.

Consider first a single market for a good, as illustrated in Figure 5.1.

Figure 5.1 A single market with imported goods

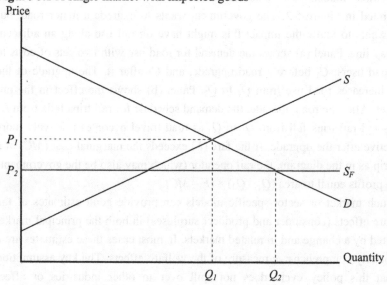

In this figure, demand is depicted with a downward sloping curve, D; demand increases as price falls. The upward sloping curve, S, shows domestic supply as a function of price. With no imported goods, Q_1 goods will be consumed at price P_1 (where demand and supply are equal). The horizontal line, S_F, represents the price at which foreign goods can be imported. With foreign trade, the price falls to P_2 and domestic consumption rises to Q_2.

The key parameters in a market-specific model are the estimates of demand and supply/cost and, in particular, estimates of demand and supply elasticities. The price elasticity of demand (supply) is the percentage change in quantity demanded (supplied) as a function of the percentage change in price. These elasticities may be estimated as part of the development of the model, or generated from other studies and then used as an input to the market-specific model.

A market-specific model can examine the effect on the airline industry of route-specific events such as the entry of a new airline on particular routes, the merger of two airlines, or the liberalisation of particular air services agreements. Such models, with appropriate demand and supply functions, can provide projections for passenger numbers, air ticket prices, and expenditure on airline travel on a route-by-route basis arising from such changes. They can also provide projections for airline revenues, costs and profits.

Market models can also consider interactions between markets, as illustrated in Figure 5.2. The government wants to upgrade a major road, but also wants to know the impact this might have on rail use along an adjacent railway line. Panel (a) shows the demand for road use with two sets of costs to the road users: C_1 before a road upgrade, and C_2 after it. The upgrade of the road increases road use from Q_1 to Q_2. Panel (b) shows the effect in the rail market. After the road upgrade, the demand schedule for rail trips falls from D_1 to D_2 and rail trips fall from Q_1 to Q_2 as road travel becomes relatively more attractive after the upgrade. If the fare (F) exceeds the marginal cost (MC) of a rail trip as in the diagram, the rail operator (which may also be the government) loses profits equal to area $(Q_1 - Q_2) \times (F - MC)$.

Such market or sector-specific models can provide good estimates of the welfare effects (consumer and producer surpluses) in both the principal market affected by a change and in related markets. In most cases these estimates are a reasonably comprehensive measure of the welfare effects. The key assumption is that this policy event does not spill over to other industries or affect household incomes in a major way. In effect it assumes that prices in other sectors are close to marginal cost so that in so far as consumers spend their savings (or producers their profits) in other sectors, the generated surplus in other sectors is small or negligible. This is a common assumption where changes are small and employment high. However, if there are major spillover effects across numerous sectors, a multi-sector model may be required to take these spillovers into account.

Figure 5.2(a) A model of related road and rail markets: road market

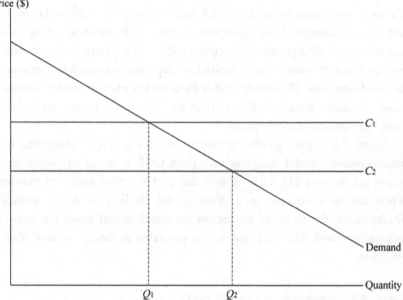

Price ($)

C_1

C_2

Demand

Quantity

Q_1 Q_2

Figure 5.2(b) A model of related road and rail markets: rail market

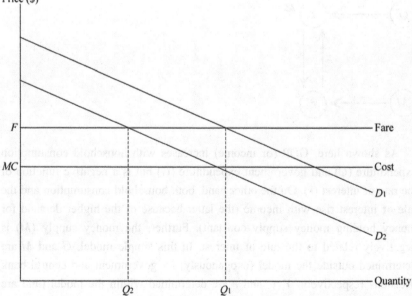

Price ($)

F Fare

MC Cost

D_1

D_2

Quantity

Q_2 Q_1

Macroeconomic models

Macroeconomic models, unlike market-specific models, are designed to explain and forecast economy-wide aggregates such as GDP, inflation, employment, interest rates, exchange rates and imports and exports. Macroeconomic models vary from simple models with a handful of equations up to models with several thousand equations. The simple models focus on key macroeconomic variables. More detailed models address relations between output, employment investment and other variables.

Figure 5.3 (<www.geoffwyatt.com>) provides a simple illustration of a macroeconomic model designed to explain GDP in terms of output or its equivalent, income (Y). GDP is a measure of the total value of economic production in a country in a given period. Subject to minor statistical discrepancies, the value of production generated should equal the value of income generated. This includes income generated to foreign owners of local resources.

Figure 5.3 A simple macroeconomic model

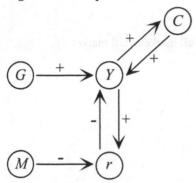

As shown here, GDP (or income) increases with household consumption expenditure (C) and government expenditure (G) but is a negative function of the rate of interest (r). On the other hand, both household consumption and the rate of interest rise with income (the latter because of the higher demand for money holding money supply constant). Further, the money supply (M) is negatively related to the rate of interest. In this simple model, G and M are determined outside the model (exogenously) by government and central bank decisions respectively. Y, C and r are determined within the model (and are described as endogenous variables).

Modern macroeconomic models consist of a large system of simultaneous equations relating macroeconomic variables. Australian examples include the Treasury's model (TRYM), the Monash and Econtech (Murphy) models, and the McKibbin and Sachs MSG multi-country model. The number of equations varies according to the level of disaggregation required. For example, the TRYM model consists of 26 behavioural equations, three behavioural identities, and 102 accounting identities. (The exact numbers vary as the model is modified.) These equations are generally specified according to some economic theory.

However, these macroeconomic models generally do not have a sector or industry breakdown. To relate macroeconomic changes to specific industries, such as tourism, macro models can be used in conjunction with sectoral models, with the macro-economic elements providing aggregate economy controls. Alternatively, as noted later in this chapter, they can be integrated with computable general equilibrium models so that the consequences of macroeconomic changes for the aviation and tourism sectors can be traced.

Multi-sector input–output models

An input–output (I–O) model shows the demand and supply of goods in dollar terms across industries, and includes the household sector and imports and exports. In an I–O model, an increase in output by an industry requires an increase in inputs purchased by that industry. This then requires an increase in output by those industries supplying the inputs for the first industry, and these industries then require increases in their inputs to production. An I–O model traces and estimates these input requirements among industries.

Table 5.2 shows a simple transactions model with three industries and household and trade sectors. Such tables are typically developed from industry survey data for a particular historic period. The sales (outputs) are shown along the rows and the purchases (inputs) down the columns. For each industry, the sales to other industries, households and exports must equal the purchases from other industries, labour and imports. Likewise labour sales (wages) must equal household purchases, and in equilibrium, exports equal imports.

Thus additional demand for output from industry A, due say to more tourists, will require extra inputs from industries B and C and extra inputs from labour as well as extra imports. The extra sales by industries B and C and the extra labour income will require in turn more inputs from each industry and more labour, and thus generate another round of expenditure.

Table 5.2 A simple input–output transactions table

	Sales					
Inputs	Industry A	Industry B	Industry C	Households	Exports	Total
Industry A	0	300	100	600	0	1000
Industry B	100	0	100	400	1400	2000
Industry C	100	300	0	600	0	1000
Labour	600	1200	400	0	0	2200
Imports	200	200	400	600	0	1400
Total	1000	2000	1000	2200	1400	

This process continues while industries can meet additional demands, and labour and other resources are available to increase production to meet this additional demand. Total generated output may be twice as high as the initial increase in expenditure on the output of the first industry. This ratio of the total output across industries to the initial increase is called a multiplier, which in this instance has a value of 2.0, or even higher.

Input–output models can be constructed for an economy as a whole or for regions or local areas. They can provide information about a range of variables of interest to decision-makers. In particular, they provide information about how values of industry outputs might change in the face of a *pre-specified* increase in demand in one particular industry, *assuming* that the required labour and capital is available to support this expansion. However, an I–O model does not explain where the extra labour and capital services come from. It simply computes the requirements. In so far as the results are interpreted as forecasts of output, it is assumed that the resources are available with no loss of output.

Input–output models cannot provide other types of information that might be of interest. For example, they cannot provide projections for numbers of tourists, expenditure per tourist or gross expenditure on tourism activities. On the contrary, they require assumptions to be made about these variables in order to provide the pre-specified increase in demand for tourism services. Nor do input–output models provide measures of economic wellbeing at the national or regional level.

Computable general equilibrium models

Computable general equilibrium (CGE) models combine a national accounting framework, as described by a macroeconomic model, with an industry-level input–output model. The macroeconomic equations provide a balancing framework to ensure that the model satisfies resource constraints. Under the macroeconomic equations, there are numerous equations linking the industries to each other and specifying how production is determined (the production function) in each industry. The production function specifies how output varies with inputs, notably capital and labour. CGE models also have equations to explain household and business demand for goods, and allow for changes in relative prices, substitution in consumption and production between industries, and supply-side constraints.

A CGE model is typically estimated from a base year set of data with a large number of relationships between the variables in the economy. The model is generally assumed to represent an equilibrium economy. Changes to key variables are made and the effects chased through all sectors until another macroeconomic equilibrium is reached.

CGE models can explain:

- where the extra demand for an industry's services comes from;
- where additional labour and capital services might come from to meet that demand (including the industry they may come from); and
- how input ratios may change if the prices of those inputs change.

CGE models specify how demands and supplies for goods and services, capital and labour are kept in balance via price adjustment. For example, an increase in tourism demand can lead to an increase in supply of tourism services by allowing providers of these services to raise their prices and to attract more workers into their businesses.

Resources used in one sector have to come from another sector or, if there is unemployment, from an unemployed pool. A CGE model specifies the supply of labour and capital available. If there is significant unemployment, a small tourism expansion may not lead to skills shortages. But if labour markets are tight, skills shortages may occur and hotels and other suppliers may need to offer higher wages to bid workers away from other parts of the economy. Assumptions about the availability of resources are critical to CGE forecasts.

Within CGE models, assumptions vary greatly. Critical assumptions are the nature of unit costs (whether industries have constant, falling or rising unit costs as the volume of production increases); whether additional capital comes from domestic saving or foreigners; and the availability and real opportunity cost of local labour.

CGE models can provide all the information that an input–output model can. They can also provide estimates of value added, wages and profits in an industry. They can model an industry-level impact and show the interactions *between* industries (or sectors). However, usually they do not show what happens *within* an industry or market. In such circumstances, a market-specific model is required.

Most CGE models can produce regional as well as national outputs. However, estimates of regional output can vary greatly as a result of different assumptions about inter-regional labour and capital mobility.

Generally CGE models focus on measures of economic activity rather than on explicit measures of economic welfare. However, it is usually possible with care to decompose changes in the model into the value of consumer surpluses; producer surpluses; terms of trade effects; technical change effects; endowment effects; and net payments to foreigners (these effects are similar to those from market-specific models). However, CGE models generally do not account for the real opportunity cost of labour (when workers have leisure or occupational preferences) or for non-market (environmental) effects.

Strengths, weaknesses and applications of the models

Table 5.3 provides a summary of the major strengths and weaknesses of the major types of models. Important summary points contained in this table are as follows:

- Univariate time series models are used for forecasting variables where the past structure of that variable is likely to dominate outcomes. They can also be extended to test causation and its direction with other variables.
- Multivariate structural models trace impacts and outcomes of major events, activities and changes through an industry and for different components of the industry. They can be used for analysis and forecasts. They do not provide welfare measures.
- Market-specific models are the most direct and cost-effective models for analysing effects in a single market and some related markets. They can provide forecasts and estimate welfare effects. They can also produce inputs to CGE models and use outputs from CGE models.

Table 5.3 Summary of major features of models

Model type	Strengths	Weaknesses	Applications
Time series models (univariate and multivariate)	Do not depend upon theoretical structures or upon data beyond the variable of interest.	Not directed at comprehensive analysis of behaviour and relationships.	Major use is for forecasting variables where past structure may dominate outcomes.
Multivariate structural estimation models	Provide estimates of magnitude of underlying relationships within an industry and assess the model's accuracy in representing past behavior.	Miss any flow-on effects and feedbacks outside the industry; subject to a range of problems in measuring and isolating all relevant variables.	Trace impacts of major events and changes through an industry. Can be used for analysis and forecasts. Do not provide welfare measures.
Market-specific models	Market-specific models focus on key details and primary effects. They use well-understood demand and cost functions and produce transparent results. Welfare effects are readily estimated.	May miss flow-on effects and feedbacks outside the industry. Relies upon external, rather than own, estimation of the magnitude of the internal relationships.	These models are the most direct and cost-effective way to analyse and forecast effects in a single market. They can produce inputs to CGE models and use outputs from CGE models.
Input–output models	The models track inter-industry relationships and knock-on effects.	Models contain no prices or resource constraints and assume effects are fixed with no behaviour adjustments. Poor for forecasting as too many variables kept constant.	May be used to estimate impacts of major events and regional impacts, but only with considerable caution and explicit notes on limitations.
CGE models	Good CGE models track inter-industry relationships, are based on realistic behavioural assumptions, and allow for resource constraints and prices. Can provide fully simulated economic impacts.	CGE models require substantial detailed modelled inputs. Model assumptions regarding scale effects, adjustment mechanisms, and labour supply need scrutiny. Modelling often seems black box to non-expert users. May be overkill for small changes	Can model industry-wide effects, regional or national impacts of major changes. Good for conditional forecasting, but less so for unconditional forecasts and for time paths. Can provide welfare estimates but only with much care.

- Input–output models may be used to estimate impacts of major events and regional impacts, but only with considerable caution and explicit notes on limitations.
- CGE models can model industry-wide effects, inter-industry effects, and national or regional impacts of major economic changes. They can also provide welfare estimates, but these need to be decomposed and explained. However, the results are often very sensitive to externally imposed economic assumptions.

Using a combination of models

We emphasised early in this chapter that the model of choice depends on the task at hand. For example, if the task is to forecast tourist numbers or expenditure for commercial purposes, a multivariate structural estimation model or a time series model is likely to be the model of choice. If the task is principally to analyse the economic and welfare effects of a change in one or two sectors with minimal spillover effects to other sectors, as is the case for minor policy changes in the aviation sector (such as a change in night curfew hours), a market-specific model is appropriate. However, this may still draw on a structural estimation or time series model to provide some inputs.

Matters are more complex when multiple sectors are involved (as may occur when a new airline is added to a route or a new route is introduced to an airport), and when both forecasts of economic activity and estimates of welfare effects are required. Here, as shown in Figure 5.4, there are three main approaches. These approaches do not have formal names. For convenience they are labelled below as the traditional approach, the mixed approach, and the comprehensive integrated approach. Importantly, in each case the starting point is likely to be estimates derived from a primary market-specific aviation model, drawing on relevant estimation methods.

Figure 5.4 Approaches to estimating economic activity and welfare effects

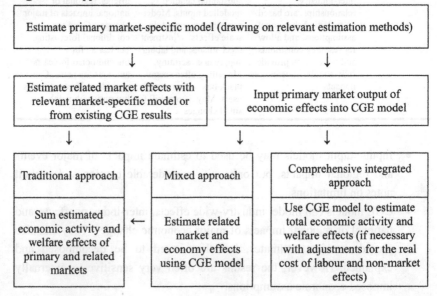

Traditional approach

In this approach, the analyst estimates the consumer and producer surpluses in the principal market and, separately, the net benefits in the related tourism markets from other sources, and adds these effects together. Other sources may be the analyst's own estimates of the net benefits in the tourism market using a market-specific model for that sector or estimates derived from results from existing CGE model work. This approach is commonly used in multi-modal transport studies, where estimates of effects in the primary mode (say aviation or rail) are estimated first and the estimated spillover effects on other modes are added in.

For many applications this approach provides robust, reasonably accurate and comprehensive answers. However, a market-specific analysis of the tourism sector does not pick up the spillovers, and reliance on existing CGE outputs may not pick up the circumstances of the particular case under study.

Mixed approach

Under this approach, the analyst inputs the estimated primary market effects into a CGE model and takes the outputs of the CGE model for the tourism sector back into account in summing the primary and related effects. A simple model of the relevant primary markets can be estimated, using information about airline costs, elasticities of demand for air travel and tourism, and tourism expenditure levels and patterns. This model can also provide estimates of changes in tourism demand etc. as inputs to a CGE model. The changes in tourism expenditure can be fed directly into a CGE model with a tourism sector. If the CGE model does not possess this sector, the impacts on individual industries must be specified as inputs. The CGE model will produce estimates of changes in key variables such as Gross Domestic Product, Gross National Product (GNP) and Gross Social Product (GSP). Further adjustments is required to estimate changes in net benefits with changes in factors used.

The estimates provided by the aviation and CGE model can then be combined to obtain estimates of overall changes in welfare, consumer surplus, employment and other variables of interest. This approach can produce the same range of outputs as the more comprehensive approach below, though some estimates are less rigorous and more approximate. The mixed approach is useful when modelling the full secondary effects is important and an existing CGE model can be readily used.

Comprehensive integrated approach

Under this approach, the estimated primary market effects are used as inputs into a CGE model; the CGE model is then used to estimate the full economic activity and welfare effects. This approach involves a detailed industry-specific model, such as an aviation model, linked in with an advanced CGE model. The aviation model would incorporate demand and cost functions, along with the capability to explore behavioural issues (such as how airlines compete). The CGE model would incorporate an explicit welfare measurement module as well as shadow prices of any inputs, like labour, which might vary. It would also incorporate a detailed tourism sector.

Such a model could incorporate a detailed aviation industry, but detail at the level necessary for useful analysis may make the model expensive and cumbersome. It would be better to tailor aviation models to the problem at hand. Thus the aviation model used would differ if the issue were one of extra flights from China rather than of a trans-Tasman strategic alliance.

However, the aviation and the CGE models would be closely linked. The aviation model would provide, inter alia, estimates of the changes in inbound and outbound tourism numbers and expenditures, including, if necessary, estimates of direct arrivals and departures through a gateway and the impacts on indirect flows through other gateways. It would also provide estimates of the change in the demand for home-provided aviation industry services.

Combining the results of these linked models could give a range of outputs of interest, including:

- estimates of the welfare gains to Australia or a state as a result of the change;
- gains to consumers of air transport (home and foreign) as a result of the change;
- impacts on the airline industry in terms of demand and profits;
- impacts on national and state GDP/GSP and employment;
- impacts on tourism industry output, profits and employment; and
- changes in federal and state taxes.

This approach may be regarded as the gold standard, especially for major economic events or policies. However, it requires sophisticated analysis of large numbers of assumptions, and the welfare affects must be analysed carefully.

Thus, the different types of economic models are not mutually exclusive. Outputs from forecasting models are often inputs to market-specific and general economy models, and outputs from market-specific models are often used as inputs to general economy models. Applications by government or industry may draw on more than one of these kinds of models.

Modelling of the aviation and transport industries illustrates the way that models are used in combination to generate desired outputs. Many studies of air transport liberalisation are based on a market-specific approach to estimating outcomes and assessing the gains. The reports by the Productivity Commission (1998) and by Gregan and Johnson (1999) are examples of a market-specific approach. The latter constructed a model of airline activity along a particular international route structure. Its treatment of demand and supply along those routes was considerably more complex than it would be in a typical CGE model. However, these studies did not evaluate welfare effects. On the other hand, Forsyth (2005b) provides a market-specific analysis of the aviation sector supplemented by estimates of tourism benefits derived from CGE modelling.

Traditionally, input–output models were the most common form of model used to estimate the economic activity effects of aviation and tourism (separately or combined), both nationally and, more especially, at regional levels. Dwyer et al (2000) cite numerous of input–output studies of the economic effects of tourism, especially in the 1980s and 1990s.

Structural models have been used in tourism and aviation analysis from time to time, such as Gregan and Johnson (1999) for the Productivity Commission and the Tourism Forecasting Committee for its regular forecasts for international visitor arrivals, domestic visitor activity, outbound departures and export earnings. Another study by Oxford Economic Forecasting (1999) is a hybrid work. The report straps an input–output set of estimates for the aviation industry on to a macroeconomic model with standard consumption and investment regression equations and time series regressions relating air travel to GDP.

But the potential for use of univariate time series analysis and other non-structural models has apparently yet to be picked up in this area. In the tourism and aviation industries, the method could give precise short-term forecasts on key variables such as fuel prices or consumer expenditure in aggregate or, especially, for market segments, particularly where there are no major known changes in train in relation to structure of the market or impacts on the market. Superior accuracy in 'business as usual' forecasts, where only the forecast itself is needed (for example, for inventory management or casual workforce hiring) can be provided usefully and economically by univariate methods.

A range of regression-based estimation models have been used in tourism and aviation analysis. A common model is the discrete choice model used to analyse customer responses to different product characteristics, for example, flight frequency, in-flight service characteristics, plane size and configuration (Louviere, Hensher and Swait 2000). This is especially appropriate for business planning by service providers in public and private business spheres. Rail corporations, government airlines and private transport operators, for example, need to know what aspects of the bundles of service they offer are valued in what ways by consumers. Focus groups and other qualitative market research techniques can assist, along with the intuition and experience of executives, but for major reconfigurations by major organisations it can be helpful to move to more precise formal methods.

The tourism and aviation literature has also occasionally called upon estimated regressions prepared for other purposes to impute impacts from the sector. Oxford Economic Forecasting (1999) adapts a general purpose macroeconomic model for the whole economy to incorporate a detailed tourism and aviation component, which uses results from direct estimation studies elsewhere to establish that aviation has had a positive effect on the productivity of other sectors.

In terms of multivariate models, the work of the Tourism Forecasting Committee should be mentioned. Tourism Australia releases detailed forecasts of a range of variables or activities of relevance to industry and governments (Tourism Forecasting Committee 2005). The forecasts are described as 'consensus' forecasts of activity across international, domestic and outbound tourism sectors, based upon a first stage of economic modelling looking at income, seasonality, as well as significant events impacting on source markets. This involves direct structural estimation, and subsequent 'qualitative' adjustments made after expert evaluation of the model forecasts, particularly in relation to matters not easily represented in the formal modelling process.

In Australia there has been active development of CGE models for estimating aviation and tourism effects. The Industry Commission (1996) estimated output results of the Monash CGE model for moving the Grand Prix from Adelaide to Melbourne. This did not include a formal welfare evaluation. Econtech (2001) used its in-house model to estimate the GDP effects of the decline in flying due to the 11 September 2001 New York attack and the collapse of Ansett. But, again, there is no welfare analysis. Woollett, Townsend & Watts (2002) developed a one-off CGE model specifically to estimate the effects of tourism in Queensland. The consulting firm NECG (2002) also made extensive use of CGE modelling to present the case for the Qantas/Air New Zealand alliance across the Tasman, although not without criticism.

Conclusion

For many policy evaluations, including for modelling aviation and tourism, market-specific models are the most direct and useful models. When spillovers are small, market-specific estimates can provide practical and robust results. These results may be combined with existing CGE results to estimate secondary effects.

In any case, an industry-specific model is generally needed to capture the specifics of proposed changes, such as the changes in inbound and outbound air travel and the change in profitability of the airline industry, as inputs to a multi-sector CGE model. Where there are significant sectoral spillovers, a CGE model is needed to capture the full changes nationally or regionally. Input–output models are not sufficient for this purpose in most cases, although they may be relevant in some regional analyses.

6 Scenario analysis for strategic thinking

Gary Saliba and Glenn Withers

Too many forces work against the possibility of getting the right forecast. The future is not stable; it is a moving target. No single 'right' projection can be deduced from past behavior. The better approach is to accept uncertainty, try to understand it, and make it part of our reasoning. Uncertainty is not just an occasional temporary deviation from reasonable predictability; it is a basic structural feature of the decision environment (Wack 1985).

Former US Defence Secretary Donald Rumsfeld defined the problem of uncertainty in decision-making well, when he famously drew attention to life's 'known unknowns' and like phenomena. Essentially there is a resultant Rumsfeld Matrix of Knowledge (Figure 6.1):

Figure 6.1 The Rumsfeld Matrix

Known knowns	Known unknowns
Unknown knowns	Unknown unknowns

Decision-making almost invariably involves a blending of all of these forms of knowledge. In organisations, capacity can be built to shift the weight of knowledge more into the known categories. This is the task of various evidence-based methods, including qualitative and quantitative information and its processing by formal methodologies, such as statistical analysis and modelling. But at any given time these states are given and a blending of these forms of knowledge is required for planning or decision purposes.

A requirement for such blending may emerge suddenly. There are a myriad of factors shaping the nature and direction of private and public sector organisations. Many of them appear to be disconnected and distant, and yet all too suddenly what is appearing in the news and in the background 'ether' embroils decision-makers. The focus for decision-makers is then reactive to reduce any damage to the credibility of an agency and the government of the day.

To maintain public confidence in public sector agencies, decisions often have to be made quickly and the urgency of the situation does not always allow decision-makers the opportunity to reflectively and systematically consider the magnitude of the problem or the options available. To anticipate and be pro-active is therefore a helpful management skill. In some cases the decision-makers are not emotionally prepared to confront the issues. Such stasis is compounded when the issues are complex, poorly defined and characterised by many factors and time-dependent relationships. Nevertheless decision-makers are inevitably forced to make decisions without fully understanding the systemic consequences over time of what is to be done. In these situations agencies can be at risk of developing and implementing inappropriate policy and corresponding interventions.

One approach that seeks a way to make decisions that distil complexity and blend all information states, and which are consistent with today and tomorrow, is to rehearse the decision-making process (before one has to make those decisions) through futures or scenario techniques. This is akin to pilot training in a simulator. Landings, take-offs and crashes are all simulated and practised, with the learning integrated into the pilot's skills set. When an event happens, decision-makers then know how to respond. In the context of decision-making in an organisation, rehearsing what and how decisions are made can be facilitated using decision scenarios.

The scenarios are the decision-makers' version of the pilot's simulator. They allow decision-makers to test their thinking, challenge assumptions and practise decision-making before they have to do it in a real situation. If and when a situation arises, decision-makers have rehearsed what sort of decisions are to be taken and how they can be implemented.

This chapter outlines how scenarios can be used to enhance decision-makers' ability to consider more broadly the external contextual environment and its potential evolution and, with knowledge of organisational capacity (strengths and weaknesses), be able to make decisions that are more informed, focused and effective.

What are scenarios?

Scenarios are alternative visions of potential futures, including conceptualisation of the path by which those possible futures unfold, emerge or are reached. They seek to define the major elements of the future that determine that path and outcome, condition the basic environment of the decision-maker and, where relevant, respond to or interact with the decisions-maker's choices. Where outside the scope of decision-maker influence the elements are exogenous, and where they are open to influence, endogenous.

Attention to formal and systematic scenario analysis is often attributed to its particularly successful development and use by the Shell Company; and its use during the transition to post-apartheid South Africa is seen as a major contributor to the success of that process (see Schwartz 1991). Another recent use was in the formulation of the Malaysian government's Human Resource Development Masterplan, as embodied in that country's current five-year economic plan. The OECD fosters such approaches through its Millennium Project (<www.millennium-project.org>), and one major public use made of the technique in Australia in recent times is the Business Council of Australia (2004) *Aspire Australia 2025* study.

In Shell's case, its prescient consideration of corporate strategies under alternative oil price and supply scenarios position made the company better placed than its less imaginative competitors during OPEC oil shocks. In South Africa's case, joint participative development of alternative social and political scenarios post-apartheid assisted materially in encouraging cooperation strategies for the country's future. Malaysia's scenario process helped to convince government to build in educational enhancements in national strategies as a way of providing flexibility to deal with uncertain futures and capitalise on those possible futures by turning threats into opportunities.

Consider three very different future scenarios from the Business Council of Australia (2004), stated in deliberately stark form in Table 6.1.

Table 6.1 BCA *Aspire Australia 2025* scenarios

Scenario	Characteristics	Policy issues
Riding the Wave	• Global economic growth • In Australia – reform fatigue and complacency; loss of faith in institutions • Loss of competitiveness leads to economic decline and social crises • Government becomes discredited and ineffective • In 2021, new Constitution with two levels of government – small, powerful central government plus large local governments (no state governments)	• Trust in institutions • Avoiding short-termism • Pressure on government resources • The suitability of Australia's political system to new challenges
Stormy Seas	• After initial high growth, sustained decline in Asia–Pacific stability and security • Pacific island instability, China turns to Russia for resources, terrorism around Asia • Taiwan, North Korea, Kashmir flashpoints • Australia becomes more nationalistic and cohesive • High security issues, low economic growth	• Influx of refugees • Escalating defence requirements • Maintaining regional relations • National identity, developing export markets • Engagement of US and Australia in the region militarily and economically
Changing the Crew	• Assumes globalisation trends and international cooperation • Focuses on generational and social forces for change in Australia • Value tensions between baby boomers (now retirees) and new generation of pioneers who favour opportunities and competition • Australia more connected to rest of world economically and culturally • Sydney becomes dominant but divided city	• Pace of change • Widening gaps • Competition for government resources • Dominance of Sydney

As senior decision-makers view each of these worlds, they can find different and sometimes similar implications as they test the robustness of current policies, implementation plans and other agency-based strategies, initiatives and projects. It is from these insights that the decision-makers can begin to assess the appropriateness of the agency's strategy for the future, using these stories as a means to enrich the thinking. They can test whether some strategies remain firm irrespective of environment and whether some require development or change. They can also test whether any of these strategy options change that environment itself.

The scenario stories are not necessarily extrapolations of current patterns or trends. Rather the stories represent the interaction of the uncertain forces that unfold to define different descriptions of the contextual environment in the future. Thus the scenarios describe different versions of the contextual environment in the future. Indeed one way to consider scenarios is to imagine a future (desired or otherwise) and see if a plausible path to it can be defined.

Nevertheless scenarios must to a degree be grounded in the present. This is an important criterion when scenarios are being developed. If the scenarios are too unrealistic they are almost always dismissed as irrelevant. Consequently, when reading a scenario one will notice elements of today sprinkled throughout images of the future.

Pulling this together, scenarios are a framework to assist with:

- analysing and understanding emerging complexities;
- exploring areas of uncertainty – things that we don't expect;
- assessing interdependence and coherence; and
- assessing 'what if' events.

That is, scenario analysis is a way of making decisions under uncertainty.

What are the advantages of scenarios?

There are four main advantages to the use of scenarios.

Affecting mental models

We often see what our minds allow us to see. Our minds dictate what information we capture and make sense of. If what we are exposed to does not make sense, we tend to dismiss that and look for what draws our attention. In an organisational context, this can be risky because the very issues we dismiss could in time be very relevant in relation to strategy.

The aim of scenarios is to affect the thinking of decision-makers and stakeholders such as public sector senior managers and key opinion shapers, so that they have a perspective that allows them to encounter the myriad of dynamics that could influence the performance of the agency system either now and/or in the future. With this in mind, scenarios can indeed be used wherever there is a need to exercise people's minds over how they view the world.

Because of the increasing complexity and change in the contextual environment, there is now a greater recognition that current and/or past approaches to decision-making may no longer be totally appropriate for the conditions that are now enveloping public sector organisations. An agency's success will depend on the extent to which people understand the dynamics that shape the contextual environment, and are aware of the mental models that they have which filter the information they receive and present to the world.

The more 'tuned-in' are the collective mental models that can emerge from a scenario process, the better is the agency's ability to sense new trends and forces which could be affecting performance now and into the future. Scenarios provide the means to enhance the flexibility of mental models so that people are in a better position to be conscious of the issues that are confronting them and are prepared to adjust.

Decision-makers sometimes develop policy and strategies and make decisions without a full appreciation of the underlying beliefs and assumptions of the individuals and stakeholders with whom they interact. Decision-making processes all too frequently progress with the assumption that there is a shared belief system for the issues at hand. The use of scenarios, and even the process of developing them, can enhance the decision-making process by providing the means to bring mental models to the surface, and challenge and explore them so that there is a common understanding of the basis for making decisions.

New thinking and innovation

A powerful approach in developing new thinking and innovation is the 'visualisation' process. Scenarios represent an effective means to enhance people's ability for visualisation because they expose people to totally different temporal and spatial frames to what exists today.

As people explore future worlds described by the scenarios, they begin to construct and develop visual images of different versions of how the future of their contextual environment could evolve. Through the process of comparison and definition of images, people begin to make new connections between different ideas that are stimulated by the scenarios and draw new conclusions for policy development and implementation by exploring potential opportunities and possibilities.

This is achieved by: comparing the images within a future world to today and identifying the associated learning; comparing the images between two, three or four different worlds to also gain learning; and by comparing the images from two, three or four different worlds and using the results to make distinctions from the present world.

Such 'comparison' and 'distinction' represent key approaches that people can use to develop new thinking and innovation in their organisation.

Folding the future back into the present

The demands of day-to-day pressures on decision-makers can force them to focus mostly on today and even yesterday ('generals who fight the last war'). It can provide the illusion of safety and comfort. Consequently there is limited thought given to the future because of the lack of energy and time, and because it is risky and 'outside the comfort zone'. This increases the risks in policy development including lack of alignment with societal needs and demands.

The use of scenarios assists decision-makers to fold the future back into the present and past to provide a reference so that they can shift their focus of time from yesterday and today to today and tomorrow. In this way the future rather than the present and the past is used as the context for thinking and innovation. Decision-makers are able to take their learning about the future and intertwine it with the fabric of today. Decisions about policy, projects and government initiatives become more focused on the interplay between today and tomorrow, enabling decision-makers to be much more aware of developments in the contextual environment and respond quickly, or even anticipate or influence these developments.

Contextual cues about future events

One way to become more informed about developments in the contextual environment is to be aware of emerging trends that are in their early stages of evolution. Scenarios provide contextual markers that allow decision-makers to pay attention to events that could be initiating an emerging trend. These markers, commonly called 'flags', highlight to decision-makers aspects of the scenarios that are currently in play. The flags could identify events and trends that are concurrently emerging in one and/or a number of scenarios. This becomes especially useful in developing policy and advising ministers of emerging issues prior to their becoming mainstream. Ministers, along with senior agency officials, are able to lead an informed public debate.

Because decision-makers have rehearsed their response to such events and trends, they are more able to quickly make informed decisions about current and evolving issues and influence that evolution. Their approach becomes instinctive, informed and consistent with the dynamics of the contextual environment, ensuring and enhancing organisational performance in a time of turbulence. This contrasts with the performance of others who are trying too late to make sense of the turbulence!

Using scenario analysis

Many people tend to focus only on forces that are shaping the internal dynamic of an organisation. Scenarios take people out of the internal environment and enmesh them into different future contextual environments. This process encourages people to undertake a journey in the contextual environment where they begin to explore the world and their mental models of it, and then creatively use that to review, challenge and enrich their internal environment too. Some ways for this to be achieved are outlined in the following four beneficial uses of scenarios. Each relates to aspects of cognitive processing, which makes clear the limitations to simple individualistic rationality assumptions and how such limits can nevertheless be transcended in a disciplined way, as with these scenario tools.

Defining critical issues

It has been found that in some instances, a group of decision-makers may not always share a common understanding of the critical issues, let alone how they may play out. Further, there are occasions when sole decision-makers are not able to define the critical issues that are/could affect the organisation. These are the issues where people wonder about what would happen if they 'took this approach or that approach'. If they actually had a crystal ball, it is these issues that they would like to gain insights about. But before the crystal ball is interrogated, it is necessary to determine the issues of interest! Failure to clarify the critical issues can lead to decisions about policy development that are not always congruent with the needs of society.

Hence one of the first steps in scenario development is to identify and gain a shared understanding of the critical issues in the contextual environment: what are the issues capable of 'keeping decision-makers awake at night'. The process provides the opportunity for people to undertake meaningful interactive discussions at a mental model level. This directs the group of decision-makers along a journey of raising their mutual consciousness and awareness of how they work together and share their perceptions of the contextual environment.

By working through the issues together, individual mental models are exposed, explored and challenged. Through this process decision-makers' different perspectives of the contextual environment begin to be shaped and shared. This is important when policy and strategy are being developed, as people are then able to focus on their shared perspective of factors in the contextual environment that can have dramatic impacts on organisational performance. Decisions can then be developed which will take into account these critical issues or, when they differ, an active process of reconciliation or explicit recognition and understanding of alternative possibilities can be used.

This part of the process is effective in reducing tensions and contrary approaches often seen in organisations, providing common understandings of possibilities, and even giving a productive common language. People sometimes undertake processes that are unaligned with other areas of the organisation, simply because assumptions about direction are not articulated. By sharing and prioritising the critical issues, different organisational units can work more systemically towards jointly optimising organisational performance.

Understanding the dynamics of the contextual environment

The presentation of emerging trends and mental models in the contextual environment can sometimes highlight for decision-makers the need to develop their understanding of the forces which are shaping their organisation. For some this can be a challenging experience, as their mental models have not been shaped as quickly as the changes in the contextual environment. But the process can be rewarding, developing people's mental models to allow for greater flexibility in decision-making.

Through regular briefings about the trends in the contextual environment, decision-makers begin to stand back from the pressures and details of the day-to-day to consider the organisation from higher up. It is akin to walking away from within a dense grouping of trees and walking up to a high point to view the forest – that is, avoiding the problem of 'not seeing the wood for the trees'. Decision-makers suddenly realise that the view from the hill indicates to them that some of the decisions that have been taken are not consistent with each other and hence they may not provide the optimal outcomes for the future.

Being on the metaphorical hill also allows decision-makers to identify other forces that are imminent and could be of importance, or could be of major significance at a later stage. As a group, decision-makers can even assimilate this information to ensure that decision-making is synergetic with the dynamics of the forces that are/could shape the agency. The process is about learning. Individuals learn and, as a group, undertake organisational learning. Decision-makers can then return to the 'trees' to communicate and translate the strategy for implementation.

Transcending temporal and spatial boundaries

The mental models that people hold in relation to interpreting space and time can have an important influence on their decision-making ability. For some their temporal frames of reference are in the past and present while for others it can be the present and future. Spatial frames of reference can vary from local to global. Whatever the frame a person holds, it will act as a filter to allow in information that is aligned with the reference frame.

Thus a person who has a filter with a local/regional frame focusing on the future, will still to some extent be 'blind' to the dynamics on a national/global level in the present and future. People with such an orientation and who hold senior decision-making roles in relation to broader policy development and implementation can pose a major risk to the delivery of government services.

Scenarios can be used to challenge people's mental models about time and space. The shift in focus from today to tomorrow surfaces and challenges different mental models on how the future could be, and the forces that are influential in creating it. The dialogue undertaken is sometimes boundaryless as people explore the extreme horizons of the contextual environment and the business of the agency and the forces that could shape it. The issue of boundary therefore becomes an important component of the dialogue because it highlights the temporal and spatial scope of decision-makers' mental models of the contextual environment. For some the scope is reduced while for the others it is increased. This can happen differently for each of the time and space parameters.

Decisions for the whole organisation

In some agencies the rewards system, responsibility and accountability guidelines often force people to primarily focus on their immediate business portfolio with only limited awareness of other parts of the agency and their delivery capabilities and priorities. This approach to working and making decisions tends to help optimise for component parts of the organisation. However, it does not necessarily optimise for the agency as a whole.

Working in this limited context can influence people's mental models so as to view the wider environment from the unique dynamics of their own portfolio only. Consequently this focus directs a search toward those variables that are influential to their portfolio rather than the agency as a whole.

In wider decision-making forums, discussions about issues happen from different contexts. Scenarios can be used by people to view their portfolio from the perspective of the external world that immediately and directly influences their part of the organisation, and also from the perspective of the contextual environment of the whole agency. The ownership and reward issues some people hold in relation to their portfolio can make this challenging. Over time, people's mental models about the scope of their activity can shift and the group of decision-makers can begin to shape a shared mental model, which considers the organisation as the entity comprised of interdependent portfolios. Decision-making is then based on the agency as a whole and outcomes are considered with regard to the systemic implications for the portfolios.

Scenarios and strategic planning

The process of developing scenarios is one of conducting an environmental scan of the contextual environment. However a distinct difference between this process and traditional approaches is the way the data are used to create futures and influence mental models. Scenario development transforms data/information in the present to insights about what the future may look like. These insights can be then be used as context to develop a strategic plan.

In contrast, many traditional approaches make use of the data/information from the contextual environment to understand the present through such tools as a SWOT (Strengths, Weaknesses, Opportunities and Threats) analysis. Although this is extremely valuable, it limits the use of the data and defines the context for the strategic plan to be in the present. By the time the plan is implemented, the context could very well have changed!

If, however, the opportunities and threats are treated as the contextual environment, and the strengths and weaknesses as an assessment of organisational capability, a more forward-looking and holistic analysis can be adopted to transition SWOT into scenario insights for strategic planning.

The following sections describe how scenarios can be used to provide a futures context for the development of strategic plans.

Scenarios as 'windtunnels' to refine the strategic plan

The exterior design of the late 20th century automobile has been influenced by constant testing and design in windtunnels. The prototype models are placed in a windtunnel to determine their aerodynamic efficiency. As the controls in the windtunnel are varied, the environmental conditions change and the aerodynamic capabilities of the design are assessed as various probes monitor the flow of air over the vehicle. The windtunnel experiments provide invaluable information for making design changes to the automobile so that its performance is enhanced.

Scenarios can be thought as mental windtunnels. Each time a different scenario is considered one is changing the control settings of the windtunnel, creating a different set of test environmental conditions. It is within the windtunnel of the scenarios that an agency's policy, initiatives and strategic plan can be conditioned, tested and evaluated.

Decision-makers can use scenarios to test how well policy, initiatives and a strategic plan can stand up to the environmental conditions of the scenario. The windtunnnelling process requires decision-makers to ask the question: 'if the elements of this world were to come true, to what extent would today's policy and strategic plan be relevant and effective?' The answers to this question could be different in each scenario and they can range from totally relevant and effective to totally ineffective! There is also the possibility that parts of the plan are very effective in one scenario and totally ineffective in other scenarios.

The purpose of the windtunnelling exercise is to take the implications and use them to challenge the assumptions, thinking and mental models that created the plan. It is from this perspective that decision-makers use the results to learn about themselves and the process that they had used to develop the plan. The learning can then be used to refine the thinking and correspondingly the plan, so that it is more robust for future worlds.

Note that the windtunnelling exercise can be used to test a range of other organisational models and tools, such as mental models, financial plans, business plans, business design, just to name a few! As in the windtunnelling of the policy documents and strategic plans, implications will emerge for each of these items leading to refined approaches that will be more aligned with the dynamics of the emerging contextual environment.

Scenarios as the basis of a new strategic plan

For some people the opportunity arises to be able to develop policy, government-led initiatives, and strategic plans afresh without any previous formats or influences. Scenarios can serve an important role in this process by providing the context to develop models and frameworks anew. Each future world provides a different context in which people are able to explore patterns in areas such as technological innovation, shifts in social values, the political and regulatory environment, economic and financial changes, and ecological issues. Box 6.1 provides a challenging analysis of how one US agency, the National Security Council, might have acted very differently had it used scenario analysis pre-September 11, and how it has incorporated such analysis since then to be better prepared for such events (Bobbitt 2003).

Box 6.1 Could futures scenario analysis have prevented September 11?

Question: Was the Administration blindsided because of poor work by the intelligence services, or was the problem poor co-ordination by the National Security Council?

Answer: None of these were complete surprises. The problem was not foresight but forethought.

Explanation: The National Security Council has for 50 years relied upon 'strategic planning' that chooses the desired result and organises to achieve it. This worked in a two-power arms race but not for a non-linear future.

Solution: Augment strategic planning with scenario planning: the creation of alternative narratives about the future based on different decisions – by many players – as each scenario progresses.

Argument: Replace the single likeliest story – applying the past to the future – by how forces may push the future along different paths –creating a learning framework for decisions by applying the future to the present.

The scenarios reflect visual language, which stretches people's imagination to contemplate how the futures can manifest themselves. The richer the language, the stronger the image about the future world that appears in people's minds. Through the visualisation process people are comparing the images conjured by the scenarios with what they perceive of today. They are also able to compare the images that appear between different scenarios. It is through comparison and distinction that people begin to learn and ask questions about the contextual environment. They begin to imagine what the future could be like and through that, the future they want to create. People can use the imagery in their minds as rich information for developing a new policy, initiatives and a strategic plan. The consistency and relevance of these would be determined by first considering each in today's world, and subsequently exploring the robustness of each under different scenarios.

Scenarios help identify new possibilities and opportunities, which provide a context to enrich policy development, implementation and a range of initiatives. One way of seeing this is to position scenario analysis in the context of related techniques. To assist, two broad approaches to the future can be distinguished: 'whitewater rafting', which takes basic trends or direction as given but allows for turbulence, and 'alchemy', whereby mixing of ingredients allows for major future change to be envisaged, often far removed from present trends. Scenario methods can include whitewater trends as a scenario but can also envisage massively different futures better seen as alchemy, and so can be distinctively placed there.

Whitewater rafting (trends) can involve the following:

- *Quantitative trend analysis (projections)*. This requires taking current numerical trends and extrapolating them into the future based on certain assumptions. Quantitative trend analysis can be useful if the assumptions are not too restrictive. They can provide a sense of scale and behaviour. However they can be easily seduce people into defining what will be as opposed to what could be. Many studies have shown the inaccuracy of quantitative projections.
- *Qualitative trend analysis (trend spotting)*. This approach can alert decision-makers to emerging factors that can have major effects in the future. In a similar vein to the quantitative trend analysis, the qualitative approach can mislead decision-makers that the identified trends will be the future. A recent example of this has been the emergence of e-business. In the early days this trend was extrapolated to the point that there would be major downturn in buildings where people were able to buy goods and services. Purchasing would be made over the Internet and goods would be delivered to homes and commercial locations.

- *Delphi survey (expert/stakeholder iterative consensus).* This requires interviewing a range of experts and stakeholders, synthesising the material and returning to them for verification and refinement. This is a powerful approach when the stakeholders/experts have an enriched mental model about the contextual landscape, and also when a large sample with wide diversity is considered as part of the process.

Alchemy (change) can involve the following:

- *Scenario methods (holistic narratives).* Although qualitative in nature the scenarios provide the context to identify key variables with boundaries, which can then be used for quantitative simulations. A large degree of diversity can be introduced into the scenarios through the story writing and the means by which the scenarios are presented. A potential issue for this approach is the extent of the research that has been conducted to identify the current and emerging uncertainties that are used to design the scenarios. The mental models of the scenario writer can limit the richness and complexity of the story. This can be a major limitation to the effectiveness of the process.
- *Wild cards (big impact shocks).* Wild cards are a useful approach to awaken decision-makers to large scale and scope issues that would affect the contextual landscape. The impact of this approach is heightened when the wild cards chosen are directly related to the business and are relatively plausible. In some instances wild cards are raised for discussion that are in the realm of doomsday and in many cases this situation loses its value in challenging thinking and developing options.

Moreover there are sub-groups within these approaches, with greater nuances thereby possible. Some examples for whitewater rafting are as follows:

- *Contingency planning: base case and plan B.* In a world of increasing complexity the use of contingency planning is relatively limited unless the contextual environment is narrowly confined. However the approach can provide important contexts for challenging thinking to inspire innovative approaches. The presentation of an alternate approach creates a difference. It is this difference that when constructed well, can provide the difference for powerful idea generation.

- *Sensitivity analysis: one uncertainty at a time.* Changing one uncertainty at a time assists decision-makers to develop a sense of the degree of influence a variable has in shaping a system. In some instances what would have been perceived as a highly influential variable has limited impact on the system and vice versa. A limitation of this process is that systems are highly interconnected and that changes in one variable will affect others and through the connectedness of variables, high degrees of non-linearity can be developed that multiply the effects of changes to one uncertainty. Thus such an approach can potentially lead to misleading perceptions. The importance of sensitivity analysis is to enable the decision-maker to gain a visceral experience of how change can manifest itself and the implications it will have for decision-making.
- *Simulation models: 'what if' quantification.* Similar to the sensitivity analysis described above, this approach is aimed at enabling decision-makers to develop visceral appreciation of simultaneous change to multiple variables. Decision-makers are able to ascertain the sensitivity of a range of variables and the system as a whole to change. It is through comparison of visceral responses and cognitive analysis that decision-makers begin to 'connect the dots' to develop new ideas and/or refine current approaches that will assist in policy and strategy development.

For alchemy some specific sub-groups of analysis include:

- *STEEP analysis: environmental scanning.* STEEP refers to Society, Technology, Economy, Environment and Politics. Trends and possibilities in each can be examined. A STEEP analysis provides a useful filter for collecting information that will assist in the discovery of critical uncertainties that will affect the performance of the agency. The utility of a STEEP analysis lies in the requirement to continually conduct scanning to develop an updated source of information. When compared with previous sources of information, patterns or trends can be identified that provide the basis for an early warning system that enables decision-makers to reshape policy and/or intended interventions.
- *SWOT analysis: self-appraisal.* When used with a STEEP, the SWOT analysis provides a comparative self-appraisal that combines internal capability with external possibilities. Like some of the other approaches described above, this approach utilises the concept of difference to challenge thinking and enable the development of new ideas.

- *Backcasting – tracking futures.* Backcasting is a technique that describes the history from a defined future back to the present. The factors and events that are described in the backcast are designed to challenge mental models and promote the development of new approaches and possibilities for policy development and planning. The approach has many similarities with developing scenario stories.
- *Visioning – preferred futures.* The development of a preferred future, a future that is desired, provides a creative tension between what is happening today and a future state. The *difference* in context establishes a mechanism for decision-makers to explore possibilities for future policy development and projects as well as the refinement of current approaches.

In more recent times there is the emerging art of using Internet 'virtual worlds' for some of this analysis. A decision-maker can be represented by an 'avatar' and social, political, economic and environmental worlds can be created online. Decisions can be tested using these multimedia resources, including allowing for reactions by other Internet users.

Irrespective of what approach is taken, decision-makers need to be mindful that the aim of the exercise is the development and/or refinement of policy and plans that will be effective in the contextual environment. The approaches are tools for challenging thinking and broadening mental models. To view these techniques as ends in themselves devalues the rationale for their development.

Scenarios and day-to-day management

The hectic day-to-day life of decision-makers usually forces them to focus on today and yesterday as opposed to today and tomorrow. Their work mode tends to be reactive, dealing with the issues that flare up within their current temporal and spatial context. Talking about futures is, on occasions, like 'raising a red rag to a bull!'

One challenge with decision-makers at any position in an organisation is therefore to introduce the concepts and practices of futures work into their day-to-day repertoire of skills. This can be achieved if the scenarios and their outputs are presented in a form that is relevant and useable in a day-to-day context, and allows decision-makers to improve the performance of their own portfolio.

In a time of increasing uncertainty, scenarios can assist decision-makers to be aware of possible current trends and emerging patterns in their business context. This is achieved through the use of 'flags'. The flags help managers to navigate the contextual environment in a way that does not require a great deal of time or resources. The use of flags allows decision-makers to be much more responsive to environmental changes, reorganising resources to ensure that their activities are in sync with the emerging trends in the contextual environment. If decision-makers view the world from this frame, such change would not be disruptive and would be a natural part of organisational life.

From a resource planning perspective, the scenarios provide decision-makers with the opportunity to develop a strategy that would assist them to obtain, and coherently manage, finances, equipment, technology, networks, structure, work and job design, human resource development, and the number of people to do the work under a range of different and challenging business environments. The scenarios provide the context to determine the implications of the diversity of decision-makers' current mental models about resources, and how those mental models may need to change to ensure that the agency is able to deliver the government's agenda through responsible resource management.

Testing the current resource management plan in each of the scenarios also provides the context to conduct a quantitative modelling exercise that illustrates the implications of different approaches. These numerical simulations help to contextualise the meaning of the scenarios to the issues that are faced by decision-makers on a day-to-day basis, allowing them to quickly make sense of the results and use them to navigate in a hectic and uncertain environment.

Conclusion

The steps needed for effective scenario analysis can be summarised as follows (Schoemaker 1995):

- *Define scope*. Setting the timeframe and scope for crafting the scenarios provides an important reference point in relation to the workload that will be required to complete the project. The timeframe will depend on the dynamics of the contextual environment for the agency. The greater the degree of uncertainty and turbulence then the greater is the requirement to craft scenarios within the near future rather than the longer term. The scope of the scenarios will determine the extent of research required to ensure that the stories are rich in content. The key decision-makers and stakeholders who are the clients of the process determine the scope. Start by asking decision-makers: 'what are their unstructured concerns?' and 'what knowledge would be of greatest value to your organisation?'. Such an approach will assist to set the scope of analysis in terms of areas and subject matter.

- *Identify major stakeholders*. Who will influence events? And who will be affected? Stakeholders who can affect the performance of the agency and the external policy landscape are sometimes well beyond the usual group. It is useful to stretch beyond the obvious set of influential stakeholders and explore others who could provide an insightful view about the performance of the agency and the influence that they can have on policy development.
- *Identify basic trends*. Explain why they are important to your organisation. Trends provide a benchmark for decision-makers to determine the relevance of policy and initiatives and ensure that they are developed to align with the dynamics of the contextual environment. The articulation of current and emerging trends will help decision-makers to determine what really matters in the exploration of the scenarios.
- *Identify key uncertainties*. Which events could substantially affect you organisation? Identify relationships (combinations) between uncertainties. The uncertainties provide the basis for the crafting of the scenarios. The usefulness of the scenarios will depend upon the uncertainties chosen and how they are explored in the scenario stories.
- *Construct initial scenario theme*. Note the role of the theme and key issues under it. The theme becomes an organising principle for the development of the scenario story. A range of ideas about how the story unfolds will be determined by the scenario theme.
- *Check for consistency and plausibility*. Tests include internal inconsistencies (possibly in relation to timing), dealing with trends, outcome combinations, and reactions of major stakeholders. Try to describe a stable end-scenario.
- *Develop learning scenarios*. Refine scenarios for plausible strategically relevant themes, which are useful for learning and research purposes.
- *Identify research needs*. Identify blind spots. The art of exploring ideas and concepts to draft scenarios sometimes raises challenges about the information base that will enable the rich writing that is required to craft

the scenario. Blind spots can easily emerge and their identification provides a very important window into exploring more deeply issues that are shaping the agency's contextual landscape.

- *Develop quantitative models.* Certain interactions may be formalised via a quantitative model. Quantitative analysis can be presented in a number of ways. First, quantitative information provides a very powerful source of information to challenge mental models within a scenario. Second, quantitative analysis can be used to provide the information to construct aspects of a scenario. Third, the qualitative descriptions that are presented in the scenarios provide the context to develop quantitative analysis of the scenario as a whole. In some instances whole computer simulation models are developed for each scenario that is constructed.
- *Evolve towards decision scenarios.* Converge towards scenarios that can be used to test strategies and new ideas.

The resultant scenarios should be:

- relevant – they must connect to mental maps of users;
- internally consistent – not contradictory;
- archetypal – describe generically different futures;
- an equilibrium or state that must exist for some length of time – evolutionary or revolutionary but not ephemeral.

The scenarios approach is best used when:

- change is high relative to trend;
- surprises are costly;
- the organisation is routinised;
- common understandings are needed;
- contending worthy opinions need examination.

However, there are important weaknesses. In particular, process can overtake substantive analysis; it can prove difficult to link theory to implementation; precision through quantification is difficult; linkage to other complementary techniques can be token; and continuous updating and evaluation becomes readily neglected.

Scenario analysis is being used increasingly by Australian and overseas organisations as a means to gain better understanding and manage uncertainty.

The most ardent managers and decision-makers will use well-developed scenarios, as long as they are able to make use of them today. The major use for scenarios today is to challenge people's mental models by exposing them to the myriad of factors that unfold from today into different plausible futures. This is both intellectually challenging and emotionally confronting, but managerially rewarding.

If people in organisations have the courage to challenge how they view the world, individually and as a group; if they are willing to shape their views and correspondingly engage in action; then it will be those people and their organisations that will emerge to be better leaders, not only in the future but in the present.

PART B
Gathering and analysing evidence

7 Using consultants to gather evidence
Leo Dobes

It is often the case – in work requiring cost–benefit analysis, for example – that public servants need to supplement in-house skills or the number of staff available. Where a temporary increase in resources is required to marshal evidence in support of new program or project proposals, or to evaluate existing programs or policies, consultants offer a ready means of extending available resources. However, the engagement of consultants itself requires a degree of skill – or at least a knowledge of major potential pitfalls – to ensure that outcomes reflect value for money.

Most government jurisdictions have developed their own comprehensive legislation or guidelines to assist their employees in the task of selecting consultants. The Australian government, for example, issues the *Commonwealth Procurement Guidelines* (Commonwealth of Australia 2004) and subsidiary, more detailed guidance.

But procurement guidelines are usually just expressions of minimal, formal requirements designed to ensure adherence to financial accountability and other managerial imperatives. They invariably cover only the rationale for choosing consultants and the formal processes involved. What is generally not provided in any detail is advice on the practical aspects of working with consultants. In fact, the personal and professional relationship with a consultant is often equally, if not more, important to the success of the work in hand.

Some public service myths and prejudices

Public servants have been trained to deal well with personal relationships, and are generally good at doing so. It is therefore ironic that some of them seem to lack the same degree of empathy when it comes to consultants. The following is a list of some of the underlying myths and prejudices that occasionally surface.

- 'Consultants are grossly overpaid, often earning in a day what a public servant gets for a week's work.' Often true, but it is equally true that much of the consultant's fee goes to cover the overheads of the large firms they work for, or, in the case of smaller operators who may not have a steady income or paid leave, the annual earnings can be less than that of a public servant with a steady job.
- 'Consultants are happy to work through the night to finish a task.' While consultants will, in fact, sometimes work through the night to deliver work required by a client, it is remarkable that some public servants almost expect this by requesting work at short notice, when they themselves, or their staff, would not countenance working under similar conditions.
- 'Consultants are greedy because they work for more than one client at once.' Because of the uncertainty of obtaining work, consultants will often put forward bids for more work than they can actually handle. If too many bids are successful, or if clients do not stick to their original timeframes, 'bunching' of workloads can cause problems for both the consultant and a client.
- An occasional complaint is that 'consultants cheat because it is often necessary to teach them before they can produce any work.' This belief is based on a misunderstanding: consultants are usually hired for specific skills such as quantitative analysis, rather than knowledge of specific subject matter. Begrudging time to explain the background facts or issues to a consultant may mean that their output is less than optimal, so that it is ultimately the client who suffers in terms of value for money.

- 'Consultants can't produce work to the same high standards as public servants.' If this is true, then do the work yourself, and don't pay a consultant. Otherwise, be careful to select one who can produce high-quality work, and manage them in a way that produces the results that you need.

Despite the prejudices of some public servants, value for money can ultimately be maximised only by treating consultants as human beings.

Ninety-nine per cent preparation, one per cent perspiration

Experienced managers may find it tiresome to be reminded (yet again) that good planning is essential to any project, including hiring a consultant to assist with the collection and analysis of supporting material. But real-life experience does demonstrate that even a few hours of quality thinking time invested at the outset can reduce effort later. Indeed, many consultants point to lack of clarity of purpose as the key reason for lack of success in work commissioned by the public sector.

One consequence of a lack of clarity may be the need to redefine the task after the contract has been let. Apart from the risk of engaging a consultant who is not fully suited to the (redefined) task, a change in scope of the work will probably require variations to the contract. Depending on their nature, contract variations can be expensive, especially if they involve long extensions of time.

Although some hard thinking – possibly combined with internal debate and discussion – about the output required from a consultant is virtually unavoidable, large or complicated projects may justify bringing in a specialised project manager or consultant who can help define the terms of reference (usually called the Statement of Requirement). Specialised consultants can also be used by a selection panel to identify a preferred tenderer from the bids submitted.

A concisely written business case is a good place to start. Not only does it help to clarify thinking about the actual need for a consultant, but it also generates a paper trail that may later be useful for evaluation purposes. And if signed off by a delegate (someone with authority to commit expenditure of government funds) or a supervisor, it helps put in place the first link in the chain of accountability for moneys appropriated by Parliament.

Preparing a business case

A business case can usefully address issues such as:

- an explanation of the issue or problem being analysed or solved;
- the relevance of the work to broader government policies or program outcomes;
- why a consultant is preferable to undertaking the work in-house (for example, lack of staff, lack of appropriate specialised skills, or the need for an independent external opinion);
- stakeholders who will benefit, or may be affected by the consultancy (for example, will it attract media attention that is not welcome to the Minister?);
- the scope and quality of outputs required from the consultant (work can be minimised by framing this part as a Statement of Requirement that can be used directly in tender documentation);
- a timeframe for completion and whether the timeframe is consistent with the needs of any broader project needs;
- likely costs and whether funds have been budgeted and are available for the consultancy;
- the form of contract to be used: many government departments use short and long forms of their standard contracts, depending on the scope of the consultancy;
- who will manage the consultant on a day-to-day basis (contract manager);
- whether there would be merit in requiring the consultant to transfer any skills to employees of the government agency as part of the contract (if this is the case, it is necessary to ensure that the employees will be available during the proposed timeframe);
- security considerations, including access to classified material;
- an analysis of the key risks involved in hiring a consultant (for example, if there is a shortage of capable consultants who would be available within the timeframe required), and any potential strategies that can be employed to mitigate the risks;
- the form of the tender: open tender (for example, advertised in the media), select tender (restricted to consultants already known to the agency), or sole source (direct approach to one consultant considered likely to provide best value for money); and

- an assurance that the proposed method of tendering meets all government and agency regulations and requirements (some agencies have supplementary instructions for procurement activity, sometimes embodied in the Chief Executive's Instructions).

Saving time and costs with panels

Government agencies can face considerable costs in conducting selection processes to obtain consultancy services. Many now routinely establish panels of consultants through a single Request for Tender, in order to reduce costs.

A panel is effectively a group of consultants who are selected to be available to provide services over some period of time (often three to five years), but with no specific work being promised to any of them. Often, panel members are chosen on the basis of fee quoted, as well as their skills. When the government agency needs work done, it simply rings one or several panel members to obtain a quote quickly, rather than going through a full tendering process. Where panel members have been chosen on the (per hour) fee quoted, the only need is for them to quote how long they expect to spend on the task.

Where guaranteed access to a specific but busy consultant is required, it is worth considering the possibility of a retainer fee that gives the government agency some degree of priority in access to advice. A retainer fee is probably a useful approach where advice is required frequently and at short notice, particularly if the arrangement specifies some minimum level of availability (for example, ten hours per week) of the consultant's time for a fixed fee.

Uncertainty regarding scope of project

Where the objectives or likely scope of a project are difficult to determine with any certainty at the outset, a decision-tree approach may be appropriate. For example, the project can begin with a short feasibility and scoping study, at a fixed price of a few thousand dollars, which is limited to identifying possible analytical frameworks, the likely project timeframe and costs.

Upon completion of an initial scoping study, a government agency is better placed to decide whether to proceed with the next, more substantive stage of the project, such as data collection. The same phased procedure can be applied again, with a subsequent stage (for example, analysis and interpretation of data) being contingent on successful data collection. This 'decision-tree' approach ensures that options to cancel the project are maintained without committing all available funds to the project at too early a stage.

In the case of large projects in particular, a so-called 'gateway process' (Box 7.1) may prove useful. Because it involves the use of peer-review, a gateway process offers scope for input from other perspectives and by experienced procurement personnel. While gateway processes are generally used for large projects, there is no reason why a similar approach, appropriately scaled-down, could not be used for smaller tenders.

Box 7.1 Peer review through a gateway process

The gateway review process originated in the United Kingdom in 2000, and the method is now used by the state governments of Victoria and New South Wales, and by the Australian government. The gateway process acts as a form of peer review of the conduct of large procurement projects in order to provide assurance about the quality of the underlying approach and methodology. Because they use significant resources (up to five or six days may be devoted by a group of experienced people), they are generally used only for expensive or mission-critical projects. The Australian government (Commonwealth of Australia 2006, p 10), for example, requires reviews for projects (other than information technology) whose value exceeds $20 million. Reviews are undertaken at each of the key steps, or so-called 'gates', or decision-points, of a procurement process. In the case of the Australian government, there are six different stages or gates (0 to 5) where reviews may be conducted:

- *Business need.* Determines whether scope and purpose been adequately assessed, communicated to stakeholders, and aligned with expected outcomes and timing.
- *Business case.* Assesses different options, feasibility, scope of project, likely interest in the market, likelihood of achieving desired outcomes, and so on.
- *Procurement strategy.* Confirms business case and availability of funding, and the type of approach to procurement.
- *Investment decision.* Provides assurance that business needs are likely to be met and that contract management controls and processes are in place.
- *Readiness for service.* Confirms existence of appropriate contractual arrangements, and plans for risk, training, communication, roll-out and commissioning.
- *Benefits realisation.* Final check of relevance of business case, end-user satisfaction, contingency arrangements, and so on.

A similar, scaled-down concept can be applied to smaller projects. For example, a 'research auditor' – a specialist consultant or academic – can be brought in by either the consultant or the client agency to advise on the procurement process or on technical aspects of any work undertaken.

Preparing tender documentation

Just as clarity in specifying the objectives of a consultancy helps ensure relevance, and hence value for money, well-presented tender documentation saves time and money for both consultants and clients. It also sends a positive signal about the professionalism of the agency letting the tender.

There are no hard and fast rules, but tender documents that include clearly delineated sections such as the following can facilitate evaluation of responses. And the lower the burden on the consultant of responding to a tender, the more competitive the field is likely to be, with a wider range of fees and potential solutions or approaches to choose from.

1. *Tenderer's details.* A formatted cover sheet can help ensure capture of tenderer's details. Information such as the full name of the company, ABN number, trading name, referees, contact person, and so on, make it easier to keep track of tender bids. It can also assist further investigation, including checking the financial viability of short-listed tenderers, where appropriate.
2. *Statement of Requirement.* If a business case has been prepared, it should be possible to simply cut and paste relevant sections into a statement that informs potential bidders of the precise nature of the consultancy. Use of the business case ensures consistency of purpose, and saves effort.
3. *Mandatory conditions of tender.* It is generally worthwhile making some conditions of the tender mandatory. For example, a deadline for submission of bids, or a limit on the number of pages submitted, can be useful to test a tenderer's ability to write concisely, or to limit the amount of time a selection panel needs to spend reading bids. A fairly common mandatory condition is the provision of a statement by the bidder of their willingness to accept a contract like the draft (see below) that has been appended to the tender documentation; or else to propose specific amendments to the contract terms and conditions.
4. *Evaluation criteria.* Separate inclusion of the evaluation criteria to be applied (perhaps accompanied by a table showing the weight to be attached to each criterion) with clearly delineated space for a response, helps reduce room for error and ensures more targeted and comprehensive responses by bidders. Good formatting reduces

confusion about exactly what is required: this is often essential for first-time bidders or for professionals (for example, an academic statistician) who may not be as used to responding to tenders as consulting firms.

5. *Tenderer's declarations.* Where it is desirable to seek a specific assurance of some sort (for example, absence of conflict of interest, willingness to abide by an agency's ethical standards, or confidentiality provisions) it is a good idea to obtain written statements at the time of the bid. Analogous to mandatory conditions of tender, such statements can indicate early on – before time is spent assessing a bid – whether the bid will ultimately be acceptable to the agency.

6. *Draft contract.* Making available a draft contract as part of tender documentation is a practice that has become more common in recent times, partly because it ensures that both the bidder and the agency are clear about the terms of the future relationship, and partly because it allows a bidder to propose alternative clauses (for example, with respect to copyright of the work produced – a matter that academics often address) that can be taken into account by the client government agency when considering bids. Note that taking contractual differences into account when assessing bids requires that one of the selection criteria specifically includes the extent of acceptance of the contract.

Thinking ahead

It is easy to fall into the trap of issuing tender documentation as quickly as possible because of time pressures. But undue haste can mean having to repent at leisure.

Words and phrases that are crystal clear to those preparing the tender documentation can be ambiguous and open to misinterpretation by outsiders who are reading the documents in isolation. Using colleagues in another area to prepare mock responses and to question the meaning and intent of the tender can pay handsome dividends later.

In particular, ask someone to help check the following:

- Is the requirement clear? (It sometimes helps to specify what is not required.)
- Does the request documentation allow for (or discourage) innovative solutions or approaches? Where possible, avoid specifying inputs or analytical approaches: focus on the output or outcome required.

- Is it written around the capabilities of an identifiably specific consultant? If so, you may be open to accusations of bias or discrimination.
- Does the draft contract contain clauses that provide sufficient flexibility to alter specified outputs (but without changing the nature of the overall tender process)?
- Will you be able to judge quality of output? You may need to specify existing technical standards (such as the Australian *Style Manual*) in the contract.
- The timeframe specified: clients often underestimate the time required to complete work, and consultants may take more time than either party expected.
- Are your specified outputs really important? It can add to costs if you are overly specific about your needs.
- Have you given your agency's legal and probity advisers or procurement manager enough time to check the documentation?
- Is the project consistent with relevant government policies?
- Have you provided a web address or other means of disseminating information (for example, responses to questions by potential bidders) so that all potential suppliers have equal access to new information after the request documentation has been issued? Is there a close-off date for questions by potential bidders?
- Make sure that a specific person is responsible for emptying your tender box at exactly the time specified. (Under the *Commonwealth Procurement Guidelines*, there is no discretion to accept late tenders, unless the tender is late solely because of the agency's own mishandling.)
- How and where will bids be registered and stored to avoid compromising commercially or personally sensitive information?

What are the key risks?

Busy public servants often wish to have a preferred tenderer start work even before a contract has been signed. The temptation is an understandable one, but potentially risky because even preparatory background work by the consultant may be sufficient to establish a premature de facto contract. Where time is pressing, it is best to consult the agency's legal area in order to enter into accelerated, but less risky, interim arrangements.

The other key risk lies in differential treatment of potential bidders. In order for a bidding process to be fair to all bidders, a process is required that enables all potential bidders to be informed of any information released after tender documentation has been made public. For example, if a potential bidder telephones the contact officer to clarify some aspect of the tender documentation or process, then it is essential that the question and the answer provided are also made available to all other potential bidders to ensure equal treatment. Otherwise, the agency is open to allegations of bias and discrimination.

Some government agencies have electronic tendering sites that automatically allow for presentation of questions and answers (so-called 'variations' to the tender) in a publicly accessible manner. Equity of treatment is preserved where all potential bidders are made aware of the site, and are able to access it to check on any variations made while the tender is open. Where an electronic tendering site is not available, tender documentation can specify a dedicated temporary web site, or allow potential bidders to register for emailed notification of tender variations.

Fees and expenses

Unfortunately, there is no magic formula for determining what level of fees will provide 'value for money'. Hence the use of competitive bidding processes, to establish 'market' prices as a reflection of the 'right' cost for a given output.

Fixed price contracts help reduce the budgetary risk to a government agency. But, unless provision has been made in the tendering process for potential additional work, a fixed price contract correspondingly increases the risk to the agency of output being less, or of a lesser quality, than expected. The risk of a fixed price contract is therefore reduced with increased clarity about the nature and quality of the outputs specified in the tender documentation.

A perennial question is whether to indicate an expected budget in a tender process. While a specific price risks attracting tenders bunched around a single fee, specifying a range such as $30,000 to $60,000 can signal to consultants that the scope of the work expected is not $1 million or $1000; and can therefore increase competition from a greater number of realistic bids.

Comparatively little use appears to be made of 'profit-sharing' schemes to reap the benefits of lower than expected costs. In a fixed price contract, for example, it may be worthwhile specifying that, if the consultant produces the required outputs at a cost below the fixed price, then any savings will be shared in some proportion with the government client. Both sides stand to gain from such an arrangement.

So-called 'pass-through' costs such as for accommodation or travel expenses incurred by the consultant tend to be reimbursed directly and do not form part of the overall fee. Contractual provision is usually made for such expenses, and a rate of reimbursement specified, often in the form of a per diem allowance plus economy airfares.

One issue that has received little attention to date is the standard of ethical behavior by some public servants towards consultants. Consultants have been victims of late payment for work done, or have been expected to attend extended meetings (a favorite pastime of some public servants, but a loss in income for consultants) without pay, as well as 'scope creep', where public servants have demanded additional amounts of work without commensurate compensation. A charitable interpretation would be that many public servants are innocently oblivious of the implications of such behavior, but the fact that large consulting firms with legal clout are not treated in the same cavalier manner as small consultants suggests otherwise.

Unfortunately, mistreatment of consultants is likely to be detrimental to government agencies in the longer term. Potential consultants who are discouraged from bidding because of negative experiences in the past represent a loss of competitive pressure on tender costs, and a loss in valuable corporate knowledge and skills (in the case of retired public servants engaged in consulting work).

Choosing the consultant

Choosing consultants is analogous to a staff selection process. Tender documentation is like an advertisement for a position that provides information on the type of person required and the process and criteria that will be used to select the successful candidate. Rules of equitable treatment are established and followed, both in staff selection and when choosing a preferred tenderer. Interviews (or presentations, in the case of bidders) and selection panels are usually a common feature of both processes, although more care is required in the case of consultancies to ensure that the presenters will also be the people undertaking the actual work. And debriefing is often provided to unsuccessful candidates in both processes. Questions that might be asked at interview are listed in Box 7.2.

Box 7.2 Checking the consultant's capabilities

For larger contracts, it is worthwhile interviewing bidders as part of the selection process. Some of the questions that might be asked include the following (adapted from Shenson 1990, p 47):

- What do you regard as our principal need or problem?
- Can you please analyse for us the principal strengths and weaknesses of your proposed approach or methodology?
- What alternative methodologies could be used? (This is a check on whether the consultant will only apply preconceived ideas or methodologies.)
- What specifically can you offer us that others cannot?
- How will we measure or evaluate your success in meeting our needs?
- Are you willing to work on a performance basis: that is, to be compensated on the basis of results produced?
- What related experience have you (the actual personnel nominated, not the firm as a whole) had in working with similar organisations, or with other organisations in this industry or field?
- What guarantees can you offer regarding the availability of nominated personnel?
- How do you plan to maintain communication with our contact officer?
- What related experience have you had in working on similar issues?
- If you plan to use sub-contractors, what are the arrangements to ensure that they also comply with the terms of the tender and the contract?
- From your (consultant's) point of view, what are the major risks in the project, and what strategies do you intend to adopt to mitigate them? What risks do you see facing us (the client)?
- Can you confirm that your stated fees (and expenses) are likely to represent all costs to be incurred? If expenses are based on cost recovery, then what is the likely overall expense to be incurred? How do you propose to charge for meetings, time spent travelling, telephone calls, taxis and so on?
- Do all quoted costs and fees include GST?
- What penalties should be imposed on you for under-performance?
- Do you have the capacity to meet the timeframe specified?
- How do you propose to work with our nominated resources (where some of the client's staff will be working on the project with the consultant)?
- What quality assurance procedures do you have? What procedures do you have in place to ensure that files are maintained adequately?
- Do you have any conflict of interest (name a few obvious parties to provide a prompt), and how will you handle this situation?

Public servants often complain that large consulting firms roll out their A-team to make the 'sales pitch' presentation, but then send in more junior staff to do the work. Consultants tend to respond by pointing out that work produced by junior staff is subject to review by the A-team, which has a strong interest in ensuring a high degree of quality in order to gain repeat work from the client. In fact, it is probably more important for government agencies to be aware of any sub-contractors (who are not directly under the control of the A-team) that will be used. For example, a sub-contractor responsible for data collection may not train interviewers adequately, or store survey material properly so as to protect sensitive commercial or personal information.

A useful approach that is often neglected is a 'belts and braces' questioning of referees about a candidate – either in job interviews or when choosing consultants. It is often the case that referees, when asked what they think of the candidate will present only the positive side. To balance the picture, it is usually a good idea to also ask the referee to identify the candidate's three major weaknesses. Although this may sound negative, it is essential information that may not otherwise be obtained, and which may otherwise jeopardise an important project.

As a result of free trade agreements with a number of countries in recent years, there may now be an obligation on government agencies to ensure explicitly that there is no discrimination on the basis of a bidder's foreign affiliation or ownership, location or size. Submissions must be considered on the basis of their suitability for their intended purpose, not on the basis of their origin. Because the legal position of each jurisdiction will differ in this regard, it is worth checking with the legal office of the government agency letting a tender.

Probity

It is easy to fall, albeit unwittingly, into the trap of a potential conflict of interest. Avoid accepting hospitality during a tender selection process, including seemingly innocuous offerings such as a cup of coffee in a coffee shop. Even if there is a long-established relationship with a bidder, or the hospitality is part of another project, probity demands not only impartiality but also the need to avoid being seen to be compromised in any way.

For large tenders, it is useful (and is often an agency requirement) to engage a probity adviser as well as a legal adviser. Probity advisers are used to offer independent advice on the ethics of proposed actions. An example might be the case where tender documentation has omitted a request for certain crucial information. A probity adviser can best advise on how to remedy the situation in a way that maintains equitable treatment of all potential bidders. Such probity advice complements legal advice. In this situation, for example, it would focus on ensuring that the information sought was phrased in a way that would allow it to be used concretely in the selection process, and perhaps in a subsequent contract.

Executing the contract

Legal and probity advisers can be expensive. Nevertheless, the contract-signing stage is not the time to stint on making use of either legal or probity advice. Careful review by both types of advisers will help minimise subsequent problems, particularly any residual ambiguities about the respective rights and obligations of the parties to the contract. Legal advisers should also double-check that all government requirements have been covered: for example, ready access to a consultant's premises for audit purposes.

Too often, government agencies rely on the hope of being able to terminate a contract if a consultant does not perform to expectations. One of the many pitfalls of such an approach is illustrated by the case of Amann Aviation, where termination of the contract backfired on a government agency seeking proactively to forestall what it saw as an impending problem.

In March 1987, Amann Aviation won the contract to provide coastal surveillance services in northern Australia. Its tender had indicated that acquisition of resources was feasible, but it was soon apparent that the company was not in a position to begin operations by the start-up date, so the Commonwealth terminated the contract. In a subsequent court case, damages of over $5 million were awarded against the Commonwealth.

Seddon (2004, p 31) points out that wrongfully terminating a contract is itself a serious breach of a contract, 'which then provides the other party with the right to terminate and seek damages'; and 'in the Amann Aviation case the mistake made by the Commonwealth was to by-pass the show cause procedure that was written into the contract. The Commonwealth proceeded straight to termination without giving the contractor an opportunity to show cause [why the contract should not be terminated for breach of contract by Amann]' (Seddon 2004, p 31, footnote 115).

Seddon (2004, p 12) also draws attention to judicial authority supporting the principle that 'the government is required to adhere to higher standards of conduct than is expected of private sector entities [Government as a 'moral exemplar']'. The principle may be interpreted in particular cases as posing a dilemma for government (Seddon 2004, p 15) because it must act both in the interests of the beneficiary (the people it represents), as well as the contractor (a citizen, or a business that could be destroyed if the full force of a contractual remedy were exercised).

Managing consultants during the project

While most government manuals specify, in a fair amount of detail, formal rules and requirements for letting tenders, they are far less forthcoming on how to manage consultants successfully once a contract has been entered into. This is not surprising, given that successful management of contracts and consultants is primarily a case of managing human relationships. And the definitive manual for the perfect management of relationships is yet to be written.

A good contract, which includes clauses on arbitration, payment on the basis of clear milestones, termination, and scope for graduated incentives, is an essential foundation. However, good consultants need to be managed, not closely supervised or controlled. Their desire for repeat business will generally ensure that they are receptive to a client's needs. But clarity of purpose and good, regular communication on the part of the client are also essential ingredients to a successful project.

Project Charter

No matter how good the initial Statement of Requirement in the tender documentation, it pays to have the consultant prepare a Project Charter (project plan) before commencing work on a large project.

The Project Charter should be based on discussion with the client. Beginning with a statement of the purpose of the project and expected outputs, it should include details of any analytical frameworks or methodologies to be used, a schedule of milestones and payments, a schedule of review meetings to allow both sides to take stock of progress, any required clarification about respective roles and expectations and any additional information about the project. The Charter then becomes the basic operational reference document for both parties and forms the basis for managing the project.

A key advantage in asking the consultant to prepare the Charter is that it will help confirm that their understanding of project objectives and requirements accords with those of the client. Given that the client's own views and nuances about project aims and outcomes may have changed since release of tender documentation, a restatement will be doubly useful. Care needs to be taken, however, to ensure that the project does not change materially in scope from the one described in the tender process: if it does, it is worth discussing the implications with the legal and probity advisers as soon as possible.

Contract variations

Any material changes to the scope of the work involved in the contract – including any introduced in the Project Charter – may constitute variations to the contract. However, a variation to the contract may arise even if not agreed in writing. A trap for the unwary is an informal discussion or agreement between a client and a consultant which is not treated at the time as a formal variation because of the positive spirit of co-operation that may exist, or because it does not seem to be important enough. If in doubt, seek legal advice at an early stage and ensure that file notes are kept of all discussions.

Milestones

Contracts usually contain or append a schedule of major milestones to be achieved by the consultant. For example, the schedule may list the dates of expected delivery for items such as the Project Charter, production of the first (and subsequent) draft reports or chapters, finalisation of any surveys or data compilation, and so on. Good contracts also ensure that payments to a consultant are linked directly to achievement of milestones.

Maintaining an issues log

An issues log is a useful means of keeping track not only of issues that require resolution, but also of discussions that may constitute a variation to the contract. It also provides a ready-made agenda for regular meetings with consultants, and can be used to keep records of such meetings.

A simple table – divided into 'open' (current, yet to be completed) issues and 'closed' (finalised, resolved) issues – is all that is required. As open issues are resolved, they are moved (cut and pasted in electronic form) to the 'closed' section of the table to maintain a historical record (as shown in Table 7.1).

Sign-off

Where a cooperative relationship exists between the client and consultant, and where progress has been documented throughout (for example, in an issues log), there should be little difficulty in agreeing when the project has been completed. If the client has 'signed off' progressively on milestones, there remains only a final 'sign-off' to indicate completion.

Table 7.1 Issues log: open and closed issues

No.	Date	Open issue	Resolution	Date
21	12 Jul	Budgetary implications of recommendations need to be assessed before Additional Estimates.	13 Jul meeting: keep under review.	
28	14 Jul	Consultant requested to attend special meeting with another agency.	20 Aug: difficulties in arranging meeting due to interagency policy differences.	
51	15 Oct	Agency asked consultant to confirm specifically that project is on track, and that no extra work was being done that would lead to a claim for additional fees.	15 Oct: on track. 23 Dec: reconfirmed.	

No.	Date	Closed issue	Resolution	Date
1	15 Jan	Consultant requires clarification of process for claiming expenses.	15 Jan: agreed that tax invoices to be submitted to Mr Smith.	15 Jan
2	23 Jan	Consultant raised problems regarding database.	23 Jan: agreed that Ms Jones will check data.	26 Feb
			25 Feb: IT section requested to provide software to enable transfer of revised data to consultant.	
			26 Feb: consultant confirms receipt of data.	
3	12 Feb ...		...	...

The term 'sign-off' to a consultant means final acceptance by the client of work done. It implies fulfilment of the contract, and the consultant would normally expect full payment of any residual owing under the contract. So it is important for government clients to appreciate the significance of the term 'sign-off' if serious misunderstandings are to be avoided.

For example, one central government agency engaged a consultant to produce a manual to a very tight timeframe. The material was to be prepared in stages, agreed by the agency and then printed professionally prior to delivery of a training course by the consultant. Asked by the consultant to sign off on the chapters of the manual as they were completed, the agency's contact officer did so, but subsequently requested major revisions, well after the material had been sent to the printer. The consultant suffered considerable embarrassment because course participants were left with the impression that the consultant had been unable to deliver the manual in time for the course and was therefore at fault.

On the other hand, a major risk for a client providing sign-off is that it will be given without a reconciliation process first being undertaken to check that all agreed outputs have in fact been delivered. A project reconciliation should take into account the record shown in the Issues Log, the contract itself, and any contract variations.

Evaluation

Evaluations of projects seem to be more the exception than the norm. However, a quick evaluation of the process that was followed, from drafting of the initial business case to final sign-off, can be useful in terms of lessons learned for the future. Additional value can sometimes be extracted by actively involving the consultant in the evaluation process to ensure that all perspectives have been covered.

Data capture

One of the great tragedies of devolved government is the lack of ready access to data and corporate knowledge. One consequence is that research projects or policy studies may duplicate previous work, wasting resources. Or a potentially expensive project may not proceed for apparent lack of data that have actually been collected in the past.

Government agencies and private researchers can archive their studies and the data upon which they are based at the Australian Social Science Data Archive at the Australian National University (<assda.anu.edu.au>). This public archive is discussed in greater length by Argyrous in chapter 8. New Zealand's Statisphere facility makes available statistics collected by government departments (<www.statisphere.govt.nz>), but not research data.

A research project may generate a wealth of information, but the amount that can be gleaned from it is limited by time, money, skills, and inclination of the research team working on the project. By lodging the data with public archives, others that are interested in the topic area can analyse them to a depth that may not have been possible, and with skills that may not have been available, when the data were first gathered.

Warning signs of potential problems

Any number of things can go wrong at any stage of a project. There is no 'cookbook' that can reliably inform us of potential problems.

Assuming that care has been taken to put in place mitigation strategies to cover major identified risks, that a rigorous selection process was followed in choosing the consultant, that a viable and realistic contract is in place, and that every effort has been made to foster a cooperative relationship with the consultant, there is little else that can probably be done. Nevertheless, a degree of continued vigilance can pay further dividends in terms of avoiding unforeseen problems.

If the consultant appears to adopt an exclusive approach of the 'just leave it to us, we'll fix it' type, or intimates that the client's staff do not understand the requirements of the project, then a serious and detailed discussion is warranted to ensure that the project stays on track from the client's perspective. One symptom noted by an agency that experienced this attitude was persistent late arrival for scheduled meetings without apology or explanation, a problem that was quickly remedied by protesting to the firm's hierarchy.

However, the corollary of government agency staff adopting a dismissive or contemptuous attitude towards a consultant can equally harm an otherwise productive relationship. Good people-management practice will ultimately generate better results, be it directed at consultants or the government staff themselves.

A degree of judgment and balance is required when monitoring the work undertaken by a consultant. Consultants are not staff and should not be supervised in the same way: they are hired for their specialist skills and abilities. Some consultants are happy to just go away and complete tasks, delivering to milestone dates. If they have demonstrated this ability before, it is probably a good modus operandi for both parties. At the other extreme, some agencies exercise micro-control, expecting consultants to sit at their assigned desks and report regularly to a 'supervisor': most consultants would be driven to the point of exasperation at such behavior by the client, and are unlikely to produce their best work in these circumstances.

Good consultants make a point of checking regularly with a client that everything is proceeding to the client's satisfaction. Such checking may take place once a week, or even on a daily basis in the case of a large project. If the consultant does not make a practice of communicating regularly with the client, or noticeably reduces the amount of communication, then it pays to find out why. The corollary from the consultant's perspective is when the clients begin to distance themselves from the job, either by losing interest or by suggesting that the consultant take charge and finalise the project.

Excessive 'library research' may indicate a lack of expertise or an inability to come to grips with the project at hand. Alternatively, an excessive focus on producing a report, rather than dealing with people or investigating issues, may presage a quick report that will have little lasting relevance or effect.

If a written report is an important output of the consultancy, watch out for consultants who use 'guru language'. If the consultant recommends 'leveraging off the knowledge base to achieve optimal organisational alignment in a contextual framework', you may need to find a translator. Similarly, beware the 'package bender' who is familiar with only one technique or approach and seeks to adapt all issues and problems into the one pre-packaged framework. A good check is to ask the bidder during the selection process to present several alternative ways of approaching an issue or problem.

The role of 'small' consultants

Consultants come in various shapes and sizes, both physically and in their professional capabilities. Large companies – such as the 'big 4' accountancy and professional services firms – employ relatively large numbers of people in various locations across Australia. They are therefore able to draw, if necessary, on a large pool of talent that includes a range of experience and expertise. They can also substitute staff, if required – for example, if a key person falls ill. And their size and reputation means that their reports are often perceived as being more authoritative. All of these characteristics understandably make them particularly attractive to risk-averse public servants.

But 'small' consultants – those working alone or in groups of several people – are also available to provide advice on a range of specialised areas. As baby boomers retire from the workforce, many of them take on part-time consulting work, and academics often supplement their incomes or their research funds with consulting work. There are good reasons why public servants should consider hiring 'small' consultants in appropriate circumstances.

Retired public servants who turn to consulting in order to remain mentally active, or to supplement other income, are often repositories of substantial corporate knowledge. Even where their knowledge is not specific to an agency, their ability to write in a 'public service' style, and to understand the policy context of work undertaken, can enable them to make a valuable contribution.

More importantly, a ready reserve of academics with specialised skills and retired public servants with policy experience and first-hand knowledge of government processes helps maintain competitive pressure on the larger firms. This pressure helps keep fees lower than they would otherwise be (at the margin, as economists are wont to say), particularly for smaller jobs. In the longer term, therefore, fostering the continued availability of small consultants helps public service agencies to continue to obtain value for money.

Reducing red tape

A number of initiatives could help reduce the administrative and resource burdens on consultants; but particularly on small consultants. Four examples are provided below.

1. *Harmonisation of tender documentation.* Significant amounts of time are spent by consultants in responding to tenders. Familiarisation with the contents of a Request for Tender, undertaking background research to ensure that the bid is 'pitched' correctly, locating any supporting documentation required, formatting the bid in the manner required, and physically delivering a bid, is time-consuming: it can take a couple of days, even for simple tenders.

   Small consultants in particular need to invest proportionately greater effort, or to seek assistance, to understand the idiosyncratic formats and styles of the many sections and divisions of the various government agencies in Australia and New Zealand. The different requirements of each agency partially explain the diversity in form: but while flexibility is essential, some degree of standardisation could also be beneficial.

   Even a very simple format based on the sequence of steps outlined in the section above on tender documentation, with explanatory and guidance notes inserted in each part, would facilitate harmonisation of content and of responses.

2. *Standardised contracts.* Resource savings could also be achieved by standardising contracts across government agencies. In 2002, the Australian Government Solicitor developed a set of three (long form, short form, and minimalist) standardised funding agreements to reflect the contractual nature of grant funding made available by a number of Commonwealth agencies to eligible recipients (Australian Government Solicitor 2002). Unfortunately, they appear to have gradually fallen into

disuse. Despite the fact that each clause had been agreed by participating agencies, in-house lawyers and program areas within each agency gradually reverted back to preferred words.

One possible solution that merits consideration in the future is to adopt an agreed standard contract, but with a covering note or a schedule that draws the reader's attention to the difference between its own formulation and clauses contained in the standardised contract. Contract users would be able to quickly ascertain whether a specific contract differed materially from the standard one.

3. *More flexible panel arrangements.* Panels are excellent flexibility mechanisms that ensure value for money because they are based on competitive selection while minimising the resource costs of the selection process. The disadvantage is that arrangements are fixed for several years. New consultants (for example, firms expanding their operations from other cities) are effectively locked out of contention until the initial panel period expires. Similarly, if consulting fees generally fall, an agency can end up paying more than the market rate until expiry of the panel period. And if fees generally rise, then agencies may find it difficult to obtain panel consulting services in a tight market because consultants will tend to accept jobs from agencies that are paying higher fees. An intermediate approach might be to incorporate in the panel arrangements a mid-term or annual 'window' that allows a pre-specified number of new members to be selected and placed on the panel.

4. *Excessive insurance cover.* Agencies probably fail to appreciate the negative consequences of requiring high levels of professional indemnity insurance. The cost of insurance is inevitably passed back to government as consulting fees rise to recover some of the additional cost. Worse still, discouraged small consultants will dropped out of bidding processes, thus reducing competitive pressures. High levels of insurance may be justified if a rigorous risk analysis indicates a need for it. But such analyses do not seem to take place very often, if at all. And few agencies seem to take into account the difficulty of actually suing a consultant for damages in a court of law unless tangible harm has been incurred; unlike commercial operations where the harm can be readily assessed in terms of loss of profit.

Conclusion

Busy managers and researchers often need to supplement the skills and resources available to them, and consultants offer a ready means for doing so. However, there are many potential pitfalls in engaging consultants, not least because of the formidable body of public service rules and case law that govern the area (see Dobes, 2006, for more detail).

A structured, considered approach is an obvious prerequisite to ensuring a smooth tender process. However, the golden key to ensuring value for money is ultimately to treat consultants as professionals, rather than as servants or slaves.

8 Sources and uses of secondary data

George Argyrous

Secondary data are an abundant resource for the policy researcher. The amount of information available to researchers has exploded in the past ten to 15 years, partly as a result of better information collection and storage systems and partly as a result of the development of the Internet, which connects many of these stores of information. Yet Australian texts on research methods are strangely silent on this ever-growing body of research material.

This chapter fills this gap by exploring the various sources of secondary data and the uses to which they can be put in a research project. The starting point is the definition of *secondary data*: 'existing data, collected for the purposes of a prior study, in order to pursue a research interest which is distinct from that of the original work' (Heaton 1998). Two examples may help to understand this definition. Information from a survey I conduct to explore how a local government policy has affected local residents constitute primary data for that research question. If I then make the survey data available for other researchers with a different question in mind, the survey provides secondary data for these other topics. Similarly, a public sector agency may keep records of the demographic profile of its employees to help it monitor its own 'equity in hiring' program. If the agency then makes these records available to me to address my research question as to whether the age profile of employees in the public sector has changed over time, these employment records are secondary data for my project.

The term 'secondary data' is usually synonymous with 'someone else's data', but this is not necessarily so. I may have collected survey data for a research project into recreational habits of a community in 2003. In 2008 I am asked to investigate the factors that affect gambling behavior and remember that I included some questions on gambling in the 2003 survey, so I extract the results and reanalyse them in light of this new question. From the standpoint of my current project on gambling behaviour, the survey results from 2003 constitute secondary data, even though I collected them. The important point is that because they were not collected with my current project in mind there are special issues and concerns that need to be addressed.

Advantages of secondary data

There are a number of advantages to secondary data analysis as compared to primary data collection methods such as interviews and questionnaires. According to Procter (1996) these advantages include:

1. *Cost.* It is often impossible for individual researchers or small policy units to undertake surveys on a scale to match large public and private organisations. Apart from incidental costs such as the purchase of data, secondary data can be obtained as easily as clicking on a web link.

2. *Time.* Secondary data are available for analysis relatively quickly. With digital data storage and retrieval systems, secondary data are available almost instantaneously. However, it is important to recognise issues related to secondary data that may actually slow down a project, such as the time needed to find the data and to arrange data in a format suitable for analysis, especially when using multiple data sources.

3. *Quality.* Secondary data are often collected by trained, experienced field staff, samples carefully selected, and question wording refined through stringent pilot-testing.

4. *Access to 'difficult' populations.* Some groups of interest may not be easily accessed (such as indigenous groups living in remote areas) other than through an agency that has a special connection with them and has

the resources to collect data from them.

5. *Availability of longitudinal data.* Many secondary data sets are collected at regular intervals to give comprehensive time series. If you are interested in changes over time, secondary data can cover a very long period.

Alongside these advantages there may be a number of disadvantages to using secondary rather than primary data to answer a research question:

1. *Validity.* The major concern that researchers have when using existing data relates to the validity of the variables that make up that data set. A common example is the definition of employment and unemployment in official statistics. The classification of people by official statistical agencies into the broad categories that make up 'employment status' depends on very specific criteria. For example, anyone who works for payment for at least one hour in the two weeks before the Labour Force Survey is conducted is considered 'employed', thus capturing people who worked for one or 100 hours. Conversely, someone who worked long hours in their home cleaning, cooking and caring for children. but who is not paid to do so, is not classified as employed, nor are people doing voluntary work. Moreover, someone who would like to work, but has not been actively looking for work because they feel there is no prospect for them of finding employment, is not officially classified as unemployed, but rather is considered as 'not in the labour force'.

2. *Limited quality control.* It can be very difficult to check the extent to which the people who collected secondary data followed proper practices in important areas such as the training of data collection teams. We often take it on trust that secondary data have come out of a process that followed appropriate procedures, but this trust can rarely be guaranteed.

3. *Limited familiarity with the data.* Collecting data for yourself can give you a thorough sense of what the data 'mean'. Primary researchers are more 'in tune' with fine points such as the precise questions that generated a series of data, the scales upon which responses were recorded, and the sequence in which questions were asked. While secondary data can be obtained quickly, a great deal of time can subsequently be involved in 'getting to know' the data.

4. *Data gaps*. It is rare that any single existing data set will contain all the information you need to answer your research question. These gaps in the data may render any one set of information useless on its own, requiring the information to be supplemented by either other secondary sources or by primary data collection methods. Other problems then arise from the fact that data were obtained from different sources, using different methods, and at different points in time.

Sources of secondary data

The biggest problem confronting researchers who wish to use secondary data in their own research is the amount of data 'out there'. Our ability to store vast quantities of information, and to make these available across the world via the Internet, can make a search for relevant data overwhelming: how do we know where to start and when to finish? Specialists in information management and retrieval, such as librarians, can assist this search. Employing such specialists in the early stages of research to conduct a search for relevant material can save time, energy, and expense.

There are four potential sources of secondary data for your study. The first source is *individual empirical studies* that are discovered through a literature search. This task has been made much easier than it once was by the development of online databases of journals and other publications that can be searched using appropriate keywords. Academics, consultants, public sector agencies and private researchers produce such studies, and the study authors can be approached for access to the data upon which the studies were based.

A second source of secondary data are the *administrative records* routinely collected by government, business, and community organisations as part of their operations, but which may be of interest to others conducting research. An approach to organisations that operate in the area relevant to your study may turn up information you did not realise existed. For example, a study of welfare recipients in a particular area may include an approach to the Department of Community Services or not-for-profit charities operating in the area.

The remaining two sources of secondary data also are official statistical agencies and public archives of secondary data. The importance of each of these sources requires us to discuss them in some detail in the following sections.

Official statistical agencies

Most nations have official agencies whose main task is to collect information on a wide range of topics and issues; in Australia this is the Australian Bureau of Statistics (ABS). Such agencies have been in operation for many years, ans so provide comprehensive time series data for many topics. These agencies also use international standards of data collection and concept definition, so the data they provide can be used for comparative analysis across countries.

Relevant national data from the official agencies are also brought together by international data collection agencies to facilitate cross-country comparisons. The World Bank (<www.worldbank.org>) is especially worth noting, since it provides a comprehensive set of data across countries, and these are organised by topics. It also generates some data series that are not available at the individual country level.

The ABS makes available a collection of statistics that is too extensive to even begin to detail here. But a sense of it breadth can be gleaned from the themes into which the data sets are classified. Table 8.1 presents these themes and the broader classifications into which the themes are grouped. To illustrate the kind of information that exists within these themes, Figure 8.1 provides a snapshot of the ABS home page for the Crime and Justice theme.

One feature stands out about the ABS web site: the ABS does more than provide data. In particular, it provides:

- discussion of a theme's development as an area of data collection, and future plans for data collection;
- publications that describe in detail the methods of data collection and their limitations;
- publications that describe in detail how a concept such as 'crime' is defined and measured;
- links to other sources of related information, so that if you do not want to restrict yourself to official statistics, the ABS can still be a useful starting point for your search; and
- for-a-fee consulting services to assist researchers conduct their own study or to access unpublished data tailored to their needs.

Table 8.1 Australian Bureau of Statistics themes for statistics collections

Economy
- Business Indicators
- Balance of Payments
- Business Demography
- Finance

- Foreign Investment and
  Foreign Debt
- Foreign Trade
- Prices

- Government Finance
  Statistics
- National Accounts

Industry
- Agriculture
- Building and Construction
- Innovation, Science and
  Technology

- Manufacturing Statistics
- Mining
- Retail

- Service Industries Statistics
- Tourism
- Transport

People
- Ageing
- Census
- Children and Youth
- Crime and Justice
- Culture and Recreation
- Demography

- Disability, Ageing and
  Carers
- Housing
- Personal, Family,
  Household Finances
- Education and Training

- Family and Community
- Health
- Indigenous
- Labour
- Migrant and Ethnicity
- Social Capital

Regional
- Regional Statistics
- New South Wales
- Victoria

- Queensland
- South Australia
- Western Australia

- Tasmania
- Northern Territory
- ACT

Environment and Energy

Figure 8.1 ABS Crime and Justice theme home page

Themes - National Centre for Crime and Justice Statistics

Crime and justice statistics provide measures of the levels and effects of criminal activity, as well as people's perceptions of their safety. These are issues that impact directly or indirectly on the quality of people's lives, and are seen as key indicators of, and contributors to, the wellbeing of society. They are of value to users in government involved in policy development and decision-making, the administrators and practitioners within the crime and justice sector, researchers and the community as a whole.

This theme page provides a guide to both ABS and non-ABS crime and justice data, with statistics and information available on aspects of crime and criminal justice. Included are links to further sources of information. Many of these links will take you to the Main Features or Media Releases of publications which you can view online, or follow further links to purchase additional information.

Noticeboard
Information on what's new, newsletters, work in progress and latest updates.

Other Related Sources of Information
Non ABS links and sources of information.

Crime and Justice Releases
Release information including statistical publications, upcoming releases, media releases and other relevant indicators.

Frequently Asked Questions
Answers provided to frequently asked questions about crime and justice statistics.

Using Crime and Justice Statistics
Information for interpreting statistics.

Contacts
Contact details for Crime and Justice inquiries.

This page first published 5 August 2005, last updated 5 June 2008

Using the Census

The most important data made available by the ABS (and similar agencies) come from the Census of Population and Housing, held every five years. The most recent Census in Australia was held in 2006 and data from this Census are now available.

There are three interrelated choices involved in accessing Census data:

1. Determine the geographic region of interest.
2. Determine the form of presentation.
3. Determine the topic for which information is to be presented.

The data collected from the Census come from households and the people that occupy them, either on the night of the Census, or that usually reside in the household. These households need be clustered into geographic areas; due to confidentiality restrictions it is not possible to obtain data on individual households. The smallest geographic area for which data can be obtained for Australia is the census collection district (CD). In the 2006 Census there were 34,500 collection districts, each of which comprise, on average, about 220 dwellings. The largest area for which data are available is the whole of Australia. Between the collection district level and the national level are various aggregations of collection districts, including local government areas, urban centres, and state and federal electorates.

Data for a given geographic region can be presented in various ways:

- *QuickStats*. QuickStats is a summary of a selection of general topics relating to persons, families and dwellings for a chosen area, benchmarked against the data for Australia; it is not inclusive of all Census topics. QuickStats also contains a small textual description of the statistics contained within the tables. QuickStats presents the tables of information in your web browser window, which limits the ability to extract the tables and manipulate them for further analysis and presentation.
- *Census Tables*. Census Tables are individual tables of Census data, available for a range of topics. These individual tables are available as downloadable spreadsheets for manipulation on your own computer.
- *Community Profiles*. A Community Profile is a large collection of individual tables for a selected area. Each Community Profile provides

key Census characteristics relating to persons, families and dwellings and covers most topics on the Census form. Box 8.1 briefly describes the different Community Profiles available.

Box 8.1 ABS Census Community Profiles series

The ABS Census data can be presented in any of the following profiles for specified geographic area:

- *Basic Community Profile.* Basic demographic information for an area, including age, ancestry, income, education, family type and more. The data are based on place of usual residence.
- *Indigenous Profile.* Key Census characteristics of Aboriginal and Torres Strait Islander persons, families and dwellings. Includes comparisons with non-Indigenous people. The data are based on place of usual residence.
- *Time Series Profile.* Contains tables similar to those in the Basic Community Profile, comprising comparable data from the 1996, 2001 and 2006 Censuses. The data are based on place of enumeration.
- *Place of Enumeration Profile.* Basic demographic information for an area, including age, ancestry, income, education, family type and more. The data are based on place of enumeration.
- *Expanded Community Profile.* This is the most comprehensive Community Profile in the series, providing extended data on key Census characteristics of persons, families and dwellings. The data are based on place of usual residence.
- *Working Population Profile.* Labour force and employment characteristics of people who are employed in a particular geographic area. The data are based on place of employment.

- *MapStats*. The MapStats product is designed to provide users with quick and easy access to thematically mapped Census statistics. The maps depict selected population, ethnicity, education, family, income, labour force and dwelling characteristics. An example of MapStats showing people born overseas as a percentage of the total population in the New South Wales State Electoral Division of Fairfield is presented in Figure 8.2. This electorate is divided into the collection districts that fall within its boundaries, and each collection district is colour-coded according to the percentage of people born overseas. This provides a visual assessment of areas of relatively high or low concentrations of people according to this characteristic.

Figure 8.2 People born overseas as a percentage of the total population, based on place of usual residence, 2006. Fairfield State Electoral Division by Census collection district.

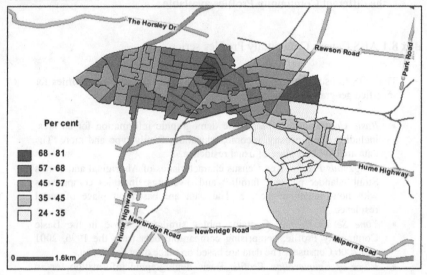

For the Census Tables and MapStats products we also need to choose the topics for which information is to be presented (QuickStats and Community Profiles provide data on a predefined set of topics; for these formats users do not get a choice of topics). The amount of information that can be obtained varies according to the geographic area selected. For some individual collection districts only a limited amount of information is available, due to the difficulty of maintaining confidentiality if detailed breakdowns are given at such a small area level. The most complete set is for Australia as a whole.

Public archives

The daunting task of finding other people's research data has been simplified by the emergence of well known and highly regarded repositories of secondary data. The vast amount of data available has led to the development of *public archives* that bring together data from various sources, both public and private. These public archives catalogue data sets by topics and use a consistent system for releasing the data and their associated information, such as the original survey instrument and codebooks used for entering the data into electronic format. They also provide a search tool that can quickly find data in the archives that may be relevant to your question.

The major public archive in the world is the Inter-University Consortium for Political and Social Research, at the University of Michigan, <www.icpsr.umich.edu>. This archive is misnamed, as it houses data on more topics than just political and social research, such as health data.

In Australia the main data repository is the Australian Social Science Data Archive, <assda.anu.edu.au>. This site houses official statistics from the ABS, as well as data sets from public sector agencies, university-based researchers and the private sector. Lodgment of data is voluntary, so it is not a comprehensive archive of all data, but despite this it contains a wealth of information. The ASSDA catalogues all the data it holds in a systematic and comprehensive way so that not only can we find useful data, we can also assess its quality and background information, and compare this to other useful data sets. The catalogue entry for each data set contains the following information:

- *Metadata*. These give information about the research that generated the data, including the bibliographic citation; study scope; methodology and processing information; data access conditions; and other study description materials such the codebook, questionnaire, and other studies that have used the data set. The metadata also include descriptions of the data, such as the number of cases and variables.
- *Variable descriptions*. Each variable in the data set is listed and a frequency count for each variable is presented.

These public data archives, and the official agencies discussed earlier, now provide tools that allow users to undertake online statistical analysis of data sets. The tools for this analysis are accessed through the web pages for each site, so no special software is needed, although most data sets are also available for download so that they can be analysed using software located on your own computer such as Microsoft Excel and SPSS. At the very least, simple frequency counts and graphs can be generated for the variables in the data set, but other more advanced options are sometimes available, such as crosstabulations and correlation analysis.

Uses of secondary data

Secondary data can play a number of uses in a research project. But before listing these, it is worth mentioning one important practical point: never work with the only copy of data you have obtained. You should always make a duplicate of the data set in the form in which you received it. As you work and analyse data, the set may change: you might change the labels, or create new variables based on recalculations of the existing ones, or add annotations of your own. However, it may be necessary to go back and see what the data set looked like in its original form. A backup of a data set that has taken time and money to obtain is also an obvious insurance policy against loss.

Once the data have been obtained, duplicated and a backup made, the data can be then put to a number of uses. First, they can form the substance of the project. For example, a local government agency may want to construct a demographic profile of its local area to better assess the needs of the population and the services it provides. A detailed analysis of Census data for the local area is thereby undertaken, with these data being the sole inputs into the analysis. Second, secondary data can form a benchmark against which primary data can be compared. A local government authority, for example, may plan a large survey of its service users, and the survey data will form the main data for analysis. The authority may in addition to this primary data analysis, obtain Census data for the demographic profile of the local area and compare these with the survey of service users to ensure that the survey respondents are representative of the community. Third, an investigation of previous research can be an important part of the exploratory stage of primary research. Reanalysing existing data can help focus a prospective study, and identify gaps or inconsistencies that primary research can then address.

Last, a major use of secondary data relates not to the data as such, but rather the questions or methods by which they were obtained. If a public agency wishes to survey its users and as part of this survey wants a measure of ethnic diversity, it can, for example, find the actual questions that were used in the Census to measure this variable, rather than invent a suitable question itself. Figure 8.3 provides one such question from the 2006 Australian Census, which asks respondents about languages other than English spoken at home, which can be used as an indictor of ethnic background.

Drawing on the work of experienced researchers who have already tested methods for gathering data such as question wording and scale construction can minimise work for yourself, as well as increase the ability to benchmark results against past research. In this example, the ABS has carefully determined which languages are worth explicitly stating, due to their prevalence in the community, and also has provided clear instructions for respondents who speak more than one non-English language at home.

Figure 8.3 2006 Australian Census question on ethnic background

16 Does the person speak a language other than English *at home*?	No, English only – **Go to 18**
• Mark one box only	Yes, Italian
• If more than one language other than English, write the one that is spoken most often.	Yes, Greek
	Yes, Cantonese
• Remember to mark the box like this: ▬	Yes, Arabic
	Yes, Vietnamese
	Yes, Mandarin
	Yes, other – please specify

Questions to ask when using secondary data

When you have identified a data source, you need to ask a number of questions about its relevance and quality before using it in a study. Some of these questions are asked of the agency or individual providing the data, while others are questions you might 'ask' of the data themselves. The following is a checklist of such questions (the first four points come directly from Nicoll and Beyea, 1999, pp 432–3):

1. *Who collected the data?* What is their reputation? Did they have adequate resources for data collection?
2. *Why were the data collected?* Are the interests of the collecting person, agency, or institution congruent with the purpose of the proposed research?
3. *Are there any geographic or demographic limitations to the data?*
4. *When were the data collected?* Are the data out of date?
5. *How were the data collected?* Was the study design a survey or case study, and what was the actual method of data collection (for example, questionnaires, interviews, observation)?
6. *How were the variables defined?* Do these definitions suit my study?
7. *For longitudinal data, have the methods of collection and variable definitions changed over time?* For example, in 1978 the ABS made a major change to the way it collected information on employment and unemployment, adopting a monthly survey format. This had the effect of making it difficult to compare data before and after this change.

8. *In what format are the data available?* If data are only available on paper the savings accrued by not having to gather primary data may be counterbalanced by the cost of data entry where computer analysis is required. Even if the data are available in digital format, is the format compatible with the software you plan to use for analysing the data? To avoid these issues, especially when purchasing data, you may wish to specify the program that you will be using for analysis, or else specify that the data are stored in a generic format such as a tab-delimited ASCII file.

9. *What is the size of the sample?* What was the sampling frame and the response rate and do these suggest any kind of bias in the data obtained?

10. *Are the data collection instrument* (for example, questionnaire, interview schedule) *and the field team instructions available?*

11. *What restrictions, including ethical concerns, are there on the use of the data?* Did the people who originally contributed responses consent to the use of the data thus obtained in future studies, and if not, does this limit your ability to use the original data?

12. *Are the data in 'raw' form (unit records) or summarised into higher aggregates?* For example, an agency may only be able to provide highly aggregated data such as the number of welfare recipients for each state, whereas you may need these numbers broken down to the local government area.

13. *Was the data collection process itself based on previous research?*

14. *What are the costs for purchasing data?*

Conclusion

The availability of data from a wide range of sources and periods of time make secondary data analysis an attractive option when compared to the costs and practical problems of gathering data for oneself. The resources now provided by public sector data collection agencies and public archives have made such data easier to access and use, making them even more attractive. However, the use of secondary data is not without its own issues and potential pitfalls, which may result in hidden costs.

9 A user's guide to sample surveys
Australian Bureau of Statistics

A major aspect of any research is the gathering of information, and there are a number of alternative methods for doing so. These include focus groups, controlled experiments, secondary data sources, and sample surveys. There are a number of factors that need to be considered before deciding to commission or undertake a survey, whether the survey results will be used as the basis for decision-making, to allocate funds, to analyse the outcome of policies or programs, or to determine the direction of future operations. This chapter will assist researchers and managers identify some of these factors, analyse their requirements and select appropriate methods of collecting the information.

Populations and samples

Before undertaking any research or study it is essential to define the purposes of the study and to translate these into specific information requirements. The first consideration is to define the *target population*. The target population must be an identifiable group that is relevant to the study. Examples of target populations are persons aged 65 and over, retail businesses in a specific urban area, and motor vehicles produced in a given year.

Having defined the population or group under study, the next step is to decide what information needs to be collected. For example, a study may be aimed at describing a target population in terms of specific characteristics such as age, sex, income or employment group, or may be far more subjective in nature, collecting information on such factors as background, community attitudes or opinions.

A survey is a means of collecting this type of information – called *data* – through the use of a standardised collection instrument such as a questionnaire. In a *census* the objective of the survey is to collect data for every member of the population under study. The advantages of a census include:

- data will be truly representative of the whole population;
- data are generally available at highly disaggregated levels, for example, for small geographic areas or sub-sets of the population. This breakdown of data allows detailed cross-tabulations, such as age by sex by country of birth; and
- benchmark data may be obtained for future studies, for example, a census of retail establishments may yield data on stocks, turnover or employment. This census can then be used to determine a suitable sampling frame (or list of the members of a population or group) for future surveys, such as a survey of part-time/full-time employment.

The main disadvantages of a census are:

- resource costs are large, both in staff and monetary terms;
- the number of questions asked has to be kept as small as possible, so as to minimise both the reporting burden on data providers and costs;
- it may be difficult to approach all members of the population within a reasonable time; and
- processing time is slow, so the results may become available too late to be useful.

A full enumeration of the target population may be a very large project with associated logistical problems. This can lead to errors in the resultant data output that could be avoided in a smaller *sample survey*. Thus, a small survey conducted effectively may result in higher quality results than a full-scale census where available resources can be stretched too far.

In a sample survey, only a part of the total population is approached for information on the topic under study. These data are then 'expanded' or 'weighted' to represent the target population as a whole. Advantages of sample surveys include:

- resource costs are generally significantly lower than for a census;
- more, or more detailed, questions can be asked; and
- results can be available far more quickly.

The major disadvantages of sample surveys are:

- data may not be representative of the total population, particularly where the number of respondents is small; and
- finely classified data (for example, small area data) are generally not available.

Survey data collection methods

There are a number of methods for collecting survey data and the choice between these depends on a number of factors. It should be stressed at the outset that the success of the survey will depend to a large extent on the suitability and appropriateness of the collection method chosen.

The nature of the questions, and in particular the depth and complexity of the topics to be covered, will in many cases dictate the collection method to be employed. Similarly the quality of responses sought may determine the choice of an appropriate collection method; for example, it is difficult to obtain detailed answers to complex questions by telephone or mail survey, whereas personal face-to-face interviews generally yield a greater depth of response.

The quality and reliability of survey data can be affected by the degree of response to a survey. Although it is rare to achieve a 100 per cent response rate for any survey, choice of collection method can influence the response rate obtained. For example, telephone interviews usually achieve a far better response rate than mail questionnaires.

Where staff and/or financial resources are limited the researcher may be constrained to use, for example, mail-out techniques for the collection phase of the survey because of the lower cost. Often this will conflict with the quality requirements of the survey. In these circumstances the researcher must try to achieve an acceptable compromise, or seek resources or cost savings elsewhere.

As with resources, the time constraints on the survey may dictate the choice of methodology. Telephone surveys (particularly using computer-assisted telephone interviewing) are much quicker than mail-out surveys or personal interviews. However, savings in time often necessitate sacrifices in the complexity or sensitivity of the questions asked, and the depth of responses received.

The type and quality of the sampling frame (the list of 'members' from which the sample is to be selected) may influence the choice of collection method. For example, to conduct a mail survey it is necessary to have a list of the names and addresses of all elements in the sampling frame. If this is unavailable there may be no option but to use personal interviews and an area-based frame for the survey.

The commonly used collection methods can be divided into two basic types: *personal interview* and *self-enumeration*. These in turn can be further divided, and some methods use a combination of the elements. In choosing a collection method for a survey, the advantages and disadvantages of each type of method should be assessed in the light of the influencing factors discussed above.

Personal interviews

There are two types of personal interviewing: face-to-face and telephone interviews.

As the name suggests, the *face-to-face interview* method involves having an interviewer visit each 'member' selected for the survey. This form of data collection is highly effective in terms of establishing rapport, boosting response rates and data quality, and collecting sensitive or complex data. However, the disadvantages of personal interviews are the costs (in staff, time, and money required to obtain, train, and manage an interviewer workforce), the possibility of bias being introduced by interviewers, the cost of supervision, and the cost of 'call backs' when respondents are unavailable.

Telephone interviewing has a number of advantages over face-to-face interviewing: costs are usually lower because fewer staff is required; interview times are generally shorter and there are no travel costs; supervision may be centralised; and 'call backs' and follow-up are quick and inexpensive.

The disadvantages of telephone surveys include the difficulty of establishing rapport with respondents, which can lead to lower response rates. Other disadvantages include the ease with which the respondent can terminate the interview, thus leading to problems of partial response; the need for questionnaires to be brief and simple to avoid boredom or fatigue on the part of the respondent; and the obvious limitation that only people with telephones can be surveyed. The exclusion of people without telephones may introduce a slight bias into the survey, if the researcher is investigating topics such as income distribution, socioeconomic groupings or employment status. There is also the issue of respondents screening calls using answering machines, which may reduce response rates and bias results. Another drawback of telephone surveys is the need for a frame of applicable telephone numbers. For example, not all private numbers are listed. This can be overcome by the use of random digit dialing (RDD). This can be inefficient, however, and can result in a large number of non-contact and out of scope calls.

Self-enumeration surveys

Self-enumeration surveys are those in which it is left to the respondents to complete the survey questionnaires. Although these are primarily postal, or mail-out surveys, they can also include hand-delivered questionnaires, and, increasingly, surveys distributed digitally via the web or email.

In many situations postal surveys can provide an effective and efficient method of data collection, particularly where information is to be collected regularly or over a long period. Postal surveys are a relatively inexpensive method of collecting data, and it is possible to distribute large numbers of questionnaires in a very short time. Other advantages of postal surveys include the ability to cover a wide geographic area, the opportunity to reach people who are otherwise difficult to contact, such as people away from home or out on business, and the convenience that it affords respondents to complete the questionnaires in their own time.

The major disadvantage of postal surveys is that they usually have lower response rates, leading to potential problems with data quality and reliability. Other disadvantages include the need for questionnaires to be kept simple and straightforward to avoid confusion or errors, the difficulties faced by respondents with only limited ability to read or write in English, and the time taken to answer correspondence or resolve queries by mail.

For surveys including businesses, a particular problem with a post-based approach is the need to ensure the appropriate person within the business receives the questionnaire. Failure to ensure that the right contact within the business receives the questionnaire can result in both low response rates and poor quality information.

An alternative form of the self-enumerated survey is where questionnaires are delivered to, and/or collected from, the respondents personally by an 'interviewer' or collector. This method usually results in improved response rates (compared with a postal survey) and is particularly suitable where information needs to be collected from several members of a household, some of whom may be unavailable when an interviewer calls. Disadvantages of this methodology include the cost, the need for the questionnaire to still be relatively straightforward and the difficulty of achieving a sufficient level or quality of response.

Computer-assisted interviewing

Computer-assisted interviewing (CAI) is a technique applying modern computer technology to telephone and, sometimes, personal interviewing. It involves the use of a computer to collect, store, manipulate and transmit data relating to interviews conducted between the interviewer and respondents. Advantages of computer-assisted interviewing include:

- *Timeliness*. CAI speeds up the whole survey process by integrating data collection, data entry and data editing and by allowing data to pass directly from data collection to analysis, therefore enabling users to receive analysed data more quickly.
- *Improved data quality*. With CAI, sequencing of the questionnaire based on an individual respondent's answers is automatic; respondents thereby only receive the questions that are relevant to them. Furthermore, errors can be automatically identified during interview, and inconsistencies in the respondent's answers can be more readily queried, thereby allowing corrections to be made to answers during the interview stage.
- *Flexibility*. CAI questionnaires can be altered and added to relatively quickly, allowing faster response to users' needs.

A particular strength of CAI is the capacity to handle complex surveys and, for repeated surveys, to offset high development costs through repeated application of the survey.

The main disadvantages of CAT are the high start-up and maintenance costs for equipment, software, site preparation, and so on, and the need for interviewers with computer or typing skills involving consequent training overheads. The CAI instrument needs to be completely specified and coded before survey enumeration commences. This includes instructions that would be common sense to an interviewer working with a printed questionnaire. For example, interruptions to interviews must be planned for and the capacity to move back through the questionnaire to revisit a question must be provided.

Questionnaire design

An integral part of any sample survey is the questionnaire through which information is to be gathered. The design of the questionnaire can influence the response rate achieved by the survey, the quality of responses gained, and the reliability of conclusions drawn from the survey results.

The central aim of a questionnaire is to collect accurate and relevant data. In order to achieve this, the questionnaire should:

- enable respondents to complete it accurately within a reasonable time;
- be properly administered by the interviewers;
- use language that is readily understood by respondents;
- appear uncluttered on the form or screen; and
- be easily processed by both people and machines.

Since the first four considerations may conflict with the fifth, it is important to use a well-designed form to reduce this conflict. To facilitate respondents' completion of the form, a researcher first needs to ascertain whether the information sought is readily available from the respondents. Next, the questions should be designed to prevent confusion arising in the mind of the respondent. A number of actions can be taken that will avoid respondents being confused by the questions:

- maintain a logical order in the sequencing of questions (Figure 9.1);
- minimise and simplify instructions and explanatory notes;
- provide clear instructions or explanations before rather than after directing respondents to 'jump' to a new question;
- make any sequencing instructions very obvious;
- provide for all possible response variations, including not applicable, zero, and non-response;
- avoid 'leading' questions, which assume a certain response to a question not explicitly asked (for example, 'which cinemas do you attend?' assumes the respondent goes to cinemas);

Figure 9.1 Example of a question sequence

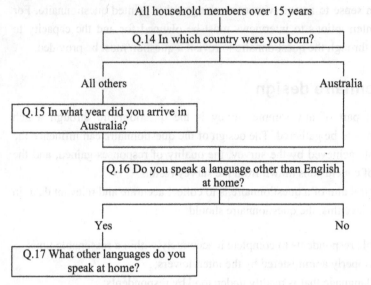

All household members over 15 years

Q.14 In which country were you born?

All others

Q.15 In what year did you arrive in Australia?

Australia

Q.16 Do you speak a language other than English at home?

Yes

Q.17 What other languages do you speak at home?

No

- making questions simple–complicated or double-barrelled questions increase the likelihood of errors and non-response, as well as making responses difficult to interpret; and
- trying to reduce memory bias. Respondents tend to remember what should have been done rather than what was done, and they tend to include in a reference period events that occurred outside the reference period. Where possible, framing questions that relate to respondents' own record-keeping improves accurate reporting. Minimising the recall period can also reduce memory bias. For example, recalling events that happened 'last month' is easier than for 'the same month one year ago'.

It is also important to consider how the answers on the form will be processed to produce statistics. To facilitate accurate processing of the survey data, space should be provided on the form for coding answers. If the data are to be entered into a computer system directly from the questionnaire, the codes for each type of answer should be displayed clearly on the form.

Questionnaires should be tested during the development stage. It is essential that questionnaire testing be implemented for all new surveys, and for existing surveys on which substantial modifications have been made, to determine whether the objectives are likely to be met by the proposed questionnaire.

Question types

Questions may generally be classified as one of two types – open or closed – according to the degree of freedom allowed in answering the question. In choosing question types, consideration should be given to factors such as the kind of information that is sought, ease of processing, and the availability of time, money and personnel.

Open questions allow respondents to answer in their own words. The answer box or area should allow sufficient space for a high percentage of the likely answers (Figure 9.2).

Figure 9.2 Example of an open question

What is the main kind of activity carried out by this department?	

It is often a good idea to provide some directions or examples on how to answer an open question and to make it clear how the respondent should answer if a 'not applicable', 'zero', or 'non-response' applies (Figure 9.3).

Figure 9.3 Example of an open question

How many full-time staff work in this department? (write NIL if there are no full-time staff)	

The questions need to be understood by all respondents in the same way. Even an apparently simple question can be understood in different ways. For example, the question 'How much diesel fuel did this business use in the year 2008?' may be answered in several ways: in 'litres', 'gallons' or as a 'dollar value'. A more precise way of asking for this information, where quantity could be derived from value, is shown in Figure 9.4:

Figure 9.4 Example of an open question

What was the amount in dollars spent on diesel fuel in 2008?	$

The advantages of open questions are that they allow many possible answers and they can collect exact values from a wide range of possible responses. Open questions are often used in pilot testing to determine the range of possible answers and the availability of the data being sought.

The disadvantages of open questions are that they are more demanding than closed questions both to answer and to process. In particular, processing problems arise from the need to create a coding frame to interpret a variety of responses. Processing errors can also arise from the difficulty of reading poor handwriting.

Closed questions can be of several types, reflecting the style of response permitted. They are generally cheaper, easier to answer, and easier to process than open questions. Closed questions are appropriate when the researcher can anticipate most of the responses and when exact values are not needed.

The disadvantage of closed questions is that they require significantly more effort than open questions in the development and testing stages. The different types of closed questions are listed below.

- *Limited choice* questions are those questions that require a respondent to choose between one of two mutually exclusive answers (for example, yes or no).
- *Multiple choice* questions require a respondent to choose one of a number of responses provided.
- *Checklist questions* allow a respondent to choose more than one of the responses provided. The responses to such a checklist can be improved by presenting each item in the list with a 'yes' or 'no' option, rather than 'tick all appropriate', as this demands closer attention to the items in the list by the respondent.
- *Partially closed questions* provide a set of responses where the last alternative is 'other, please specify'. Partially closed questions are useful when it is difficult or impractical to list all possible choices.
- *Attitudinal questions* generally seek to locate a respondent's opinion on a rating scale with a limited number of points. For example, respondents may be asked to rate their level of satisfaction with the service provided by a government agency, with 'not at all satisfied', 'somewhat satisfied', and 'very satisfied' as the options. Special care should be taken when designing attitudinal questions because they are interpreted subjectively and this interpretation can differ between respondents. Respondents may also have difficulty interpreting the scale correctly; if there are a large number of similar questions, respondents are likely to answer in a hurried or careless fashion; and expressions of attitude can differ markedly from actual behavior.

Choosing between question types

The choice between question types depends upon a number of factors including:

- the researcher's data requirements;
- the level of accuracy needed;
- the sort of information which is potentially available from respondents;
- the processing system to be used to code and analyse the survey results;
- the experience of respondents (that is, whether the survey is to be conducted regularly or once only);
- the position of questions on the form; and
- the sensitivity of the question (closed questions generally elicit more positive responses to sensitive topics than open questions).

Once the questions have been chosen they should be tested to determine whether the best choice has been made. Testing is discussed in more detail later in this chapter.

Sequencing

The sequence of questions should be designed to:

- encourage respondents to complete the questionnaire and to maintain their interest in it;
- facilitate respondents' recall;
- direct respondents to the information source;
- be relevant to respondents' own record-keeping, if any;
- appear sensible to respondents; and
- focus on the issue under consideration.

The questions on a form should follow a sequence that is logical to the respondents. Regardless of the method used to administer the questionnaire, the sequence should flow smoothly from one question to the next. It is a good idea to start the questionnaire with simple, straightforward questions that both promote interest in the survey and establish respondents' confidence in their ability to answer the remaining questions. In particular, the opening questions should establish (if necessary) that the respondent is a member of the survey target population.

The remaining questions should be logically structured so that the interviewer or respondent does not need to alternate between pages of the questionnaire. Questions on related topics should be grouped together and all questions on a particular topic should be asked before proceeding to another topic. Care should be taken to use a logic or grouping that reflects the understanding of the respondents targeted for the survey.

Questions that may be sensitive to respondents should generally not be placed at the beginning of a questionnaire. Rather, they should be placed in a section of the form where they are most meaningful in the context of relevant questions. In this way the format of the questionnaire can act as a buffer to help the respondent feel more comfortable with sensitive questions. For example, asking respondents about gambling behavior might be sensitive, but putting it in the context of questions regarding recreational activities more generally may make it less sensitive. Also, placing sensitive questions last minimises the impact of a possible refusal.

Filtering can be used to ensure that respondents answer only those parts of the questionnaire that are relevant. This is achieved by the use of filter questions, which direct respondents to skip questions that do not apply to them. Filter questions also help respondents to understand the sequence of questions and they are simpler to follow than conditional questions. An example of a filter question is shown in Figure 9.5.

Figure 9.5 Example of a filter question

Q1. Were you born in Australia?	Yes — Go to Q.3 No
Q2. In which country were you born?	
Q3. Do you speak a language other than English?	Yes No

This filter question in Figure 9.5 is preferable to the conditional question shown in Figure 9.6. With conditional questions it is not clear whether a blank answer represents a non-response, a 'don't know' or 'not applicable' response.

Figure 9.6 Example of a conditional question

Q1. If you were not born in Australia, in which country were you born?	

In general, filter questions should place the option likely to be answered by most respondents first to minimise respondents answering questions that are not applicable to them. In Figure 9.5 'yes' was listed first because it is anticipated that most respondents were born in Australia. If this question appeared in a survey of service users in an area with a large migrant community, the order of the answer options might be reversed. In fact, it is very common for filter questions to place the 'no' response before the 'yes' response because it is often the 'no' response that directs respondents to a subsequent question. Respondents then do not have to read the 'yes' response.

Filter questions are useful in situations where respondents are being asked for attitudinal information. They are used to ensure that the respondent actually has an attitude or a view about a particular topic or subject before asking for that view. For example, a respondent may be asked 'Do you have views about <topic>' before being asked those views, to ensure that people who have no real interest in a topic do not influence the results for that part of a survey.

Language

Careful wording of questions is essential to ensure that respondents understand questions correctly and do not misinterpret them. A number of techniques can be used to facilitate correct and quick understanding:

- Use short sentences that convey a single item of information rather than long sentences.
- Arrange clauses within each sentence in chronological order. For example, 'Read the instructions then fill in the form' is more quickly understood than 'Before you fill in the form, read the instructions'.
- Ask positive questions rather than negative ones. For example, 'Are you: married, single, ...? Tick one.' is easier to understand and can be answered more quickly than 'Place an X in the box next to those items that do not apply'.
- Use the active voice rather than the passive voice. Active voice is when the subject performs the action: for example, 'The operator is to complete this form'. Passive voice is when the subject is acted upon, for example: 'This return is to be completed by the operator'.
- Avoid making nouns out of verbs. For example, 'The Managing Director must certify this document' is clearer and more direct than 'Certification of this document must be done by the Managing Director'.

- Use a conversational style rather than omitting helpful phrases for the sake of brevity. An example of conversational style is: 'Please comment on any unusual events that affected your agricultural activity this year. Some examples are drought, flood, fires and hailstorms'. This example is clearer than 'Comment here on unusual circumstances (drought, flood, fires, hailstorms, etc.)'.
- Use words of one or two syllables rather than longer words unless the longer words are very familiar to most people.
- Provide some context for words whose meaning can change in different circumstances. For example, the set of relationships that constitutes a 'family' can be very different across respondents.
- It is important to describe briefly the purpose of the survey and how the statistics will be used. Avoid using technical and statistical terms or, if they must be used, explain them in plain English.
- Use simple punctuation such as commas, full stops, and question marks. If a semi-colon or a succession of commas is needed, the sentence should be broken into at least two shorter sentences.

In general, the wording of questions should be as direct as possible and should avoid being ambiguous, too general, or using vague words such as 'occasionally' and 'often'. The meaning a researcher attaches to a word may not be the meaning respondents attach to it. Things that appear clear to people in the know are often not so clear to the general population. The best way to find out is to test the questions with a group of respondents. If necessary, the questions can then be re-worded and re-tested until the respondents' understanding of the questions matches the researcher's understanding.

Questionnaire construction

The questionnaire should be physically set out so as to minimise the time needed to interview, respond, and process the results. Specifically, consideration should be given to the form's construction, graphics, and layout.

Construction. The number of pages should be as many as are needed for a clear layout. A small, short form may be cramped, difficult to read and complete, and may compromise the results of the survey. It is also important for the paper to be sufficiently opaque so that writing and printing on one side of the paper do not show through to the other side. If a booklet is used, the staples should be on the spine. (Printers refer to this as saddle stitching.)

Graphics. The aim should be to unclutter the page by removing all unnecessary ink. Using the following guidelines for typography, colour, and ruled lines can increase the speed and accuracy of responses:

- Line length should be no more than can be read in two or three eye fixations (about 115 mm) – an advantage for poor readers.
- Upper case text is difficult to read, and should be avoided if possible.
- Avoid ornate and decorative typefaces. Serif type fonts (for example, Times New Roman) are easier to read for questions than sans serif types (for example, Helvetica).
- The top line of questions should overhang subsequent lines to clearly separate questions.
- Left align text where possible.
- Leading is another point to consider and refers to the amount of space between lines on the form.
- The background colour of the form should contrast sufficiently with the text to facilitate reading and office processing. For example, black text should be used with white or orange backgrounds.
- Use the minimum number of lines to do the job.
- Lines should be as thin as possible to do the job.
- If using 'yes' and 'no' tick boxes, be consistent in whether 'yes' or 'no' appears first. It is generally preferable for 'yes' to appear first although when using filter questions, the 'no' response will often appear first, as discussed above.

Layout. Two basic principles should be followed when designing the layout of a form. First, the graphics standards should be applied consistently throughout the form. Second, the sequence of material presented in the form should match the sequence that respondents are expected to follow when filling out the form. Any notes to questions should appear with the relevant questions so that respondents do not have to alternate between different parts of the form. Enabling respondents to progress through the form one step at a time reduces the likelihood of errors.

Page margins should be 5 mm for the top, bottom and two side margins. The layout within these boundaries can be either full-page (single-column) format or split-page (double-column) format. These two formats should not be mixed on the one page. If instructions or explanations are to be incorporated with the questions, full-page format is preferable as there is sufficient room to allow for this. If a large number of short questions and answers are being used, split-page format offers a better use of space. Split-page format also has the advantages of being easier to read (owing to shorter lines) and of providing a clearer, linear progression for respondents to follow.

Sample design

Sample design covers the areas of sampling frame, sample size and sampling methodology. Aspects to be considered within these areas include:

- accuracy required;
- cost;
- timing; and
- strata

This section describes some alternative sample designs and how to choose the most appropriate one for a particular researcher's requirements. It should be noted that the descriptions given are outlines and additional assistance from a statistician is recommended. In particular, efficient sample design can introduce complexities that are best dealt with by an expert survey methodologist.

A *sampling frame* is a list of all members of the target population for the survey. For example, a sampling frame may be the electoral roll, the membership list of a club, or a register of schools.

For most sampling methodologies it is important to have a complete list from which to select a sample, otherwise the sample may not accurately represent the target population. In practice, however, it can be difficult to compile a complete and reliable list of all population members. Any known deficiencies in the coverage of the sampling frame should be stated when the survey results are documented. Flaws in the sampling frame can include omissions, duplications and incorrect entries. Omissions are very common and can be particularly serious as the omitted members may have a common characteristic. If there are too many flaws in the frame then the survey results should be used to generalise only about those types of population members that are included in the sampling frame.

Each member of the sampling frame should have a known non-zero probability of being selected in the sample. If a suitable sampling frame does not exist and cannot readily be constructed by the researcher, an alternative method of collecting data should be considered.

Sample size

A number of factors are involved in choosing a *sample size* for a survey, such as:

- the resources (time, money and personnel) available to conduct the survey;
- the level of accuracy required for the results;
- the amount of detail needed in the results;
- the proportion of the population with the attributes being measured;
- whether members of the target population differ greatly from one another on those attributes (that is, the variability of the attributes being measured);
- the expected levels of non-response; and
- other aspects of the sample design used.

Estimates based on information from a sample of units in a population are subject to sampling variability. That is, they may differ from the figures that would have been obtained had the entire population been surveyed. A large sample is more likely than a small sample to produce results that closely resemble those that would be obtained if a census was conducted; this is what is meant by the standard of 'accuracy' in this context. This difference between survey results, or *estimates*, and census results can be measured by the *standard error*.

When determining sample size, a researcher faces a basic trade-off. He or she may wish to minimise the size of the standard error in order to maximise the accuracy of the survey results. In this event, the sample size can be as large as resources permit. Alternatively, the researcher may wish to specify in advance the size of the standard error to be achieved, in order to minimise the costs of the survey. In this case, the sample size is chosen to produce the specified size of standard error.

The standard error is used to construct a *confidence interval* that is expected to include the 'true value'. A confidence interval is a range of values within which we believe the true population value 'falls'. For example, we might be interested in the percentage of service users who are satisfied with the service they have received. For the population of all service users there will be a specific percentage that is satisfied. From a sample of service users we construct a *confidence interval* within which we believe this true population value falls. We construct an interval of values because we need to take into account the effect that error due to random sampling can have on a sample outcome.

This trade-off between sample size (and therefore cost) and the size of the confidence interval is expressed in Table 9.1 and Table 9.2. Assume that in a sample of 200 users of a government service, 80 per cent felt satisfied with the service they had received. To be 95 per cent confident that our confidence interval takes in the true population percentage of satisfied service users, the interval will be 80 plus or minus 5.5 per cent; that is, the interval will be 74.5– 85.5 per cent (go down the 'sample size' column until you reach the row for 200, and then across the columns to the one headed 80/20). If we double the sample size to 400, the confidence interval shrinks to plus or minus 3.9 per cent; we estimate that the percentage of the whole population that is satisfied with the service falls between 76.1–83.9 per cent.

This table can be used to determine sample size in the planning stages of research by making an assumption as to what the sample result will be, and then adjusting the interval according to the result actually obtained if it does not prove to agree with this assumption (see Box 9.1 for an example). The calculations involved in determining these intervals are beyond the scope of this chapter. See Argyrous (2005, ch 17) for details. There are also many websites that will calculate the sample size needed to achieve a desired level of accuracy, given certain assumptions about the population. These can be found at <statpages.org> or by using 'statistical calculation pages' as a search term.

The other trade-off we have to make in determining sample size is the *confidence* we have that the sample results will be accurate. In the previous example, we wanted to be 95 per cent confident that the sample size will produce a result with a certain level of accuracy (measured by the width of the confidence interval). This is the conventional level that is commonly used, but there may be instances, given the importance of any decisions we may make on the basis of the survey results, where we want to be more confident that our estimates include the true population value. For example, if we want to be 99 per cent confident that a confidence interval derived from a sample of 200 people included the 'true' percentage of all service users who are satisfied with a service, the confidence interval will be plus or minus 7.3 per cent rather than 5.5 per cent (Table 9.2). Thus confidence comes at the cost of accuracy, and this may have to be compensated for by drawing a larger sample, especially if the confidence interval becomes so wide that it is of no practical use.

Table 9.1 Sampling errors for a binomial distribution (95% confidence level)

Sample size	Binomial percentage distribution					
	50/50	60/40	70/30	80/20	90/10	95/5
50	13.3	13.1	12.4	11.1	9.0	7.4
100	9.6	9.4	8.9	7.8	6.1	4.8
150	7.9	7.7	7.3	6.4	4.9	3.8
200	6.9	6.7	6.3	5.5	4.3	3.2
250	6.2	6.0	5.7	5.0	3.8	2.9
300	5.6	5.5	5.2	4.5	3.4	2.6
400	4.9	4.8	4.5	3.9	3.0	2.2
500	4.4	4.3	4.0	3.5	2.7	2.0
600	4.0	3.9	3.7	3.2	2.4	1.8
700	3.7	3.6	3.4	3.0	2.2	1.6
800	3.5	3.4	3.2	2.8	2.1	1.5
900	3.3	3.2	3.0	2.6	2.0	1.4
1000	3.1	3.0	2.8	2.5	1.9	1.4
1100	2.9	2.9	2.7	2.4	1.8	1.3
1200	2.8	2.8	2.6	2.3	1.7	1.2
1300	2.7	2.7	2.5	2.2	1.6	1.2
1400	2.6	2.6	2.4	2.1	1.6	1.2
2000	2.2	2.1	2.0	1.8	1.3	1.0
10,000	1.0	1.0	0.9	0.8	0.6	0.4

Table 9.2 Sampling errors for a binomial distribution (99% confidence level)

Sample size	Binomial percentage distribution					
	50/50	60/40	70/30	80/20	90/10	95/5
50	17.6	17.3	16.3	14.6	11.8	9.0
100	12.6	12.4	11.7	10.3	8.1	6.3
150	10.4	10.2	9.6	8.4	6.5	5.0
200	9.0	8.9	8.3	7.3	5.6	4.3
250	8.1	7.9	7.4	6.6	5.1	4.0
300	7.4	7.3	6.8	6.0	4.5	3.4
400	6.4	6.3	5.9	5.2	3.9	2.9
500	5.7	5.6	5.3	4.6	3.5	2.6
600	5.2	5.1	4.8	4.2	3.2	2.4
700	4.9	4.8	4.5	3.9	2.9	2.2
800	4.5	4.5	4.2	3.6	2.8	2.0
900	4.3	4.2	3.9	3.4	2.6	1.9
1000	4.1	4.0	3.7	3.3	2.5	1.8
1100	3.9	3.8	3.6	3.1	2.3	1.7
1200	3.7	3.6	3.4	3.0	2.2	1.6
1300	3.6	3.5	3.3	2.9	2.2	1.6
1400	3.4	3.4	3.2	2.8	2.1	1.5
2000	2.9	2.8	2.6	2.3	1.7	1.3
10,000	1.3	1.3	1.2	1.0	0.8	0.6

Box 9.1 Example of selecting sample size

A researcher wishes to measure the percentage of dwellings with electrical safety switches installed. The government safety authority believes that the percentage is approximately 40 per cent and needs to know how many dwellings should be sampled to obtain an estimate with a confidence interval of plus or minus 5 per cent with a 95 per cent confidence level that this interval takes in the true population value.

From Table 9.1, we read across the column to the one headed 60/40. We then move down the column until we reach a sampling error value of 5 per cent (or the closest to it). In this instance the value is 4.8. We then read back across the columns to the left-hand column and see that the needed sample size is 400.

If this survey was then completed with a sample size of $n = 400$ and it was found that the sample percentage of dwellings with safety switches is 30 per cent (not 40 per cent as believed), then the sampling error of this sample percentage of 30 per cent is plus or minus 4.5 per cent (refer to the column headed 70/30 in Table 9.1 and the row for sample size of 400). The 95 per cent confidence interval for the sample proportion (that is 30 per cent) would be from 25.5 per cent to 34.5 per cent.

The example we have used – of estimating the population of service users who are satisfied – assumes a simple random sample is to be selected from a population of infinite size. If more complex sampling techniques (such as clustering or stratification) are used, alternative formulas and calculations are required than those behind Table 9.1 and Table 9.2. Similarly, if we are interested in statistical properties of a population other than the percentage that meet a specific criterion, such as the mean or standard deviation, different calculations are involved. Online calculators for many of these specific situations are available from the <statpages.org> website.

If the survey seeks to produce detailed results that include cross-classifications, it is important that the sample size of each sub-group be large enough to produce reliable estimates (that is, with low standard errors) for the sub-group. A useful approach is to draw up a blank table showing all the characteristics to be cross-classified. The more cells there are in the table, the larger will be the sample size needed to produce reliable estimates. This larger sample size, in turn, will require more resources to conduct the survey.

The number of cells in a table is determined by both the number of characteristics to be cross-classified and the number of categories for each characteristic. For example, a table cross-classifying ten age categories by two sex categories by ten birthplace categories will have 200 cells, a table cross-classifying five age categories by two sex categories by two birthplace categories will have 20 cells, and a table cross-classifying ten age categories by two sex categories will have 20 cells.

Sample size should be increased to compensate for expected levels of non-response. However, the characteristics of non-respondents may differ markedly from those of respondents. The survey results could therefore be misleading even if a sufficient number of responses are obtained to produce low standard errors. The higher the non-response rate, the more accentuated this effect will be because the sample represents less of the target population. Selecting larger sample sizes to achieve target response levels may not be an appropriate means of compensating for high non-response as those responding may still be unrepresentative of the target population. The first aim should be to minimise non-response.

Sampling methodology

A number of alternative methodologies can be used to select a sample for a survey. The choice between these methodologies depends on considerations such as the nature of the target population, the nature of any supplementary information that can be obtained, the levels of accuracy desired, the availability of sampling frames, personnel, processing facilities, funds, and the time available to complete the survey. Each of these factors can influence the accuracy of the survey estimates for a given sample size. The reverse is also true – for a given level of accuracy these factors can affect the sample size required.

With *simple random sampling*, each member of the sampling frame has an equal chance of selection and each possible sample of a given size has an equal chance of being selected. Every member of the sampling frame is numbered sequentially and a random selection process is applied to the numbers. The random selection process may involve, for example, using a table of random numbers or randomly selecting numbered balls. The advantage of simple random sampling is that it is easy to apply when small samples are involved. The disadvantages are that it requires a complete list of members of the target population and it is very cumbersome to use for large samples.

Systematic sampling uses a fixed interval to select members from a sampling frame. For example, every twentieth member may be chosen from the frame. The size of the interval I is calculated by dividing the size of the target population N by the size of the sample required n, as follows:

$$I = \frac{N}{n}$$

The members of the frame must first be numbered sequentially. A random number is then chosen between one and the size of the sampling interval I. The member corresponding to that number is selected in the sample together with every following I^{th} member on the list. (Note: If I is not a whole number, then round it to the nearest whole number.) For example, a systematic sample of 300 service users from a list of 6000 would require a sampling interval of:

$$6000 \div 300 = 20$$

The starting point would be chosen by selecting a random number between 1 and 20 from a table of random numbers. If this number was, say, 16, the sixteenth person on the list would be selected in addition to every following twentieth person. The sample of service users would be those corresponding to the registration numbers 16; 36; 56; 76; ... ; 5936; 5956; 5976; and 5996.

The advantage of systematic sampling is that it is simpler and easier to select one random number and then every I^{th} member (for example, twentieth) on the list than to select as many random numbers as the size of the sample (for example, 300). It also gives a good spread right across the population if the list is ordered in a useful way. For example, service users can be ordered by day of the week they visit the service, and a systematic sample will yield a good spread of selections across the days as well as increase the accuracy (reduce the standard error) of the survey estimates. The disadvantage is that additional variability can be introduced if the list is ordered in a non-useful way. In general the list will be at worst random, but extreme cases can arise if poor ordering exists. For example, a frame that lists men and women on alternate lines would produce a sample of all men or all women if the selection interval were an even number. For this reason it is always a good idea to check the ordering of your population to see if systematic sampling is appropriate.

If supplementary information is available concerning the composition of the target population, it may be more efficient to use *stratified sampling* to divide the population into groups, or strata. Either simple random sampling or systematic sampling techniques are then applied to the strata rather than to the population as a whole. The strata should be as different from each other as possible, while members within each group should be as like each other as possible. Some examples of strata commonly used by the Australian Bureau of Statistics are states, industry size, age and sex.

When planning a stratified sample, a number of practical considerations should be kept in mind:

- The strata should be designed so that they collectively include all members of the target population.
- Each member must appear in only one stratum.
- The definitions or boundaries of the strata should be precise and unambiguous.

The five main benefits of stratified sampling are:

1. The representation of different groups within the sample can reflect the proportions that occur in the target population (for example, 60 per cent men, 40 per cent women).
2. Minority groups can be 'oversampled'. Greater probabilities of selection can be applied to minority groups than to the majority group. This is useful if the survey is focusing more on the minority groups than on the majority group.
3. The results are more accurate. Sampling error is reduced because of the grouping of similar units.
4. Different selection or interviewing procedures can be applied to the various strata. This is useful if the strata differ greatly in geography, topography, customs, or language.
5. Separate information can be obtained about the various strata. Stratification permits separate analyses of each group and allows different characteristics to be analysed for different groups. Stratification also enables control of an adequate sample in each group. However, analysis across strata is possible even if stratification occurs.

Stratification is most useful when the stratifying variables are simple to work with, easy to observe, and closely related to the topic of the survey. However, elaborate stratification should be avoided as difficulties with analysing the results can increase as the number of stratifying variables increases. For example, the sample sizes of the strata need to be large enough to support analysis where desired, so that as the number of stratifying variables increases, the total sample size can also increase. If a stratifying variable is difficult to observe at the sampling stage (for example, computer ownership in a household survey) it should be applied at the analysis stage instead; a procedure known as post-stratification. However, to apply post-stratification, it is necessary to know the distribution of the strata in the population.

Cluster sampling involves selecting members of the target population in groups, or clusters, rather than individually. Each member within a selected cluster is included in the sample. Examples of clusters are factories, schools, and geographic areas such as electoral subdivisions. The advantages of cluster sampling are that costs are reduced, fieldwork is simplified, and administration is more convenient than with non-clustered designs. Cluster sampling is particularly suitable for surveys aimed at regional, state, national, or even international coverage. Instead of the sample being scattered over the entire coverage area, the sample is localised in relatively few 'centres' (that is, the clusters). If the survey involves face-to-face interviews, cluster sampling facilitates the recruitment and teaching of locally based interviewers, and reduces travel time and costs. Cluster sampling also facilitates the administration of fieldwork and the supervision of interviewing. The lighter workload and simplified administrative procedures can lower costs such as salaries, office supplies, postage and telephone calls.

The main disadvantage of cluster sampling is higher sampling error (and therefore less accurate results) than for a simple random sample with the same sample size. This is because members within a cluster tend to be similar while differences between clusters can be large. The extent of the increased sampling error depends on how representative the clustered sample members are of the target population. In practice, cluster samples often need to be larger than simple random samples in order to compensate for the higher associated sampling error. In some cases, the lower costs of cluster sampling permit the sample to be expanded to the point where sampling error is actually lower than for simple random sampling with the same cost constraint.

Two-stage and multistage sampling involves selecting a sample in at least two stages. At the first stage, large groups or clusters of members of the target population are selected. These clusters are designed to contain more members than are required for the final sample. At the second stage, members are sampled from the selected clusters to derive the final sample. If more than two stages are used, the process of sampling within clusters continues until the final sample is achieved. An example of multistage sampling is first to select electoral subdivisions (clusters) from a city or state; second to select blocks of houses from within the selected electoral subdivisions; and third to select houses from within the selected blocks of houses.

As with stratified sampling, a number of practical considerations should be kept in mind when planning a multistage sample. Some of the main considerations are as follows:

- The clusters should be designed so that they collectively include all members of the target population.
- Each member must appear in only one cluster.
- The definitions or boundaries of the clusters should be precise and unambiguous. In the case of geographic clusters, natural and man-made boundaries such as rivers and roads are often used to delimit the cluster boundaries.

The advantages of multistage sampling are convenience and economy. As with cluster sampling, multistage sampling makes administration easier and reduces interviewing costs. Multistage sampling does not require a complete list of members in the target population and this greatly reduces the cost of preparing the sample. The list of members is required only for those clusters used in the final stage. At other stages, only the clusters need to be listed. The main disadvantage of multistage sampling is the same as for cluster sampling; that is, higher sampling error.

To compensate for this, larger sample sizes are needed. A design issue that needs to be addressed in working with multistage sampling is the number of units selected in each stage. If more first-stage units are selected, costs will generally increase while sampling errors decrease. If relatively more second-stage units are selected, the reverse applies. The optimal sampling scheme will take account of the cost and variance structures of the population and is quite complex. Raising the number of clusters selected in the first stage is likely to have greater cost consequences than raising the sampling fraction for later stages.

Sources of error

Two types of error can occur in sample surveys: sampling error and non-sampling error. Sampling error arises through selecting only part of the target population. Non-sampling error can occur at any stage of a survey and can also occur with censuses (that is, when every member of the target population is included). Sampling error can be measured mathematically, whereas measuring non-sampling error can be difficult. It is important for a researcher to be aware of the causes of these errors, in particular non-sampling error, so they can be either minimised or eliminated from the survey.

Sampling error

Sampling error reflects the difference between an estimate derived from a survey and the 'true value' that would be obtained if the whole target population were included. If sampling principles are applied carefully, sampling error can be kept to a minimum.

The size of the sampling error indicates how different the survey results are likely to be from the results that would be obtained from a complete enumeration of the target population. The following factors influence the size of the sampling error:

- *Sample size.* In general, larger samples give rise to smaller sampling error. However, in order to halve the size of the sampling error it is necessary to increase the sample size fourfold, which greatly increases the cost of the survey.
- *Sample design.* Stratified sampling generally reduces the size of the sampling error by reducing the variability of the population to that within each stratum, whereas cluster sampling tends to increase the error.
- *Sample/population ratio.* The larger the sample is as a proportion of the target population, the smaller will be the sampling error. However, non-sampling errors may increase as sample size increases.
- *Population variability.* When members of a target population differ widely in terms of the characteristic being measured, sampling error is greater than when the members are similar. Sample size should be increased in order to make the sample more representative of the target population and to reduce the size of the sampling error. Cluster sampling increases the size of the sampling error when the characteristic being measured is clustered in particular areas that cannot be identified in the sample design stage. Stratified sampling can reduce sampling error by reducing population variability within each stratum.

The section above regarding sample size discusses the impact of these factors on sampling error.

Non-sampling error

In principle, every operation of a survey is a potential source of *non-sampling error*. Some examples of causes of non-sampling error are non-response, bad questionnaire design, respondent bias and processing errors. Non-sampling errors can be classified as either systematic or random.

Systematic error (called bias) makes survey results unrepresentative of the target population by distorting the survey estimates in one direction. For example, if the target population is the population of Australia but the sampling frame is just males, then the survey results will not be representative of the target population due to systematic bias in the sampling frame. *Random error* can distort the results in either direction, but tends to balance out on average.

Some types of non-sampling error are:

- *Failure to identify the target population.* This can arise from the use of an inadequate sampling frame, imprecise definition of concepts, and poor coverage rules. Problems can also arise if the target population and survey population do not match very well.
- *Non-response bias.* Non-respondents may differ from respondents in relation to the attributes/variables being measured. Non-response can be total (none of the questions answered) or partial (some questions may be unanswered owing to memory problems, inability to answer, and so on). To improve response rates, care should be taken in training interviewers, assuring the respondent of confidentiality, motivating him/her to cooperate, and calling back if the respondent has been previously unavailable. 'Call backs' are successful in reducing non-response but can be expensive. Non-response is a particular problem for surveys of businesses. Care needs to be taken to ensure the right contact is reached in the business, the data required are available and an adequate follow-up strategy is in place. Good survey testing practices are vital for all surveys, especially those of businesses.
- *Questionnaire.* The content and wording of the questionnaire may be misleading and the layout of the questionnaire may make it difficult to accurately record responses. Questions should not be misleading or ambiguous, and should be directly relevant to the objectives of the survey.
- *Interviewer bias.* The way the respondent answers questions can be influenced by the interviewer's manner, choice of clothes, sex, accent,

or prompting when a respondent does not understand a question. Bias may also be introduced if interviewers receive poor training, as this may affect the way they prompt for, or record, the answers.

- *Respondent bias.* Refusal and inability to answer questions, memory biases and inaccurate information will lead to a bias in the estimates. An increasing level of respondent burden due to the number of surveys being conducted has resulted in considerable difficulty in encouraging potential respondents to participate in a survey. When designing a survey it should be remembered that uppermost in the respondent's mind will be protecting their own personal privacy, integrity and interests. Also, the way the respondent interprets the questionnaire and the wording of the answer the respondent gives can cause inaccuracies in entering the survey data. The non-availability of data can also prove to be a significant hurdle for a survey. Careful questionnaire design, effective training of interviewers and adequate survey testing can overcome these problems to some extent.

- *Processing errors.* There are four stages in the processing of the data where errors may occur: data grooming, data capture, editing and estimation. Data grooming involves preliminary checking before entering the data onto the processing system in the capture stage. Inadequate checking and quality management at this stage can introduce data loss (where data are not entered into the system) and data duplication (where the same data are entered into the system more than once). Inappropriate edit checks and inaccurate weights in the estimation procedure can also introduce errors. To minimise these errors, processing staff should be given adequate training and realistic workloads.

- *Misinterpretation of results.* This can occur if the researcher is not aware of certain factors that influence the characteristics under investigation. A researcher or any other user not involved in the collection stage of the data gathering may be unaware of trends built into the data due to the nature of the collection (for example, for a survey collecting income as a data item among all persons earning an income, the estimate would be different from the estimate produced by a survey conducted among persons found at home during daytime hours). Researchers should carefully investigate the methodology used in any given survey and how this might affect the results.

- *Time period bias.* This occurs when a survey is conducted during an unrepresentative time period. For example, a survey designed to collect data about the weekly entertainment expenditure of families in Sydney should not be conducted in the period of the Royal Easter Show as the results may be affected by the show itself. If it is required to collect information on people's recreational patterns, these can be affected noticeably by both the time of week and the time of year, and such factors would need to be kept in mind when designing a suitable questionnaire.

Non-sampling error can be difficult to measure accurately, but it can be minimised by:

- careful selection of the time the survey is conducted;
- using an up-to-date and accurate sampling frame;
- planning for 'call backs' to unavailable respondents;
- careful questionnaire design and adequate testing;
- careful design of the processing system, including edit checks;
- thorough training for interviewers and processing staff; and
- awareness of all the factors affecting the topic under consideration.

The problem of non-response

Non-response occurs when data are not collected from respondents. The proportion of these non-respondents in the sample is called the non-response rate. Non-response can be either partial or total. It is important to make all reasonable efforts to maximise the response rate as non-respondents may have differing characteristics to respondents. This causes bias in the results.

When a respondent replies to the survey answering some but not all questions, then it is called *partial non-response*. Partial non-response can arise due to memory problems, inadequate information or an inability to answer a particular question. The respondent may also refuse to answer questions if they:

- find questions particularly sensitive; or
- have been asked too many questions (the questionnaire is too long).

Total non-response can arise if a respondent cannot be contacted (the frame contains inaccurate or out-of-date contact information or the respondent is not at home), is unable to respond (possibly due to language difficulties or illness), or refuses to answer any questions.

Response rates can be improved through good survey design: short, simple questions, good form design and by explaining survey purposes and uses. Assurances of confidentiality are very important as many respondents are unwilling to respond due to privacy concerns. For business surveys, it is essential to ensure that the survey is directed to the person within the organisation who can provide the data sought. Call backs and follow-ups can increase response rates for those who, initially, were not available or were unable to reply.

Following are some hints on how to minimise refusals in a personal or telephone contact:

- use positive language;
- get the right contact, particularly for business surveys;
- state how and what you plan to do to help with the questionnaire;
- stress the importance of the survey and the authority under which the survey is being conducted;
- explain the importance of their response as representative of other units;
- emphasise the benefits from the survey results;
- give assurance of the confidentiality of the responses; and
- find out the reasons for their reluctance to participate and try to talk through them.

Other measures that can improve respondent cooperation and maximise response include:

- public awareness activities, including discussions with key organisations and interest groups, news releases, media interview and articles – these are aimed at informing the community about the survey, identifying issues of concern and addressing them; and
- using a primary approach letter, where possible, which gives respondents advance notice and explains the purposes of the survey and how the survey will be conducted.

In case of a mail survey, most of the points above can be stated in an introductory letter or through a publicity campaign. Other non-response minimisation techniques that could be used in a mail survey are:

- including a postage-paid mail-back envelope with the survey form; and
- reminder letters.

Where non-response is at an unsatisfactory level after all reasonable attempts to follow up are undertaken, bias can be reduced by imputation for item non-response (non-response to a particular question) or imputation for unit non-response (complete non-response for a unit). The main aim of imputation is to produce consistent data without going back to the respondent for the correct values, thus reducing both respondent burden and costs associated with the survey. Broadly speaking, the imputation methods fall into three main groups:

- the imputed value is derived from other information supplied by the unit;
- values by other units are used to derive a value for the non-respondent (for example, an average); and
- an exact value of another unit (called donor) is used as a value for the non-respondent (called recipient).

When deciding on the method of imputation it is desirable to know what effect imputation will have on the final estimates. If a large amount of imputation is performed the results can be misleading, particularly if the imputation used distorts the distribution of data.

If a low response rate is obtained, estimates are likely to be biased and therefore misleading. Determining the exact bias in estimates is difficult. An indication can, however, be obtained by:

- comparing the characteristics of respondents to non-respondents (for example, for a survey of attitudes to motor bike racing, which are known to be age-related, a comparison of the age distribution of respondents to non-respondents would provide an indication of non-response bias);
- comparing results with alternative sources and/or previous estimates;
- performing a post-enumeration survey on a subsample of the original sample with intensive follow-up of non-respondents.

In some cases, the achieved sample may not accurately represent the population. This could occur due to the random selection of the sample or due to differing response rates for separate population groups. We can use information from other sources to create a more accurate description of the population. Consider a sample of school children in which 30 per cent of the respondents are male and 70 per cent of the respondents are female. Through the school attendance records we have identified that there are actually 50 per cent males and 50 per cent females in the school. Estimates that we produce from our sample of children will not accurately reflect the entire school. To create more accurate estimates we adjust the weights of the respondents used to derive the estimates, so that they add up to the population total. In this example, the weight for males will be increased while that for females will be reduced.

Survey testing

Testing survey procedures is an important part of developing any survey. Testing is used to:

- assess the suitability of the chosen sampling methodology;
- estimate sampling error and variability in the target population;
- estimate likely response rates;
- identify weaknesses in sample framework, questionnaire design, and the method of data collection;
- assess field work and processing procedures; and
- estimate costs.

Types of testing

Five main types of testing are used to evaluate survey procedures: skirmishing, focus groups, observational studies, pilot testing, and dress rehearsals. Each type is used at a different stage of the survey's development and aims to test different aspects of the survey.

A *skirmish* or *pretesting* refers to an informal test of a questionnaire with small groups of respondents. The questionnaire used is usually loosely structured, with many open questions, thereby allowing the researcher to examine different ways to word questions. The questionnaire is tested by asking questions of participants and getting some feedback from them. A skirmish provides feedback on issues such as:

- the level of knowledge needed to answer the questions; and
- likely responses, and how answers are formulated.

A skirmish is used to detect flaws and awkward question wording, and can also test alternative designs. Skirmishes are often carried out at the initial developmental stage of the questionnaire or when there is insufficient time or resources available to conduct a focus group or a full pilot test.

A *focus group* (sometimes also called a discussion group) is an informal discussion of a topic with a small group of people from the survey population, often recruited to meet defined characteristics. It provides insight into the attitudes, opinions, concerns, knowledge or experiences of the participants. It is particularly useful for learning about the scope of a domain, the definitions of items of interest and the comprehension of key words. Focus groups also assist in learning about subgroups and cultures.

Focus groups can provide a wealth of detailed qualitative information because of the in-depth probing method used. Focus groups can help us to better understand how well respondents understand our concepts, definitions, question wording, and other issues about the topic. They are used to understand the range of attitudes or understanding, rather than gaining quantitative information.

Focus groups are a relatively cheap and easy way to obtain information in a short period of time. Participants can 'feed' off each other, with one comment causing someone to think of another point. Their purpose is to explore rather than to definitively describe or explain. Therefore focus groups are most often used in the very early stages of the survey development cycle. They are used mostly for new surveys, but can be used for testing changes to an existing survey before the questions are written.

However, group dynamics can interfere with the discussion, for example, extroverts can take over. This can also bias the results towards the dominant participants. Participants also tend to give 'public' opinions and therefore focus groups are not as suitable for discussion of sensitive issues.

Results from a focus group may be complicated by factors such as:

- people who are willing to take part in a focus group may not be representative of the target population; and
- the 'open-ended' nature of responses and hence the large volume of information makes analysis cumbersome.

Focus group research should be regarded as preliminary, with results not generalised to the whole population without further quantitative research.

Observational studies involve getting respondents to complete the draft questionnaire in the presence of an observer. Whilst completing the form, respondents explain their understanding of the questions and the methods required in providing the information. Respondents should be made aware that it is the form that is being tested and not the respondent. It is also important that the respondent is not given assistance in completing the form during an observational study.

Much can be gained from such studies including identifying problem questions through observations, questions asked by the respondents, or the time taken to complete particular questions. Data availability and the most appropriate person to supply the information can also be assessed through observational studies. In the development of business surveys, observational studies are important for identifying the records that are referred to when providing the data sought, so that advice can be provided to survey respondents about the types of records that assist in obtaining the data sought for the survey.

Observational studies and/or focus groups can be used to test respondent's interpretation of complex concepts. Particular groups of respondents, for which the researcher knows the correct response to a topic or series of questions, can be observed to assess whether members of these groups are able to respond appropriately to the questions.

Pilot testing involves formally testing a questionnaire or a survey with a small sample of respondents in the same way that the final survey will be conducted. Pilot testing is used to:

- identify any problems with questionnaire design, such as the format, length, wording of questions, and so on;
- compare alternative versions of a questionnaire;
- assess the adequacy of instructions to interviewers; and
- ascertain interview times.

A *dress rehearsal* is the final test of a survey where the chosen sampling methodology is used to select a small sample from the target population. Dress rehearsals are normally only part of large-scale surveys and are used to:

- evaluate survey plans;
- estimate survey costs per sampled unit (important for staffing and funding decisions);

- estimate interview, travel, and interviewer editing time per sampled unit;
- estimate variability within the population (that is, population variances) and hence sampling error; and
- evaluate the processing system design.

If appropriate information is available from previous surveys, it may be possible to estimate population variances and costs from this information rather than from the results of a dress rehearsal.

Conducting survey tests

The samples chosen for pilot tests and dress rehearsals should be as representative of the target population as possible. This maximises the validity of the test results and ensures that consequent modifications to the survey are appropriate.

Pilot tests can be used as a basis for choosing between alternative procedures for part of a survey. One approach to such testing could be to allocate two equal-size samples to interviewers and each interviewer uses both of the alternative procedures. The two techniques can then be compared without the interfering bias of differing interviewer performance.

The number of times survey testing should be conducted and the sample sizes used, are determined by the complexity of the survey and the availability of funds. For example, a simple, small survey may need only 50 respondents for a pilot test, whereas a larger, more complex survey may need 200 or more respondents.

Analysis of test results

The results of survey testing can bring to light a number of problems with questionnaire and survey design. Some of these problems may be identifiable during a skirmish; others may be identifiable only when the questionnaire is administered to a sample of the target population. Examples of the types of problems that could be highlighted are:

- non-response to a particular question by a number of respondents;
- multiple answers being given when only one should be chosen;
- a large number of 'other' or 'not applicable' responses to a particular question;

- lack of variation in the responses to a question; and
- general misunderstanding of a question.

The solution to these problems may lie in the sequencing of questions, the instructions accompanying questions, the wording of questions or the answer categories provided for questions. Changing the answer categories can produce more variation in the responses given to a question. Some techniques for doing this include:

- increasing the list of answer categories (while taking care not to make lists too lengthy);
- changing the order of this list; and
- changing the emphasis of the question and/or the answer categories.

In addition to problems with questionnaire design, survey testing may also uncover problems with the:

- sampling frame;
- sampling methodology;
- sample size;
- assumptions regarding population variability used in designing the survey;
- sources of non-sampling error;
- survey administration; and
- processing of the survey data, particularly testing the suitability of forms for data preparation.

Once identified, these problems can be addressed and either eliminated or minimised before the full survey is conducted. When used in this way, pilot testing is an invaluable tool for maximising, within resource constraints, the quality of results obtained from the final survey.

The results of pilot testing and dress rehearsals can also be used to provide a 'preview' of the results of the full survey. The data gained from the test can be analysed in the same way as the final survey, incorporating tables, statistical analyses (for example, correlations, scales, and son on) and discussion of the findings.

Collecting the data

The procedures to be followed in collecting survey data depend largely on the technique chosen, that is, self-enumeration or personal interview.

Self-enumeration surveys

Self-enumeration surveys include:

- those where questionnaires are sent out and returned through the post (postal surveys);
- those where the questionnaire is distributed through some electronic means, such as email or on the Internet; and
- those where questionnaires are delivered and/or returned by hand (hand-delivered surveys).

For *postal surveys* a questionnaire is generally mailed out with a covering letter and a reply-paid envelope. The completed questionnaire is then returned in the envelope provided. Outstanding questionnaires can be followed up by written reminders or by telephone.

The basic stationery requirements for postal surveys include questionnaires, covering letters, reminder letters, envelopes, reply-paid envelopes, and, if desired, adhesive address labels. It is a good idea to consult the post office on matters such as preferred article sizes, postage rates, and requirements for reply-paid envelopes.

To estimate the number of questionnaires, letters, and envelopes required, information from a previous, similar survey can be used (if available). If such information is not available, estimates must be based on the size of the sample and the expected response rate. For example, a survey obtaining a high initial response rate requires fewer reminder letters, envelopes and questionnaires than a survey obtaining a low initial response rate. Enclosing an additional questionnaire and reply-paid envelope with reminder letters can boost the final response rate, especially where the original questionnaire has been misplaced or discarded by a respondent. Estimates of stationery requirements should therefore include a component for additional questionnaires and reply-paid envelopes.

Before questionnaires are labelled and dispatched, a register (called a collection control register) listing all respondents selected in the survey should be compiled. The register should list each respondent's name, postal address, and some form of unique identification. (The identification, which is usually a number, enables outstanding questionnaires to be identified and followed up to improve response rate.)

When labelling questionnaires, the respondent's name, postal address, and identification number should appear on the covering letter and mail-out envelope (if window envelopes are not used). The identification number should also appear on the questionnaire so that returned questionnaires can be marked off the collection control. Spot-checks should be conducted to ensure that simple mistakes, such as the labels on the letter and/or questionnaire not matching the label on the envelope, or something being omitted from the envelope, are avoided.

As questionnaires are returned, their identification number should be marked off the collection control register. The control register can then be used to identify outstanding questionnaires that need to be followed up. Reminder letters and labels can also be produced from the register, either manually or by computer.

Reminder action should be timed to coincide with the due date or with a drop in the rate at which questionnaires are returned. To identify this time, the response rate should be calculated and updated regularly, for example, daily (the rates can be used to plot a graph, as a direct visual aid).

Reminders (whether by letter or telephone) should then be effective without being wasteful. The collection control register should be annotated to show:

- which respondents have received reminders;
- the date(s) on which reminder action was taken;
- any comments or queries from respondents; and
- which questionnaires have been returned as unclaimed mail.

In *hand-delivered surveys*, it is generally not essential to know respondents' names. A questionnaire is delivered personally by an 'interviewer' or collector who introduces and explains the survey to the respondent. The respondent completes the questionnaire in his/her own time and either returns it in the reply-paid envelope provided or gives it to the collector on his/her return. Outstanding questionnaires can be followed up by reminder letters, 'call backs' by the collector, or both. In other respects, the collection procedures and processes for hand-delivered surveys are basically the same as for postal surveys.

Interview surveys

Interview surveys can generally be conducted by one of two methods: face-to-face interviews and telephone interviews.

Many surveys are conducted by *face-to-face interview* because the units selected in the sample cannot be identified by name and address. In such cases, areas are selected and then, within these areas, dwellings, shops, factories, and such can be further selected, according to the nature of the survey,

Each interviewer is given a workload, or group of interview selections, to complete. When determining the size of a workload, consideration should be given to the:

- time taken for each interview;
- time available for interviewing;
- distances to be travelled;
- complexity of the questionnaire;
- number of interviewers available;
- total number of interviews to be conducted; and
- expected number of 'call backs' required.

Depending on how far interviewers live from the areas where interviewing is to be conducted, workloads can be distributed:

- at training or briefing sessions;
- by mail;
- by courier; or
- by interviewers collecting them from a central point.

It is important that interviewers are trained to follow consistent procedures to ensure consistency in data collection methods and to improve data quality. For example, interviewers should check that all necessary documents have been obtained before starting to interview.

It is a good idea to try to complete as many interviews as possible early in the interview period. This allows time both for 'call backs' to unavailable respondents and for clarifying any problems on the questionnaires.

Interviews should be conducted at a time convenient to respondents, even if this means calling back at a later date. In particular, it is wise to avoid calling before 9.00 a.m. or after 8.00 p.m.

The interviewer's opening remarks and the manner in which the remarks are made have a strong influence on respondents' reactions and their willingness to cooperate. Before any questions are asked, the interviewer should:

- give his or her name;
- explain that a survey is being conducted and by whom;
- provide an identification document and give the respondent time to read it – the document should include the telephone number of the survey manager or supervisor;
- explain that the respondent's household or business has been selected in the sample for the survey; and
- briefly explain the purpose of the survey.

In addition to the interviewer's attitude and ability to answer respondents' questions, the interaction between interviewer and respondent is crucial for gaining and maintaining respondents' cooperation. Some techniques the interviewer can use to improve this interaction are to:

- listen attentively;
- allow a respondent to relate personal experiences;
- keep the interview time short;
- refrain from any suggestion that one answer is more acceptable than another to the interview.

A well-designed questionnaire should include instructions to guide the interviewer through the questionnaire. It is also important for the interviewer to have a thorough knowledge of the questionnaire so that the interview can proceed smoothly. It is essential that all questions are asked exactly as worded on the questionnaire. This reduces the possibility of a question taking on a different meaning and introducing bias to the results. If a respondent has difficulty understanding a question, it should be repeated more slowly and, if necessary, explained further. However, the interviewer should avoid rewording the question in later interviews.

Respondents' answers should be recorded clearly so that they are unambiguous to processing staff. Answers are usually recorded by inserting a tick or a number in the appropriate boxes, or by writing an exact account of the respondent's answer in the space provided on the form.

To close the interview the interviewer should thank the respondent for his or her cooperation and check to see if the respondent has any further questions about the survey. Respondents should be advised if any additional or follow-up interviews are planned.

After each day's interviews have been completed, interviewers should check questionnaires for completeness, accuracy, and correct sequencing of questions. If necessary, 'call backs' for any missing information can then be planned. Any cases of refusal should be notified to the survey's manager as soon as possible.

The survey manager should also be notified of any questionnaires that are retained for 'call backs' after the date set for returning questionnaires to the office.

Where interviews are conducted over the telephone, a number of practical considerations need to be taken into account. The size of a telephone interviewer's workload should be determined realistically according to the:

- time for each interview;
- time available for interviewing;
- complexity of the questionnaire;
- number of interviewers;
- total number of interviews to be conducted; and
- expected number of telephone 'call backs' required.

Quality assurance

The basic aim of any quality assurance program is to ensure that, within resource constraints, errors are minimised. The key to quality assurance and improvement is to be able to regularly measure the cost, timeliness and accuracy of a given process so the process can be improved when a fall in quality is indicated. The emphasis is on process improvement rather than correction.

Quality assurance should be undertaken at all stages of a survey, to enhance the quality of subsequent stages and the final results. For repeating surveys, changes in processes and procedures can be implemented in subsequent cycles.

The key elements of quality assurance are preparation and evaluation. In developing a survey, there are elements of the process that are essential to realising quality outcomes. In terms of preparation, researchers should test their proposed methodology and survey technique to ensure that the correct tools have been selected and that the procedures specified are appropriate. It is also essential to prepare documentation covering each aspect of the survey well in advance, and to prepare comprehensive training programs for each aspect of the survey.

Continuing evaluation of strategies, techniques and procedures is also necessary to ensure that the lessons available from the day-to-day work of conducting the survey are used to enhance the quality of the survey outcome.

Auditing is the final aspect of quality assurance activities with potential to have an impact on the quality of survey outcomes. While testing, effective preparation and evaluation are the crucial components of quality assurance; some auditing of processes will provide indicators of the reliability and appropriateness of the techniques in use for the survey. This might take the form of probity checking of interview work or, perhaps, re-coding of survey responses. Both of these approaches can provide early and accurate sources of feedback about the performance of the techniques chosen to conduct the survey. This feedback can be used to improve these processes. Note that if monitoring of telephone interviews is a chosen quality assurance method, respondents must be warned that the telephone conversation may be monitored for quality assurance purposes.

A *post-enumeration survey or study* (PES) is a follow-up interview with a sample of respondents and non-respondents after a survey has been conducted in the field, with the aim of evaluating the quality of the data.

This may either be done through face-to-face interviews or by telephone, using questions about how the respondent completed the form and comparing the original responses with those obtained in the PES. A PES is conducted to uncover consistent errors made by respondents, and to find out why those errors are occurring. Particular aspects can be investigated in detail, if they are suspected problem areas.

In practice a PES sample will generally be selected from those who responded to the original survey or special study conducted. This will most likely be a list of 'potential' PES respondents from a particular area chosen to conduct respondent visits. This list should be randomly ordered so that the final PES respondents are a random sub-sample of the original sample. If there are any dimensions (for example, size of business) other than area to be considered, the profile of the final selections should be checked, as many respondents will decline.

Conclusion

This chapter has covered a wide range of issues that arise when a sample survey is to be administered or managed. Many of these issues are discussed very briefly, and for there is a wealth of more detailed texts to provide further guidance. Attention to the practical details raised in this chapter can help ensure that the data you obtained can answer the questions that you wish to answer. But ultimately it is the quality of the research question(s) that determines the quality of the research undertaken and the answer obtained.

10 Qualitative research methods
Ralph Hall

Qualitative research refers to a collection of research methods that yield non-numeric data. These data can be textual (as in interview transcripts), visual (as in photographs or videotapes), or aural (as in voice recordings).

Qualitative data are rich in content and varied in format. They can include transcripts of group discussions or interviews, field notes written by the researcher recording observations of a ceremony or meeting, or videotapes of children playing in a playground. Compared with the apparent objectivity, precision and structure of quantitative data, qualitative data are seemingly subjective, imprecise and unstructured.

These differences have sparked numerous controversies over the relative importance of quantitative and qualitative data in social research. Quantitatively oriented researchers argue that qualitative data do not meet scientific criteria of objectivity and precision of measurement, while qualitative researchers claim that quantitative data are devoid of context and meaning, both of which are essential to understanding complex phenomena.

It is not proposed to elaborate on this debate here. It is well summarised by Bryman (1988), in the edited collection by Reichhardt and Rallis (1994), and in many other places. The approach taken here is that qualitative research is an integral part of social science in general, and policy analysis in particular, so no defence of its status and role is necessary. The qualitative researcher contributes to the body of social scientific knowledge in ways not otherwise available.

Nor is it possible in the space of one chapter to present a comprehensive account of qualitative research. Readers are referred to the wide range of excellent texts on this subject, such as Flick (2006), Silverman and Marvasti (2008), and the collection of articles in the three-volume set of the *Handbook of Qualitative Research* (Denzin & Lincoln 2007a, b, c).

What will be attempted here is an account of the main features of qualitative research of relevance to policy work. The complexity of qualitative data means that turning these data into social scientific knowledge is a challenge. For the policy worker, this means producing knowledge of relevance to policy decisions. How this is done is the subject matter of this chapter.

Approaches to qualitative research

While quantitative research draws on a positivist or post-positivist perspective, qualitative research draws on many perspectives. As Denzin and Lincoln point out, qualitative research draws on multiple theoretical paradigms. It is, to use their terms, 'many things at the same time' (2003a, p 11).

These theoretical paradigms, or perspectives as they are referred to here, determine to a large extent what research methods will be used, how they will be used, and how the data will be analysed and interpreted.

Schwandt (2003) has distinguished three such perspectives in qualitative inquiry, namely interpretivism, hermeneutics and social constructionism. He omitted post-positivism from this classification to focus on those that reject the epistemological foundations of positivism and its successors. These perspectives are summarised in Box 10.1. More detailed descriptions can be found in Crotty (1998) or Benton and Craib (2001).

A post-positivist approach is distinguished from those approaches discussed by Schwandt by its commitment to explanation as a goal of research. This goal of explanation is rejected by interpretivism and hermeneutic approaches in favour of interpretive understanding, and by social constructionism in favour of

Box 10.1 Perspectives in policy research

Approaches to social scientific research differ in the assumptions made about how social reality is constituted and how it can be studied. The following is a brief description of the major perspectives.

- *Positivism.* All science is a unified body of knowledge based on observations made under controlled conditions. Social scientific knowledge gained in this way is objective and value free. Explanation and prediction are the goals of social science. The positivist policy researcher would seek to measure policy outputs, quantify policy decisions and explain policy outcomes.

- *Interpretivism.* Social scientific knowledge differs from natural scientific knowledge in that it is concerned with meaning and interpretation rather than explanation and prediction. The interpretivist policy researcher would seek to understand the meaning stakeholders ascribe to a policy and how this meaning relates to their response to the policy. The interpretivist would not be interested in measuring or quantifying policy decisions as this would be seen as trivialising the problem.

- *Hermeneutics.* Social scientists adapt the methods of interpretation of texts to the study of social phenomena. Social events are analysed by identifying their meaning to the individuals involved. The hermeneuticist policy researcher would adopt a similar approach to the interpretivist and for this reason the two approaches are often grouped together.

- *Social constructionism.* Social phenomena exist in a social context and knowledge about these phenomena is a product of this context. The goal of social science is to uncover the ways in which social reality is constructed by individuals and groups. The social constructionist policy researcher would focus on the social and political context within which policy decisions are made and how this social context is constructed by different stakeholder groups. Like the interpretivists, social constructionists do not consider quantitative methods appropriate for studying policy. They use in-depth interviews, focus groups and other qualitative methods.

- *Post-positivism.* Recognises the limitations of positivism by abandoning the view that observations must be objective and value free to count as scientific. To the post-positivist, social reality is much more complex than the positivists were prepared to acknowledge and needs a variety of methods to access it. The post-positivist policy researcher seeks to explain the complexity of policy-making by using a combination of quantitative and qualitative methods. Policy decisions are seen to be complex, consisting of many underlying mechanisms that can in principle be explained but not by simple cause–effect relationships.

- *Critical realism.* Critical realism is one version of post-positivism that sees social institutions as emergent phenomena reflecting underlying generative mechanisms which social science seeks to discover.

identifying social meaning. Explanation involves establishing cause–effect relationships or at least finding reasons for action. It entails an approach to qualitative data that focuses on the identification of such relationships and reasons. This approach to qualitative research brings it closer to quantitative research and is favoured by those who support integration of the two in the form of 'mixed methods research' (Tashakkori & Teddue 2003).

The absence of a unified theoretical perspective underlying qualitative research can be seen as a strength rather than as a weakness. It gives the researcher a range of options for conducting and interpreting research and opens up the possibility of gaining insights into a problem not likely to be achieved through the narrow focus of a single approach.

Designing qualitative research

The existence of alternative theoretical perspectives underpinning qualitative research means that there can be no agreed typology of qualitative research designs. As Maxwell (1998) points out, qualitative research involves an interactive model in which each component of the research design influences other components in an interactive process, rather than a linear model in which case the design follows a predetermined sequence of steps.

Maxwell identifies five components of a qualitative research design, all of which interact to determine the final design of a research project.

1. *Purposes*. Why is the study being conducted?
2. *Conceptual context*. What theory or conceptual framework underpins the study?
3. *Research questions*. What questions is the study attempting to answer?
4. *Methods*. How will data be collected and analysed?
5. *Validity*. What validity threats are there to the conclusions and how will these be dealt with?

It is the research questions that form the central component, or hub, in Maxwell's model. Other components feed into and in turn emanate from these questions. These components are in turn influenced by a number of contextual factors, including the perspective adopted by the researcher, the funding arrangements, previous studies in the field, and the role adopted by the researcher, among other considerations.

This model is diagrammed in Figure 10.1 (Maxwell, 1998, p 73, provides a more elaborate diagram). Note that the connections are shown as double-headed arrows to stress the interconnectedness of the components. Contextual factors are not shown in the diagram, although they feed into the various components, with the researcher's perspective feeding into all components because of its overarching influence on all aspects of the research design.

Figure 10.1 Maxwell's (1998) interactive model of qualitative research design

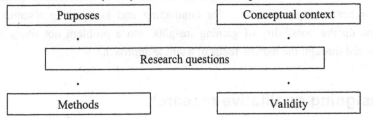

Authors such as Flick (2006), Miles and Huberman (1994) and Janesick (2003) have developed similar models of qualitative research design. All stress flexibility in design. Janesick uses the metaphor of choreography to emphasise this point. The qualitative researcher is like a choreographer, using standard procedures but improvising at points in the process.

Research questions

The central component in Maxwell's model is the research questions. They articulate what the researcher wants to find out from the study. Other aspects of the study tend to flow from the research questions, as shown in Figure 10.1.

Research questions are an integral part of any research design. In qualitative research these research questions are not fixed but are modified in response to feedback from other components of the research. This flexibility in re-evaluating the research questions is one of the strengths of qualitative research. It enables the researcher to continually monitor the research process and amend components as indicated by the outcomes at all stages of the project.

Not all kinds of research questions are appropriately addressed by qualitative research methods. As Maxwell (1998, p 84) points out, qualitative research is much better suited to answering *process* type questions, such as those concerning the meaning of events to people and the social context of those events. It is less suited to answering what he calls *variance* questions, those concerned with differences from or relationships with other events.

These differences are illustrated in Table 10.1. The broad research topic is the attitudes of male workers towards female supervisors. This broad topic can be addressed by answering more specific questions. The first research question in Table 10.1 is what Maxwell calls a variance question and is clearly not suitable for qualitative research. The second research question explores the experiences of male workers and these are not likely to be captured by a quantitative approach. Qualitative methods enable the researcher to explore many more dimensions of the issue. How this is done is the subject of the next section.

Table 10.1 Examples of research questions

Research question	Type	Appropriate method
What is the relationship between age of male sales worker and attitude towards a female supervisor?	Variance	Quantitative
What problems do male sales workers experience in working under a female supervisor?	Process	Qualitative

Collecting qualitative data

A qualitative research design consists of the research method employed and the specific data collection procedures adopted. The research method refers to the overarching design (see Hall 2008). The most common methods under which qualitative data are collected are the case study and field study methods. Some qualitative data can be collected in surveys and even experiments, but in such cases it is usually subsidiary to the quantitative data.

Primary and secondary data

In policy research much of the data exist in the form of documents such as case records, minutes of meetings, reports, memos, correspondence including emails. These are referred to as *secondary data*, and are distinguished from *primary data*, which are data collected by the researcher.

The most common methods for collecting primary data in policy research include interviews, focus groups and observational research. These methods will be described only briefly here. The reader is referred to one or more of the many detailed accounts of these methods, such as Denzin and Lincoln (2007b) or Bryman (2008).

Interviews

Interviews are a convenient way of collecting information from individuals. They can be conducted face-to-face, over the telephone or even by email. This convenience, as well as the intuitive appeal of the interview as a means of gaining information, makes it a widely used method in qualitative research.

There are many versions of qualitative interviewing, each devised to suit particular research contexts. Some of the more widely used versions are:

- *The semi-structured interview.* In this method the researcher has a set of questions or topics to be covered but the interview process is flexible enough to permit departures from these questions or topics, particularly to follow up incomplete answers or interesting leads. The main advantages of the semi-structured interview for policy researchers are that it enables the researcher to focus on the topics relevant to the issue being researched, and it facilitates comparability across interviewees.
- *The problem-centred interview.* This is a variant of the semi-structured interview described by Flick (2006). It is characterised by an orientation towards social and organisational problems and prompts interviewees about their understanding and experience of the problem area.
- *The unstructured interview.* An unstructured interview does away with formal interview schedules and adopts a conversational style. There is minimal control of the interview process by the interviewee except to keep the interview focused on the topic of the interview. The unstructured interview is useful in situations where interviewees give descriptions of life experiences such as work history or career progress.

Focus groups

The focus group method is a variant of the *group interview* in which a specific topic is explored in depth. Participants may be chosen from a homogeneous group, such as employees in a workplace, or a heterogeneous group, depending on the topic. Group size usually ranges from four to ten. The number of focus groups in any research project can vary widely (see Bryman 2004, Table 16.1) and is typically in the ten to fifteen range.

A moderator initiates the focus group discussion by introducing the topic and the participants. The role of the moderator is to keep the discussion relevant to the topic but to not otherwise contribute. The value of a focus group is to allow a group dynamic to emerge among the participants, having the effect of eliciting contributions to the topic that might not otherwise emerge. Intervention by the moderator can have the effect of inhibiting such contributions.

Focus groups can be particularly useful in policy research. Groups of stakeholders can be formed to examine issues relating to policy implementation or evaluation. These groups can be constituted either by choosing from within stakeholder organisations, or across different stakeholders. The former enables a particular stakeholder perspective to be explored, whereas the latter enables stakeholders having different viewpoints to be brought together to explore possible areas of compromise.

Observational research

Observational research involves direct observation of people going about their normal activities in their natural environment. The observations may be quantitative, such as counting certain types of activity, or qualitative, such as observing interactions between people in a meeting, or a mixture of both.

In much qualitatively oriented observational research the researcher takes on the role of a participant in the group or organisation being studied. In such cases the research is referred to as a *participant observation study*. The degree of participation by the researcher can vary from total observer, where the researcher plays no role in the group being studied, to total participant, where the researcher is in fact a member of the group. In the latter case the perspective of the insider can provide valuable insights into the group dynamics not available to an outsider. This strategy is often used in health research where, for example, nurses conduct observational studies of nursing practice.

Observational methods play an important role in policy research as they enable researchers to observe the operation of programs or the policy implementation process first-hand, as it actually takes place. This can eliminate some of the bias or subjectivity of interview or focus group research. It is, however, often a time-consuming and generates a large amount of data for analysis.

As an example of observational research, Taylor et al (1998) studied the use of open spaces by children living in urban public housing in Chicago. Courtyards were observed and the activities of children using them were recorded on four occasions. The authors found that green spaces were more conducive to creative play by the children than those spaces without vegetation.

Mixed methods research

It is common among qualitative researchers to employ more than one method of data collection in a study. This practice has become known as *mixed methods research* (Tashakkori & Teddue 2003), although it has been in existence for many decades.

Case study research and ethnographic research have always used multiple methods of data collection. Ethnography typically involves participant observation and interview methods (Boyle 1994; Tedlock 2003), and case studies can employ a range of qualitative as well as quantitative methods (see Yin 2002).

Ethnographic studies are typically extended in time as they involve intensive study of communities or groups aimed at gaining a comprehensive understanding of their culture. Most policy research has a relatively short timeframe, so traditional ethnographies have limited application. Shorter versions of ethnography have been developed that might be more suitable for policy research. Boyle (1994) describes a method she calls *particularistic ethnography*, in which the ethnographic method is applied to the study of a small group such as patients in a hospital ward. Low, Taplin and Lamb (2005) used what they call a *rapid ethnographic assessment procedure* (REAP) to study the impact of the 9/11 disaster on residents of Battery Park City, a community adjacent to the former World Trade Center Site. This method is described in more detail in Box 10.2.

Box 10.2 Using the rapid ethnographic assessment procedure

Low, Taplin and Lamb (2005) used the REAP method to study the impact on residents of Battery Park City of the attack on the World Trade Center in New York on 11 September 2001. Battery Park City is situated next to the World Trade Center and was evacuated during and for some time after the attack.

The study was conducted during July 2002, ten months after the attack, and involved interviews with sixty-five residents chosen more or less randomly from the area as well as participant observations conducted in the area. The authors tested four 'folk models' of the impact of 9/11, focusing on the sense of community existing before and after the attack and on relations between newcomers to the area after the attack and those residents who returned.

Documents in qualitative research

Existing documents are a major source of data in policy research. These documents include:

- official documents produced by organisations such as minutes of meetings, reports, memos, media releases and web sites;
- unofficial documents produced by individuals within organisations, such as personal memos, emails and text messages;
- official government documents, such as reports, policy statements, media releases and web sites; and
- media outputs from newspapers, television, radio and the World Wide Web.

Documents of the kind listed above are an important source of data in case study research, particularly when the case study is of an organisation or human services program. Documents relating to the organisation or program contain information on its history, structure, operation and management, as well as on the issues being addressed by staff. Program documents also include case records of clients of the program, details of program delivery, and, in some instances, evaluation reports on the program.

Care needs to be exercised in interpreting existing documents. They have been produced for the purposes of the organisation and not for research purposes. Organisational requirements are not the same as research requirements so documents may well be deficient for the latter. For the purpose of research, documents may be incomplete or even misleading for a number of reasons, including:

- organisational records rarely include reasons for a decision or policy. Usually just the final decision is recorded, so contextual information important to the researcher is missing;
- documents may be 'sanitised' to reflect the official view of the organisation about decisions or actions rather than the 'real' reasons behind them;
- records may be incomplete or missing due to poor record-keeping and/or filing; and
- some records may be confidential or are not made available to the researcher because of their sensitivity.

Researchers using existing documents need to be aware of these problems and take steps to find out what documents are produced, to gain access to them, and to ensure their quality. In policy research, existing documents are likely to play an even greater role than in other areas of qualitative research, so attention to the quality of the documents is of central concern.

This caution applies even more so to unofficial documents, such as letters, memos or emails, produced by individuals within organisations. These documents express the viewpoint of their author and this may not reflect the official viewpoint of the organisation. On the other hand, they may provide valuable information to the researcher on the differences between official organisational policy and actual practice.

Documents produced by government and by the mass media can also be relevant in policy research. Reports of inquiries, parliamentary debates reported in *Hansard*, and interviews with experts or critics of government policy are all sources for the policy researcher.

Analysing qualitative data

Qualitative data, whether derived from primary sources such as interviews or focus groups, or from existing documents, are voluminous and unstructured when compared with quantitative data. A set of interview transcripts, for example, can produce many pages of text for analysis and interpretation. Partly because of the complexity of qualitative data, and partly because many qualitative analysts have epistemological positions opposed to positivism, there are many seemingly incompatible approaches to analysing qualitative data.

A major division in the approaches is between those who adopt a holistic approach to the data and those who break down the data into smaller units. The former approach includes narrative analysis, discourse analysis and interpretive phenomenological analysis (Lyons & Coyle 2007). The latter includes content analysis, grounded theory and ethnographic decision models (Ryan & Bernard 2003).

This division derives more from epistemological differences than from methodological ones. Social constructionists and interpretivists favour holistic approaches so as to preserve the integrity and meaning of the data. Breaking down the data into discrete codes or categories runs the risk of losing sight of the overall meaning of the data. Carving up qualitative data into categories and sub-categories removes the data from their context and destroys their coherence, so it is claimed.

Supporters of coding see the coding process itself as capturing the meaning and context in the data, and argue that a good coding scheme ensures nothing has been omitted.

Whatever approach is adopted, a major task for qualitative researchers is to reduce a large mass of unstructured data to a manageable size by selecting content based on its relevance to the research questions without losing essential meaning. The approaches mentioned above differ on how this data reduction is done.

Miles and Huberman (1994) have identified three processes involved in qualitative data analysis, which provide a useful framework.

1. *Data reduction* refers to the process of selecting relevant aspects of the data and filtering out that which is not relevant.
2. *Data display* refers to the organisation of the data into some form of summary that presents the key features of the data.
3. *Conclusion drawing and verification* refers to the activity of interpreting the patterns emerging from the data analysis.

These three processes are interactive rather than sequential. Each activity feeds into the others to form a continuous feedback process, as illustrated in Figure 10.2 (adapted from Miles & Huberman, 1994, Figure 1.4; and Dey 1993, p 31). The data reduction process is achieved by one or more of three processes identified by Dey (1993), namely *description*, *classification* and *making connections*.

- *Description*. Description in qualitative analysis includes information about the context, intention and meaning of actions. It is important in describing qualitative data that meaning is preserved. Divorcing actions from their context runs the risk of stripping away their meaning. Descriptive methods in qualitative data analysis include memos, interim case summaries, field notes and vignettes.
- *Classification*. Classification involves assigning segments of text to categories. The categories are developed from the data to provide a conceptual framework that will assist the researcher in making sense of the data. The categories may be derived from existing theory or be built up from the data using a grounded theory approach. Methods of classifying qualitative data include coding and content analysis.

Figure 10.2 Processes of qualitative data analysis

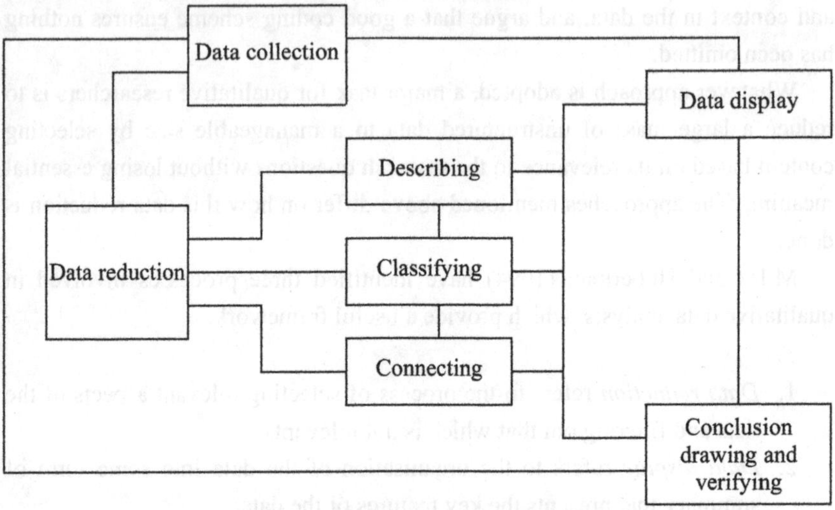

- *Making connections*. Connecting the concepts that have been established by the process of classification enables the construction of theoretical accounts of the data that hypothesise relationships among concepts. Making connections among concepts integrates the analysis and provides the basis for establishing an explanatory framework. Connections can be made among the categories by linking them through some common features.

These three processes are also interactive. There is continual movement backward and forward between the processes rather than one process being completed before the next is commenced. The lines connecting the various processes of qualitative data analysis in Figure 10.2 represent *movement that can go in either direction*. The interconnectedness of all processes involved in data collection and analysis is what gives qualitative research its flexibility to adapt to the demands of the research context.

Qualitative data analysis methods

To implement these general principles, the researcher must choose a particular method of data analysis. Unlike quantitative research, where the range of available methods is constrained, there is a wide range of methods available to the qualitative researcher.

The choice of method will depend on the theoretical and epistemological orientation of the researcher, the nature of the research questions, and the nature of the data, as well as the objectives of the analysis.

It is beyond the scope of a relatively short chapter on qualitative research to provide detailed accounts of even the major methods of qualitative data analysis available. Instead the main features of commonly used methods will be outlined and the reader referred to more detailed descriptions of these methods.

Holistic methods

Holistic methods are those that seek to preserve the integrity of the data by treating it as a whole rather than breaking the data down into components. These methods include narrative analysis, discourse analysis and interpretative phenomenological analysis. Ryan and Bernard (2003) refer to these methods as *linguistic analysis*: the text is the object of analysis. Lyons and Coyle (2007) provide detailed accounts of them, including examples of their use.

While there are differences among these methods in the focus of the analysis, they have in common an in-depth analysis of the meaning of the data, either to the individual or of the social constructions underlying the data.

In using these methods researchers search for themes that run through the data and give it coherence. These themes can be discourses, as in discourse analysis, or personal themes, as in interpretative phenomenological analysis.

Classification methods

Classification methods break the data down into categories, or codes, and sub-categories. These methods include content analysis, grounded theory and pattern coding. They all involve assigning codes to segments of the data, where the codes represent units of meaning. The aim in coding qualitative data is to identify similarities in meaning both within and across cases.

Miles and Huberman (1994) have identified three types of codes, varying in their degree of explanatory value. These are:

- *Descriptive codes*. These codes assign descriptive labels to segments that entail minimal interpretation. Such codes may be used when, for example, respondents list a set of activities in which they are engaged, without any interpretation of these activities.
- *Interpretive codes*. These codes are used when the respondent or the researcher is inferring motives or making some evaluative claim.

- *Pattern codes*. These codes are used to identify themes, relationships or explanations, and are more complex than descriptive or interpretive codes and play an important role in theoretical analysis of the data.

In policy research, coding is a useful way of extracting the main themes or points from qualitative data. Codes can be organised into hierarchical orders, reflecting increasing levels of specificity of themes emerging from the data. A hypothetical example of an interview transcript, coded using HyperResearch software (discussed below) is shown in Figure 10.3.

Figure 10.3 Coded interview transcript using HyperResearch software

	SampleInterview.txt
Page Number ◁ 1 of 1 ▷	[Font Settings...] [?]
	Interview transcript Topic: Impact of key performance indicators on workplace Interviewee: Ms Jane Coyle Position: Manager, Customer services
Impact of KPIs	I: What has been the effect on your workplace of the introduction of the new KPIs?
Negative	A: Staff here have reacted negatively to them. They feel that they are constantly under surveillance and are not trusted by management. I: Have the work patterns of staff changed? Are they more productive?
Services omitted	A: Staff here have concentrated their support to clients in the areas covered by the KPIs and have stopped providing
Increase productivity Clients disadvantaged	assistance in other areas. You might say that they are more productive in some areas but I would say that the general level of support for clients has in fact declined. I: What, if any, are the positive effects of the KPIs on your workplace?
Greater awareness	A: Well, I suppose you could say that they have focused our attention on what the Department regards as important in client
Services omitted	services, although most staff think that many important services have been left out.

In Figure 10.3 'I' refers to the interviewer and 'A' to the answer. The interviewee is a manager of a client services section in a government department. The topic of the interview is the impact of the introduction of a system of key performance indicators (KPIs) to measure output of the section and performance of staff. The section manager is being interviewed to study the effects on staff and services provided of the introduction of this new system. Only one interview is shown for simplicity, but in such a study a number of interviews would be conducted and each interview coded.

Codes are shown in the left margin of Figure 10.3 and the interview transcript is reproduced in the text box. This coding can be done manually but use of qualitative data software described in the next section makes this task easier. Codes are applied to parts of answers. The hierarchical ordering of descriptive codes used in this study is shown in Figure 10.4. Two levels of codes are shown, but more levels would normally be used to capture complexity. In this example, the first level is whether the impact of the new system is positive or negative, and the second level is the categories of positive or negative impacts.

Figure 10.4 Hierarchical arrangement of codes in hypothetical KPI study

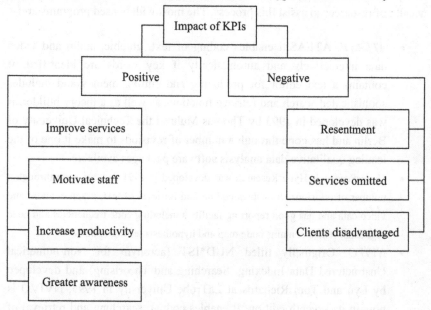

This manager has clearly regarded the overall impact of the new system of KPIs as negative, although manages to make just one (qualified) positive comment. Other managers may take a different view and the coding scheme shown in Figure 10.4 allows for this.

Once all interviews have been coded, reports can be produced showing code frequencies, all examples of a particular code and other characteristics of the coding scheme. Computer software packages for doing this are described in the next section.

The use of computers in qualitative data analysis

The process of coding and classifying qualitative data has been facilitated by the development of computer software specifically designed for this purpose. Although coding has to be done manually, by attaching codes to segments of text organised into cases as in the above example, once this is done the software enables the production of code summaries, code segment reports and in some cases builds networks of codes to enable the testing of if-then propositions.

There are a number of software packages available for qualitative data analysis. The Computer Assisted Qualitative Data Analysis (CAQDAS) network at the University of Surrey, <caqdas.soc.surrey.ac.uk>, provides a comprehensive list of programs for analysing qualitative data, as well as a wealth of resources to assist this process. The most widely used programs are:

- *ATLAS.ti*. ATLAS.ti enables coding of text, graphic, audio and video data interactively and automatically if key words are identified. It contains a text editor for producing and editing memos and includes sophisticated search and retrieve functions as well as a theory builder. It was developed in 1993 by Thomas Muhr at the Technical University of Berlin and has gone through a number of revisions to make it one of the leading qualitative data analysis software packages available.
- *HyperResearch*. HyperResearch was developed in 1991 and has gone through a number of revisions. It enables coding and retrieval of text, graphic, audio and video data and has good reporting facilities including code frequencies and code segments. It also contains code map and hypothesis testing options.
- *NVIVO*. Originally titled NUD*IST (acronym for Non-numerical Unstructured Data Indexing, Searching and Theorising) and developed by Lyn and Tom Richards at LaTrobe University in 1995, NVIVO is now in its seventh edition. It enables coding, searching and retrieval of text data and includes hypothesis testing and theory building facilities.
- *The Ethnograph*. The Ethnograph is the oldest of the computer-assisted software packages for qualitative data analysis having been developed in 1985. It enables coding of text data and includes code families, memo writing and search and retrieval functions.
- *Transana*. Transana is an open source program designed to transcribe into text, and then analyse, large video and audio data sets. It enables coding of video and audio clips, sorting of these into themes or patterns, graphing coding patterns and relating these back to the original video.

All these software packages greatly facilitate the coding, searching and retrieval processes in qualitative data analysis. They are no substitute for the coding experience of the researcher and are limited by the quality of the coding scheme developed.

Evaluating qualitative research

There is debate over whether the same concepts used to evaluate quantitative research, namely reliability and validity, are appropriate for qualitative research. Some writers (for example, Kirk & Miller 1986) use the classical concepts but apply them differently to qualitative research, while others, such as Lincoln and Guba (1985) propose alternative criteria such as trustworthiness and authenticity.

Any method of evaluating qualitative research must address the main threats to validity. Miles and Huberman (1994, p 263) have identified these as:

- *The holistic fallacy.* Making findings look more congruent than they really are.
- *Elite bias.* Involves giving too much emphasis on data from high-status informants and too little emphasis on data from lower-status informants.
- *Going native.* This refers to being too influenced by the perspectives of the informants.

Both Maxwell (1998) and Miles and Huberman (1994) set out strategies for addressing threats to validity in qualitative research. This approach appears to be more fruitful than arguing over what terms should be used. Some of the main strategies outlined by Maxwell and by Miles and Huberman are listed below.

- *Triangulation.* This term refers to the use of different methods, observers, settings and perspectives in investigating an issue. Triangulation can be achieved by combining interviews with field observations, by using different interviewers, or even by using different theoretical approaches to analyse the data. Triangulation does not necessarily provide an infallible means of validating findings as there is always the possibility of findings from different methods yielding conflicting interpretations. The researcher is then faced with the problem of deciding which interpretation is valid.

- *Communicative validation.* Flick (1998) uses this term to describe taking findings and interpretations back to the participants and checking with them that these findings and interpretations make sense to them. Some care needs to be taken here to avoid offending some participants, so discretion is needed in how this is achieved. This strategy may assist in removing some forms of researcher bias.
- *Searching for discrepant evidence.* Maxwell (1998) proposes this strategy to guard against the holistic fallacy. It makes sure the researcher does not overlook data that may not support the conclusions being reached. This is referred to by Flick (1998) as *analytic induction.* Negative evidence disconfirms a theory and forces the researcher to either revise it or discard it altogether.
- *Replication.* A valid finding should be able to be replicated in a situation similar to the one in which the finding was obtained. Validity is strengthened if the replication is conducted by different researchers using different instruments with different participants.

While implementing these strategies does not guarantee the validity of the research it does increase confidence in the findings.

Generalisation in qualitative research

Qualitative research is not designed to draw conclusions about large populations. This is the domain of quantitative research. Qualitative research deals with small samples that are studied in depth and are chosen purposefully rather than randomly.

This does not mean, however, that findings from qualitative research cannot be generalised, just that the generalisation is not to a population. Samples in qualitative research are chosen for their unique characteristics. They may be extreme or deviant cases, as in the success case method, or they may be expert or key informants. Generalisation from such cases is then made to a theory or explanation of the case findings. This generalisation may then be extended to other cases through application of the theory or explanation.

Lincoln and Guba (1985) argue that generalisation should be replaced with the notions of *transferability* and *fittingness* to apply to qualitative research. Both terms refer to the extent to which findings from a qualitative study can be applicable in different contexts.

Communicating qualitative research

The flexibility associated with qualitative research carries over into the writing of qualitative research reports. The standard format for writing research reports (to be found in most texts on social research) seems inappropriate for most qualitative research, particularly ethnographic research.

As Miles and Huberman (1994, p 299) point out, 'there are no fixed formats, and the ways data are being analyzed and interpreted are getting more and more varied. As qualitative data analysts, we have few shared canons of how our studies should be reported.'

The options for writing up research available to the qualitative researcher include the following.

- *Style.* Qualitative research is often written up in a *narrative* style, where the findings are presented as stories illustrating the themes emerging from the study. This is contrasted with the *scientific* style common to quantitative research reports. Miles and Huberman (1994) recommend a blend of the two for most qualitative research.
- *Voice.* The term 'voice' refers here not only to the grammatical form denoting active or passive, but also to the manner of expression of the author. Van Maanen's (1988) classic delineation of three 'voices' in presenting ethnographic findings illustrate the range of options available to the qualitative researcher. These are outlined in Box 10.3.

Box 10.3 Three approaches to ethnographic writing

Van Maanen (1988) outlined three forms of ethnographic writing that can be used in all qualitative research:

- *Realist tales.* The account is written in the third person and the researcher is absent from the account. This form accords closely to the scientific mode of quantitative research.
- *Confessional tales.* The account is written from the researcher's viewpoint and incorporates the experience of the researcher in undertaking the research.
- *Impressionist tales.* The account is written as stories to achieve dramatic effect, to convey the experience of the research to the reader.

- *Presentation mode.* Text and graphic displays are the usual modes of presentation but greater dramatic effect can be achieved by presenting the findings in the form of a *vignette* – that is, acting out of the findings of the research.
- *The audience.* Some combination of these styles is likely to be appropriate in policy-oriented research. Regard must be had for the audience. If the audience is likely to be politicians or their advisors then some form of summary presentation may be needed, as politicians are notorious for just reading the summary and maybe the conclusions. Alternative versions of the report may be needed to suit a range of audiences, from the scientific to the policy communities.

Implementation issues

The way in which research is reported can also have an impact on the use to which the findings are put. If the research is designed to influence policy, steps need to be taken to communicate the findings effectively, and to ensure that the findings are disseminated to the widest possible audience. This is achieved by:

- highlighting the implications of the findings and including recommendations for action where appropriate;
- gaining support from key decision-makers. Patton (1997) argues strongly for this approach. It involves identifying an individual or individuals who have influence over the implementation process and getting their support to implement findings; and
- publicising the research findings. Have the findings publicised widely in media such as newspapers, television and radio where appropriate, and in publications internal to the stakeholders.

Conclusion

Qualitative research plays an important role in policy analysis and decision-making. The concepts and questions involved in most policy issues are complex and not readily reduced to quantitative measures. At best these measures capture only some aspects of a policy issue and at worst they can trivialise issues and mislead decision makers.

Qualitative methods enable exploration of context and meaning in the policy and decision-making process allowing the complexities inherent in such processes to be revealed. To achieve this, adherence to the highest standards in the collection and analysis of qualitative data is essential. Poor quality data collection or inadequate methods of analysis will provide little useful information for decision makers.

In this chapter the main methods of collecting and analysing qualitative data have been outlined and some references given to the expanding literature on this topic. Qualitative research is better placed now to provide evidence for effective decision making. But this will only happen if policy workers are aware of the strengths and limitations of qualitative methods and are able to employ the best methods available to answer the questions being asked.

11 Basic statistical methods for policy and decision-making

George Argyrous

This chapter provides a basic introduction to statistics for analysing quantitative data. It focuses on the first step in statistical analysis – straightforward statistical description – and points the way to more advanced methods for those who wish to undertake further reading on the subject.

To illustrate the concepts that follow in this chapter, assume that a public agency is interested in how users of its service feel about the quality of the service they receive. The agency is interested in the attitudes of all its service users, which thereby constitute the *population* of interest. With limited time and resources, however, it conducts a short survey of a randomly selected group of 200 citizens who have accessed its services in the preceding year. This sub-group of the whole population of interest that is actually surveyed is a *sample*. As part of the survey, the agency asks each respondent their sex, age, marital status, how long they had to wait before being served, the number of times they have accessed the service in the previous year, and their level of satisfaction with the service they received. Each of these characteristics of the sampled users is called a *variable*. This chapter helps us communicate the information – data – we gather about these variables. We begin by discussing how we present the data we obtain from a sample using *descriptive statistics*, and then how we can generalise from the sample results to the wider population using *inferential statistics*.

Descriptive statistics are the numerical, graphical, and tabular techniques for organising, analysing and presenting data. The major types of descriptive statistics are listed in Table 11.1.

Table 11.1 Types of descriptive statistics

Type	Function	Examples
Graphs	Provide a visual representation of the distribution of a variable or variables	Pie, bar, histogram, polygon Clustered pie, clustered/stacked bar Scatterplot
Tables	Provide a frequency distribution of a variable or variables	Frequency table Cross tabulations
Numerical measures	Mathematical operations used to quantify, in a single number, particular features of a distribution	Measures of average such as the mean Measures of dispersion Measures of association and correlation

The great advantage of descriptive statistics is that they make a mass of research material easier to 'read' by reducing a large set of data into a few statistics, or into a graph or table.

Levels of measurement

The decision as to which descriptive statistic most effectively summarises a set of data involves many considerations. One of the most important is the level at which each variable is measured. To illustrate what levels of measurement mean, consider three of the variables included in the survey of service users:

1. Marital status: respondents are asked to select whether they are married, never married, widowed, or separated/divorced.
2. Satisfaction with service: respondents are asked to rate their satisfaction with the service they received as 'very dissatisfied', 'dissatisfied', 'satisfied' or 'very satisfied'.
3. Age: respondents are asked to give their age in whole years.

We call the set of responses offered to a respondent, from which they select the one appropriate to them, a *scale*. Thus the options of 'married', 'never married', 'widowed' or 'separated/divorced' constitute the scale upon which we measure the variable 'marital status'.

Each of the scales listed above provides a different amount of information for the respective variable they try to measure. Take the first scale for recording marital status. This scale only allows us to say that service users are qualitatively different according to the option they choose, and as such is an example of a *nominal scale*: it classifies cases into categories that have no quantitative ordering. We can determine this by comparing two people who choose different points on the scale: we cannot say, for example, that someone who selects 'divorced' has a higher or lower marital status than someone who selects 'single'.

Compare this to the second scale measuring service satisfaction, which is an *ordinal scale*. The four categories that make up the scale have a logical order, starting with the lowest point, 'very dissatisfied', and moving up to the highest point, 'very satisfied'. This scale allows us to talk about service users being different in terms of their satisfaction (nominal and ordinal scales are sometimes collectively referred to as categorical scales since they both use broad categories to group data). But unlike a nominal scale, we can also say that some respondents have more or less satisfaction than others. This ability to *rank order* cases according to the quantity or intensity of the variable expressed by each case makes this an *ordinal* scale. We cannot, however, measure how much more or less satisfied one person is relative to another.

The third scale above, for measuring age, does allow us to measure such differences. As with nominal and ordinal scales, measuring age in whole years allows us to classify patients into different groups. As with ordinal (but not nominal) scales, we can rank respondents according to their respective scores from lowest to highest. But unlike both nominal and ordinal scales, we can measure the differences – the intervals – between people. We now have a unit of measurement, years, which allows us to quantify the difference in age. This is therefore an example of an *interval/ratio* scale (sometimes called a *metric* scale).

Note that had we asked service users to indicate their age by selecting among a few broad age groups we would no longer have enough information to measure differences in age. Such a scale for measuring age is only ordinal. This illustrates that any given variable can be measured at different levels, depending on the particular scale that is used. It is important to be clear about the level at which a variable has been measured, since the descriptive statistics that we can use to express variation across cases is limited by this fact.

The importance of the distinction between nominal, ordinal, and interval/ratio scales is the amount of information about a variable that each level provides (Table 11.2).

Table 11.2 Levels of measurement

Level of measurement	Examples	Measurement procedure	Operations permitted
Nominal (lowest level)	Sex Race Religion Marital status	Classification into categories	Counting number of cases in each category; comparing number of cases in each category
Ordinal	Social class Attitude, satisfaction and opinion scales	Classification plus ranking of categories with respect to each other	All above plus judgments of 'greater than' or 'less than'
Interval/ratio (highest level)	Age in years Income in dollars	Classification plus ranking plus description of distances between scores in terms of equal units	All above plus other mathematical operations such as addition, subtraction and multiplication

Graphs

Graphs or *charts* are the simplest, and often most striking, methods for describing data, and there are some general rules that apply to their construction. Most importantly, a graph should be a self-contained bundle of information. This means we need to:

- give the graph a clear title indicating the variable displayed and the cases that make up the study;
- clearly identify the categories or values of the variable;
- indicate, for interval/ratio data, the units of measurement;
- indicate the total number of cases;
- indicate, where the total in the graph is less than the total number of cases in the study, why there is a difference; and
- indicate the source of the data.

The pie graph in Figure 11.1 illustrates these rules of presentation. A *pie graph* presents the distribution of cases in the form of a circle. The relative size of each slice of the pie is equal to the proportion of cases within the category represented by the slice. Pie charts can be constructed for all levels of measurement and their main function is to emphasise the relative importance of a particular category to the total. They are therefore mainly used to highlight distributions where cases are concentrated in only one or two categories. The pie chart in Figure 11.1, for example, highlights the heavy concentration of service users who are married.

Figure 11.1 Pie graph: Marital status of a sample of service users ($n = 200$)

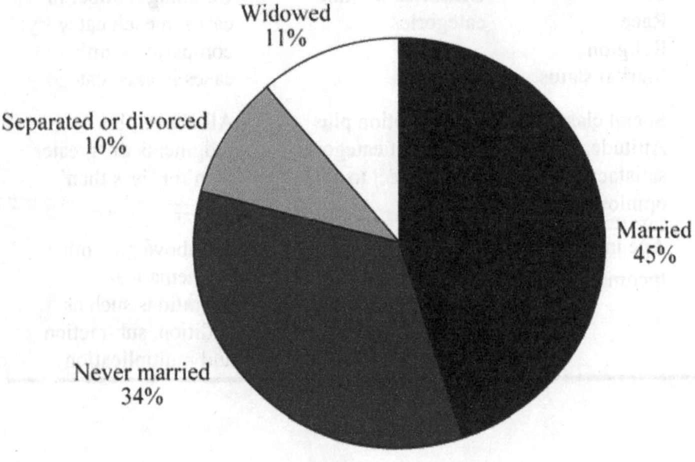

Source: Survey of service users, 2008.

Pie graphs begin to look a bit clumsy when there are too many categories for the variable. As a rule of thumb, there should be no more than five slices to the pie. Many charts achieve this by grouping together a number of categories with low frequencies into an 'other' category.

Bar graphs and *histograms* emphasise the frequency of cases in each category relative to each other. Along one axis are the categories or values of the scale. This axis is called the *abscissa*, and is usually the horizontal base of the graph. Along the other axis are the *frequencies*, expressed either as the raw count or as percentages of the total number of cases. This axis is known as the *ordinate*. This is usually the left, vertical axis. A rectangle is erected over each point on the abscissa, with the area of each rectangle proportional to the frequency of the value in the overall distribution.

The difference between *bar graphs* and *histograms* is that bar graphs are constructed for discrete variables, such as the satisfaction level of service users, which are usually measured in broad categories on a nominal or ordinal scale as illustrated by Figure 11.2.

With bar graphs there are always gaps between each of the bars: there is no gradation between the levels of satisfaction, for example. A person's age, on the other hand, is a continuous variable, in the sense that it progressively increases. As a result, the bars on the histogram for age in Figure 11.3 are 'pushed together'. Note that we have grouped the original age scores into five-year intervals for easier presentation.

Interpreting graphs

Once we have constructed the relevant graph we then need to interpret it. When we look at a graph, we generally try to identify one or more of the following four aspects of the distribution it represents:

1. shape;
2. centre;
3. spread; and
4. the existence of outliers.

There are certain common *shapes* that appear in research. For example, the histogram for age in Figure 11.3 is 'bell-shaped' or 'mound-shaped'. For a distribution that has this bell shape, we also describe its *skewness*. If the curve has a long tail to the right, it is *positively skewed*, or, as is the case Figure 11.3, the long tail to the left indicates a *negatively skewed* distribution.

To gauge the *centre* of a distribution, imagine that the bars of the histogram are lead weights sitting on a balance beam. Where would we have to locate a balance point along the bottom edge of the graph to prevent it from tipping either to the left or right? This, in a loose fashion, identifies the *average* or typical score. In the example in Figure 11.3 we might guess that the average age of patients is around 35–39 years of age.

We can also observe how tightly clustered our measurements are around the central point. Do the scores *spread* very wide across the range of possible values (that is, is the distribution *heterogenous*) or are most similar to each other (that is, is the distribution *homogeneous*)?

Figure 11.2 Bar graph: Satisfaction levels of service users (*n* = 200)

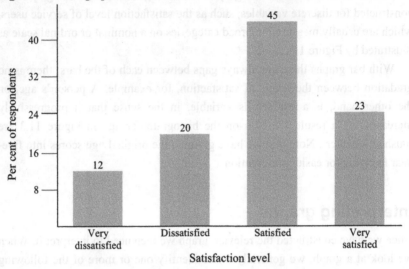

Figure 11.3 Histogram: Age of a sample of service users (*n* = 184*)

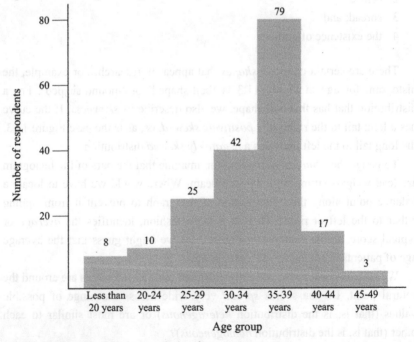

* Total is less than 200 due to missing data.

Lastly, we can note the existence of any *outliers* – cases that are not just at the upper or lower end of the tails, but are disconnected from the rest of the group. Figure 11.4, for example, presents the frequency for number of times each survey respondent accessed the service in the previous year.

Figure 11.4 Number of visits to the service in the past year (*n* = 200)

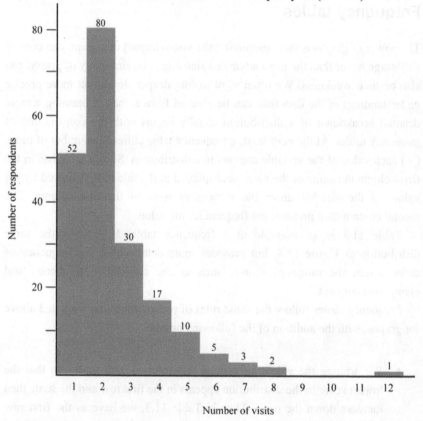

We can immediately see an outlier with 12 visits in the previous year. Where we identify an outlier we work through the following three steps:

1. *Isolate the reason why it appears*. Outliers can appear as a result of a data entry error or because of an unusual but real case.
2. *Correct the mistake if possible or exclude the outlier from further analysis*. The inclusion of any outliers in the data can distort other statistics such as the mean.

3. *Indicate that 'trimming' of the data has taken place.* If outliers are excluded some discussion of why they have such unusually high or low values is warranted and, most importantly, a statement is needed indicating that the sample size has been effectively reduced by excluding the presence of outliers.

Frequency tables

The power of graphs is their simplicity; the visual impact of a graph can convey a message better than the most advanced statistics. The simplicity of graphs can also be their weakness. We often want to 'dig deeper' to extract more precise understandings of the data than can be gleaned from a chart. Obtaining a more detailed breakdown of a distribution usually begins with the construction of *frequency tables*. At the very least, a frequency table tallies the number of times (f) each value of the variable appears in a distribution. Such a table has in the first column the name of the variable displayed in the title row, followed by the values of the variable down the subsequent rows of the first column. The second column then presents the frequencies for value.

Table 11.3 is an example of a frequency table. It presents the same distribution as Figure 11.4, but provides more detail about the frequency of cases across the range of scores, such as the cumulative frequency and cumulative per cent.

Frequency tables follow the same rules of presentation that we listed above for graphs, with the addition of the following points:

- We arrange the values of ordinal and interval/ratio scales so that the lowest score in the distribution appears in the first row and the scale then increase down the page. Thus in Table 11.3, we have as the first row those who visited the service only once, and the scale increases down the page to the last row before the total. This is the highest point on the scale, with 'more than 8' visits.
- We arrange the categories of nominal scales so that the category with the highest frequency (what we will learn to call the mode) is the first row, the category with the second highest frequency is the second row, and so on. The modal category is often of specific interest when analysing the distribution of a nominal variable, and therefore it is convenient to present it first.

Table 11.3 Number of visits to the service in the previous year

Number of visits	Frequency	Per cent*	Cumulative frequency	Cumulative per cent
1	52	26	52	26
2	80	40	132	66
3	30	15	162	81
4	17	9	179	86
5	10	5	189	95
6	5	3	194	97
7	3	2	197	99
8	2	1	199	99
More than 8	1	<1	200	100
Total	200	100		

* Do not sum to 100 due to rounding error.

Table 11.3 also provides the *relative frequencies*, which express the number of cases with each value of a variable as a percentage or proportion of the total number of cases. *Percentages* are statistics that standardise the total number of cases to a base value of 100. Sometimes relative frequencies are expressed as *proportions* rather than percentages. Proportions standardise the total to a base of 1. The formulas for calculating a percentage (%) or proportion (p) respectively are:

$$\% = \frac{f}{n} \times 100$$

$$p = \frac{f}{n}$$

where f is the frequency of cases in a particular category and n is the total number of cases. Notice that the column of percentages in Table 11.3 should add up to 100 per cent, since all cases must fall into one classification or another. The actual percentages listed in the table, however, sum to 101 per cent, as the numbers have been 'rounded off'. Where this occurs, a footnote should be added to the table that states 'do not sum to 100 due to rounding error', or words to that effect, as is done in Table 11.3.

Percentages and proportions are very commonly used summary statistics they are regularly misused. Some of the more common errors that are made when calculating, presenting, or interpreting these statistics are discussed in Box 11.1.

Box 11.1 The use and abuse of percentages, proportions and rates

Frequency counts are often converted to percentages (or their close cousins proportions and rates). This helps to compare groups that have different totals, and as a result percentages are very commonly cited statistics. However, precisely because they 'wash away' the raw numbers from which they have been calculated, percentages lend themselves to misuse. To avoid the problems we list below, it is important to always present the totals from which percentages (and rates and proportions) are calculated.

1. *Percentages calculated on small totals.* The number of people attending a pro-capital-punishment meeting may be 150 per cent greater than the number that attended the last meeting. This may actually be due to five people attending the recent meeting rather than the two who attended the previous one. This example illustrates the fact that percentages will change dramatically with a small change in either the total or the categories making up the total, when we are dealing with very small numbers. As a general rule we should not refer to percentages when working with totals of less than 30; some texts even recommend that the total must be greater than 50 for percentage values to be sufficiently stable to small changes.

2. *Percentages calculated on large totals.* The opposite problem to the previous occurs when we work with very large totals. When the total is very large, a small changes in percentage values can conceal large changes in absolute numbers: an increase in unemployment rates from 4 per cent to 4.5 per cent does not seem dramatic in statistical terms. But this 0.5 per cent may represent 50 000 people.

3. *Only citing percentage change.* It is not uncommon in media reports of health information to hear statements such as 'the new drug was effective at relieving pain but the risk of breast cancer increased by 150 per cent'. From such a dramatic statement, women might be very reluctant to take the new drug. But what if the statement was 'the new drug was effective at relieving pain but the risk of breast cancer increased by 150 per cent from 2-in-1 million to 5-in-1 million'? By including the absolute risks, it is clear that although the change is relatively great, the actual risk remains very small. A woman's decision may be very different. (Note that the rates in this example are purely hypothetical for illustrative purposes.)

4. *Confusing changes in percentage share with percentage change over time.* Media reports often present a change in percentage shares as representing increases or decreases in the incidence of events over time. For example, a headline might scream out 'Murders on the increase!', and justify this by pointing out that the percentage of all crimes that are murders has jumped from 3.1 per cent to 5.9 per cent. However, the actual number of murders may not have changed at all; the total number of other crimes may have gone down, thereby bumping up the *share* of murders. When making comparisons over time, it is more appropriate to standardise the incidence of some event with reference to the relevant population that might experience this event. In this example, if the population of all people has increased in the relevant time period, the murder rate may actually have gone down. The headline is therefore completely wrong.

5. *Adding or subtracting rounded percentages.* Assume that the percentages of particular types of crimes are 13.4 per cent, 22.3 per cent, and 42.1 per cent, In presenting these in a table, the percentages are rounded with no decimal places: 13 per cent, 22 per cent, and 42 per cent. If we sum these rounded values to group these types of crime together we also accumulate rounding errors and get a different total per cent than if we had added the unrounded values. If we want to add or subtract category totals, we should add or subtract the raw numbers and then calculate the total per cent based on this total.

With ordinal and interval/ratio data one further extension to the simple frequency table can be made, which is also illustrated in Table 11.3. This is the addition of columns providing *cumulative frequencies* and *cumulative relative frequencies*. Since ordinal and interval/ratio scales allow us to rank-order cases from lowest to highest, it is sometimes interesting to know the number, and/or percentage, of cases that fall above or below a certain point on the scale. For example, in Table 11.3 we can see that 162 respondents (81 per cent), which is the sum of the frequencies in the first three rows of the table, visited the service three times or less. By implication, this means that 19 per cent of respondents visited the service more than three times in the last year.

Cumulative frequencies are not appropriate in the following instances:

- where we have a nominal scale, as the ordering of the categories is not fixed; and
- where there are only two categories, as the simple frequencies and cumulative frequencies will be the same.

One additional point needs to be made about tabulating interval/ratio data: we often use *class intervals* rather than individual values to form the rows of the table. A *class interval* groups together a range of values for presentation and analysis, as was done in the histogram in Figure 11.3. We use class intervals if the range of values that appears in the distribution is so large that it makes presentation and analysis difficult. For example, if we have many individual ages for the patients in our study we may first group them into five-year intervals, such as 1–5 years, 6–10 years, and so on, before constructing the table or graph. Generally, class intervals should have the same width, although at the lower and upper end of the data range we often have open-ended class intervals, such as '60 years or over' (the exception is the value of zero, which is usually listed separately; it is common for readers of tables to be specifically interested in the number of cases that have a zero value for a particular variable). The actual width of class intervals depends on the particular situation, especially the amount of information required. The wider the class intervals the easier it is to 'read' the table, since this will reduce the number of rows in the table. But this increase in 'readability' comes at the cost of information, and therefore should not be undertaken if the data already come in a few, easily presented, values.

Choosing between graphs and tables

Graphs and tables can be used to describe the same distribution. For example, Figure 11.4 and Table 11.3 each describe the scores representing the number of visits to the service in the previous year. How do we choose when to use a graph and when to use a table?

The first consideration is whether we need to use either method of data description. Where we are summarising the scores for a variable with only a small number of categories, it is often best to use plain words. For example, while we can use a graph or table to represent the sex of service users, it is more succinct to state: 'our survey consisted of 112 (56 per cent) females and 88 (44 per cent) males'.

For more complex distributions, the general rule is that graphs are best used when we wish to highlight one or two distinguishing features of a distribution. For example, Figure 11.4 highlights the highly concentrated nature of number of visits, as well as the one outlier. However, where we want more detailed information about a set of scores, such as the cumulative frequencies, tables should be used rather than graphs.

Tables are also preferred to graphs when we wish to describe several distributions at once. Presenting every variable in the form of a graph can take considerable space, whereas the compact nature of tables allows us to succinctly present a large amount of information. For example, the demographic profile of survey respondents, such as their sex, age, and language background, can be combined in one 'super' table that presents these variables together. Such a table, as shown in Table 11.4, can also include the summary statistics that we discuss in the following sections, such as the mean and standard deviation.

Table 11.4 Demographic profile of survey respondents

Variable	Frequency*	Per cent
Sex (*n* = 200)		
Male	88	44
Female	112	56
Age (*n* = 184)		
Less than 20 years	8	4
20–24 years	10	5
25–29 years	25	14
30–34 years	42	23
35–39 years	79	43
40–44 years	17	9
45 and over	3	2
Mean 37 years		
Standard deviation 5 years		
Language background (*n* = 190)		
English speaking	150	79
Non-English speaking	40	21

* Totals differ due to non-responses.

Measures of central tendency

We mentioned above that graphs and tables give us a quick visual sense of key features of a distribution. But we sometimes want to be more precise about these features, such as the centre of a distribution; for instance, rather than stating that 'the scores tend to centre around an average of 35–39 years', we often need to be more precise about the average score. *Measures of central tendency* indicate the typical or average value for a distribution.

There are three common measures of central tendency: mode, median, and mean. Each measure embodies a different notion of average, and choosing the measure to calculate for a given set of data is restricted by the level at which a variable is measured.

The *mode* (M_o) is the simplest measure of central tendency, and can be calculated for all levels of measurement: it is the value in a distribution with the highest frequency. The great advantage of the mode over other measures of centre is that it is very easy to calculate. A simple inspection of a frequency table is enough to determine the mode. In Table 11.3, for example, we can see the most frequent number of times a person visited the service is 2, which accounts for 80 people. The mode has one major limitation, however, that especially arises when it is used to describe interval/ratio data that have many values. Take, for example, the following scores, which represent the time in seconds someone has to wait in a queue before being served:

36, 36, 81, 82, 84, 85, 86, 89, 91, 95, 97, 98

It is clear to the naked eye that the data are 'centred' somewhere in the 80–90 seconds range. Yet the mode is 36 seconds since this appears twice in the distribution, whereas every other score only appears once. The mode is not really reflecting the central tendency of this distribution. We should either use other measures of central tendency, such as those we are about to discuss, or else organise the data into suitable class intervals, and report the modal class interval, rather than the individual modal score.

With interval/ratio data the *mean* and *median* can also be calculated as measures of central tendency. The mean is the sum of all scores in a distribution divided by the total number of cases. The actual formula we use to calculate the mean depends on whether we have each score in the distribution listed separately or in a frequency table. If we have the raw data with each individual score listed separately, the equations for the mean of a population and the mean of a sample respectively are:

$$\mu = \frac{\Sigma X_i}{N}$$

$$\overline{X} = \frac{\Sigma X_i}{n}$$

where μ (pronounced 'mu') is the mean for an entire population, N is the size of the population, $\overline{X}$ (pronounced 'X-bar') is the mean for a sample, n is the size of the sample, and X_i is each score in a distribution. The symbol Σ (pronounced 'sigma') means 'the sum of' (or 'the total from the addition of'), so we read these equations in the following way: 'the mean equals the sum of all scores divided by the number of cases'.

Where the scores are already grouped into a frequency table such as in Table 11.3, the formula for the mean of the sample is:

$$\overline{X} = \frac{\Sigma f X_i}{n}$$

This formula instructs us to multiply each score by the frequency with which it appears in the table and to sum these products before dividing by the number of cases. For Table 11.3, excluding the one outlier with more than eight visits, the calculations will be:

$$\bar{X} = \frac{\Sigma f X_i}{n}$$

$$= \frac{(1\times52)+(2\times80)+(3\times30)+(4\times17)+(5\times10)+(6\times5)+(3\times7)+(2\times8)}{199}$$

$$= \frac{487}{199}$$

$$= 2.4 \text{ visits}$$

The mean has two major limitations, both of which derive from the fact that it is calculated using every score in the distribution. The first limitation is that it is affected by the presence of outliers, and therefore we generally exclude outliers from the calculation of the mean (as we discussed above). Thus, when calculating the mean number of visits to the service, we excluded the one 'outlier' who visited more than eight times. When presenting a 'trimmed' mean as the average we should note for the reader that such 'trimming' has occurred.

The other limitation to the use of the mean as a measure of central tendency, even where outliers are excluded, is that its value is pulled away from the centre of a skewed distribution. For example, looking at Figure 11.4, we can see that the spread of scores for number of visits is skewed to the right and this has produced a value for the mean that is higher than what we might expect from a quick visual inspection of the graph (even after we exclude outliers).

An alternative measure of central tendency to the mean, especially for skewed distributions, is the *median* (M_d). If all the cases in a distribution are ranked from lowest to highest, the median will have an equal number of cases above and below it. The actual calculation of the median will differ according to whether we have an odd or even number of scores. For an odd number of rank-ordered cases, the median is the middle score. For an even number of rank-ordered cases, the median is the mean of the two middle scores. Thus if I lined up the 200 service users in my sample according to the frequency with which they visited the service, starting with the users who came only once, the middle scores are those for the one-hundredth and one-hundred-and-first people in the order, who each have a value of two visits. We have an even number of cases, so the median is the mean of these two middle scores, which is 2 visits.

If a cumulative relative frequency table such as Table 11.3 has been generated, an easier way to calculate the median is to identify the value at which the cumulative per cent first passes 50 (that is, 2 visits). We can see that the median depends solely on the value of these scores in the middle, and is not 'pulled' in one direction or another by the long tail of a skewed distribution or the presence of any outliers, factors which we have seen affect the value of the mean.

We have seen that each of the measures of average that we have discussed can produce different values for the average of a set of scores, and specific aspects of the distribution can also affect each measure. As a result these measures of average can lend themselves to misuse. Box 11.2 discusses critically questions to ask when reading these, and other, statistics in a research report.

Box 11.2 Critically reading statistics on average and spread

When reading statistics that discuss the average and spread of scores for a variable, ask the following questions:

1. *Which average: mean or median?* The mean is the most common measure of average, but it can be a very misleading measure of the centre of a skewed distribution. For distributions that are skewed to the left (relatively few low scores) the mean will be lower than the median; for right-skewed distributions (relatively few high scores) the mean will be higher than the median. For example, the mean house price in a city will always be higher than the median house price, because there are a relatively few, extremely expensive, houses that bump up the mean. At the very least, both the mean and the median should be presented, so that the extent and direction to which the underlying set of scores is skewed can be assessed.

2. *If the mean is presented, has it been calculated with or without outliers?* Even where a set of scores is not heavily skewed, the existence of only one or two extremely high or low values will throw out the mean. It is legitimate in such instances to 'trim' the mean and exclude outliers in the calculation, but where this is done, it should be made clear to the reader. Similarly, if the mean is calculated on all the scores in a distribution, one should assess whether it is thrown out by the existence of outliers that otherwise should have been excluded from the calculations.

3. *Have measures of average been cited with information about the spread of scores?* An average is only useful it applies to a set of scores that are not spread a long way from it. For example, the average waiting time for a service may be 10 minutes, but if the standard deviation around this mean is 8 minutes, it is not really capturing the experience of a lot of people in waiting to be served.

4. *Have the authors averaged averages or percentages?* The percentage of people in New South Wales, Victoria, and Tasmania respectively that use a government service may be 10 per cent, 14 per cent, and 15 per cent. The percentage of all people in these three states is therefore 13 per cent (that is, [10+14+15] ÷ 3). Wrong! This *simple* average of the three percentage figures ignores the very different total populations in each state. As with the previous point, the aggregated figure should be calculated from the raw numbers for each state. Similarly, we cannot calculate the mean of a set of means, because these measures of average may themselves be based on different totals. Such averaging of percentages and means gives excessive weighting to groups with relatively small totals by treating them as if they were the same size as the other groups.

5. *Have the authors made the original data available?* Many of these problems with the use of statistics, and others, can be checked if the authors are willing to make available the raw data from which they are calculated (with due respect to any obligations to maintain confidentiality). This allows a critical reader to check the little nuances involved, such as whether outliers have or have not been excluded. It also allows a critical reader to check that the calculations are indeed correct. One should not underestimate the likelihood that occasionally people may simply get it wrong. I recommend that for reports that rest on a small number of critical statistical results, it is reasonable to request the raw data from which they have been generated and check that no mistakes have been made.

Measures of dispersion

Measures of dispersion are descriptive statistics that indicate the spread or variety of scores in a distribution, and most of these require interval/ratio level measurement (a measure for nominal scales, the Index of Qualitative Variation, is not covered here, but further details can be found in Argyrous 2005, p 141). The simplest measure of dispersion is the *range*, which is the difference between the lowest score and highest score. This is an easily calculated measure of dispersion, because it involves a straightforward subtraction of one score from another. This advantage of the range is also its major limitation: it only uses the extreme scores, and therefore changes with the values of the two extreme scores.

The *inter-quartile range* (*IQR*) overcomes this problem with the simple range by ignoring the extreme scores of a distribution. The *IQR* is the range for the middle 50 per cent of cases in a rank-ordered series. It ignores the top and bottom 25 per cent of scores, and as a result, unlike the simple range, the *IQR* will not change dramatically if we add one or two cases to either end of the distribution. For the data in Table 11.3 the *IQR* is 2 visits.

The *standard deviation* is a more complex measure of spread, whose value depends on the difference between each score and the mean. The difference is called a *deviation*. Take, for example, one of our sampled service users who visited the service four times in the previous year. This person has a *positive deviation* (score above the mean) of 1.4 (that is, 4 – 2.4). A sampled user who only visited the service once has a *negative deviation* (score below the mean) of -1.4. The standard deviation uses the deviations for all the scores in its calculations. Distributions that are spread out will have many scores that are different from the mean, producing many large deviations and thereby a high value for the standard deviation. Another set of scores may have the same mean, but with the scores more tightly clustered around it. The deviations between each score and the mean will thereby generally be small, producing a lower value for the standard deviation. For the data in Table 11.3, the standard deviation is 1.5 visits, excluding the one outlier, indicating the moderate amount of spread in the distribution.

Inferential statistics

We have discussed at some length various ways of describing our data. As in the above example of service users, these data often come from a sample rather than from the whole population, so we are faced with a problem: Are the sample statistics 'representative' of the population from which the sample is drawn? The operation of sampling error may cause the sample to be 'off'. Sampling error is the result of random factors that can cause us to include in our survey members of the population that have relatively low or high scores for the variable we are investigating. Sampling error causes the overall sample statistics to be different to those we would have obtained if we did study the whole population. Given the possible effect of sampling error, on what basis can we make a valid generalisation from a sample to the population?

We address this problem with *inferential statistics*. Inferential statistics are the numerical techniques for making conclusions about a population based on the information obtained from a random sample drawn from that population. We will illustrate the nature of inferential statistics by explaining the way that they are often presented in a report or policy document. For example, assume that in reporting the above results, drawn from a survey of service users, we read the following:

The government has set aside extra funding for services that cater to older populations. This funding is released to a service if it can show that the mean age of its service users is significantly greater than 35 years. Our survey respondents had a mean age of 37 years (standard deviation = 5 years), and this is statistically significantly greater than 35 ($t = 5.43$, $p < 0.001$). In fact, we estimate from the sample that our service users have a mean age between 36.3 and 37.7 years (alpha = 95 per cent). The service has therefore applied to access the extra funding.

This statement is conducting what is formally known as *hypothesis testing*. An hypothesis is a speculation or conjecture about some characteristic of the population. In this example, we hypothesise that the population has a mean age of 35 years. Note that the service really wants to show that this hypothesis is wrong so that it can tap into the extra funding. But much like the presumption of innocence in criminal law, we often begin by asserting an hypothesis, and try to gather evidence to show that this hypothesis is not justified; it should be rejected. This is the logic of proof by contradiction: we find support for something in which we do believe by disproving its opposite.

On the face of it, the evidence from the sample of service users does seem to refute the hypothesis that the whole population of service users has a mean age of only 35 years (or less). The sample mean of 37 years, however, may have come about for one of two reasons. One possibility is that the population really has a mean age of 35 years, but our sample has a mean age of 37 years because of sampling error: we just happened to randomly select a few relatively older service users. We can call this the *null hypothesis* (H_0). Alternatively, the population of all users may have a mean age higher than 35 years and our sample accurately reflects this. We can call this the *alternative hypothesis* (H_a).

The process of hypothesis testing helps us decide between these two alternative explanations by calculating the *statistical significance* of the sample result (also called the *p*-value). In our example, statistical significance is the probability that the sample did indeed come from a population of service users whose mean age is 35 years, and that the high sample mean is due to sampling error alone. This probability is less than 1-in-1000 ($p < 0.001$). Given the low probability that the high sample mean is due to random error alone, the service rejects this possible explanation in favour of one that asserts that the underlying population of service users is on average older than 35 years.

Consider what the conclusion might be if the significance level turned out to be $p = 0.4$. This would mean that, although the sample had a mean age higher than 35 years, we cannot dismiss the possibility that the population from which it was drawn only has a mean age of 35. In fact, 4-in-10 samples drawn from a population with a mean age of 35 years will have mean more than 2 years above this average. Given the likelihood that any given sample may stray this far from a mean age of 35 years, we would not regard a sample mean of 37 years as particularly unusual; it would not allow us to conclude that the underlying population was on average older than the target age.

Note that in addition to the all-important *p*-value, the report also cites a statistics known as a *t*-score. Sometimes alternative statistics called *z*-scores, *F*-scores, and chi-square statistics are cited. These statistics as such are not of any great importance; they are merely a halfway house in calculating the *p*-score.

Whether or not we choose to reject an hypothesis we need to be aware of the difference between a *type I error* (alpha error) and a *type II error* (beta error). A *type I error* occurs when an hypothesis about the population is rejected, even though in fact it is true. In the example above, we dismissed the hypothesis that the population from which our survey sample was drawn has a mean age of 35 years. The chances of selecting, from a population where the average is 35 years a sample with an average of 37 years is less than 1-in-1000. However, we may have actually selected one of those rare samples. The population of all service users may indeed have a mean age of 35, but the sample may have just happened to randomly pick up a few older people. There is always a risk of such an event, which is why we speak in terms of probabilities.

A *type II error* occurs when we do not reject the population hypothesis, although in fact it is false. Sometimes such a result is reported as 'not statistically significant.' In our example, had the *p*-value been very high, we would not dismiss the hypothesis that the population only has a mean age of 35 years. But it may be that the population does indeed have a higher mean age, and a relatively high proportion of younger people in the sample means we do not detect this higher mean age.

The relationship between these two possible error types is summarised in Table 11.5. These two error types are the inverse of each other: reducing the chance of one error occurring increases the chance of the other error occurring. It is a question of which mistake we most want to avoid, and this depends on the context of the research and how it will be applied in practice. If we are testing a new drug that may have unpleasant side effects, we want to be sure that it actually works. We do not want to make a type I error (conclude that the drug does make a difference when it does not) because the consequences can be

Table 11.5 Error types

Decision based on hypothesis test	Truth about population	
	H_0 true	H_a true
Reject population hypothesis	Type I error	Correct decision
Do not reject population hypothesis	Correct decision	Type II error

be devastating. The difference in the rate of improvement observed between a test group taking the drug and a control group that is not will have to be very large before we can say that such an improvement is not due to chance (say 1-in-1000). Thus a sample result may be significant at the 0.01 level (that is, 1-in-100), yet we are not prepared to reject the null unless the more demanding significance level of 0.001 is reached.

In other words, the 'appropriate' balance between these two alternative error types depends on the use to which the results are to be put, and this requires us to provide the exact probability when reporting results, to allow a reader to make his or her own decision about the population.

Inference using confidence intervals

The hypothesis testing procedure outlined in the previous section has one major limitation: it assesses, using the sample result, whether the population of interest does or does not have a particular characteristic, such as a mean age of 35 years. It is conceivable that we could have tested whether the sample came from a population with a mean age of 33 years or 39 years, or any value we choose. The 'test' value of 35 years was chosen in this instance because a specific funding policy is triggered if the mean age of a population of service users is older than this. The hypothesis testing procedure lets us determine what the population is not; but it does not really tell what the population is. In our example we have determined that the population does not have a mean age of 35 years; it could be any number greater than 35.

This information is provided by *confidence intervals* (readers may wish to look over the sections on sampling error in chapter 9 which also covers the concepts in this section). We do not guess an individual value for a population mean, but rather a range of values that we believe 'takes in' the true population value. This information appeared in the hypothetical report we quoted above in the form of the following statement: 'we estimate from the sample that our service users have a mean age between 36.3 and 37.7 years (alpha = 95 per cent)'. Such a confidence interval assumes that the sample mean is within the 'normal' bounds of sampling error. In other words, if we assume that the sample outcome is not greatly affected by sampling error, the sample mean must not be too far above or below the population mean. In this example we estimate the population mean to be within the range of 37 ± 0.7 (that is, between 36.3 and 37.7 years). The calculations involved in constructing such an interval are beyond the scope of this chapter, but underlying these calculations is the simple logic that random samples will rarely produce a result that is very different from the population from which they are drawn.

Note that we could be wrong. Our sample may indeed be one of the relatively unusual samples that fall very far above or below the population mean. Thus constructing a confidence interval around our sample mean is always subject to this kind of error. The risk of this error is expressed by the confidence level; in estimating the population value from the sample result we assume that the sample is not one of those 5-in-100 samples that will be very different from the underlying population from which they are drawn. Remember that this is only an assumption: we may have actually drawn one of those freakish samples with a mean very different from that of the underlying population. We can never know if this is the case, but given the very low probability of this being the case, we can be confident that this assumption is correct. We call this assumed probability the *confidence level*; in this instance it is a 95 per cent confidence level (this confidence level is sometimes reported as the alpha level).

This process of constructing a confidence interval around a sample result that we believe takes in the true population value complements the hypothesis testing procedure we discussed in the previous section. The hypothesis testing procedure allowed us to determine whether or not the underlying population from which a sample is drawn has a particular characteristic. The confidence interval gives us a range of values within which we are confident the population characteristic of interest falls.

In the example of service users we have been using, we rejected the possibility that the mean age of all service users is 35 years, using the hypothesis testing procedure. And this conforms to the confidence interval analysis that suggests the population mean age is between 36.3 and 37.7 years; a range that excludes the value of 35. In other words, a confidence interval provides at a given alpha level the full range of values against which the sample result will not be significantly different (and by implication the full range of values against which it will be significantly different).

What does it mean 'not to find a statistically significant difference'?

In the hypothesis testing procedure we begin with the presumption that the null hypothesis is true, and then proceed to test this assumption, but researchers are usually interested in rejecting the null; we believe a difference exists (that is, usually we want a low 'p-value'). Does this mean that if we fail to reject the null, the difference we are searching for does not exist? Not necessarily: failing to reject the null hypothesis of no difference simply means there is not sufficient evidence to think that the null hypothesis is wrong. This does not necessarily mean, however, that it is right. There might actually be a difference 'out there', but on the basis of the sample result such a difference has not been detected. This is like the presumption of innocence in criminal law. A defendant is presumed not guilty unless the evidence is strong enough to justify a verdict of guilty. However, when someone has been found not guilty on the strength of the available evidence, it does not mean that the person is in fact innocent: all it means is that, given that either verdict is possible, we do not choose 'guilty' unless stronger evidence comes to light. Similarly, with a verdict of 'no difference', failing to reject the null hypothesis does not mean the alternative is wrong. It simply means that on the basis of the information available, the null can explain the sample result without stretching our notion of reasonable probability.

Therefore, failing to find a significant difference should not be seen as conclusive. If we have good theoretical grounds for suspecting that a difference really does exist, even though a test suggests that it does not, this can be the basis of future research. Maybe the variable has not been operationalised effectively, or the level of measurement does not provide sufficient information, or the sample was not appropriately chosen or was not large enough. In the context of research, inference tests do not prove anything; they are usually evidence in an ongoing discussion or debate that rarely reaches a decisive conclusion.

What does it mean 'to find a statistically significant difference'?

What if our decision is the converse: we reject the null hypothesis? In formal language we say that we have found a *statistically significant* difference. So what? What have we learned about the world, and should we do anything about it? These questions are not ones that hypothesis testing as such can answer. A difference that is statistically significant simply indicates that it is unlikely to have come about by random error when sampling from a population with a pre-specified characteristic. Whether such a difference is of any practical importance – whether it is 'significant' in any other sense of the word – is really something we as decision-makers answer for ourselves.

In the example we have been using, government policy is to make funds available to any service whose users have a mean age that is 'significantly' greater than 35 years. Our sample of users had a mean age of 37 years, which we found to be *statistically* significant. But does that mean our population of users can really be considered old? The government may accept that statistically the population of users is older, but may argue that in practical terms it is not so much older that it warrants extra funding; it is not *practically* significant. (Of course, the government could have been clearer by stating how much greater than 35 years a population mean age has to be for it to be considered significant in policy terms.)

This illustrates an all-too-often neglected point. It is not uncommon for researchers simply, and blandly, to state that a result is significant at the 0.05 or 0.01 level without further comment, as if this is all that needs to be said. In fact this should just be the entry point to the more creative and interesting (but usually more difficult) research problem: what does this tell us about the world and what can we do about it? A finding may be statistically significant – but does it matter? (see Box 11.3 for further discussion on reporting inferential statistics in a way that discusses both statistical and practical significance).

Tools for analysing quantitative data

It was not long ago that statistical analysis was normally undertaken 'by hand' using pen and paper (and a calculator). Since the development of affordable desktop computers, and the Internet that connects them, hand calculations are the exception rather than the rule. There are four broad classes of alternatives to hand calculations.

1. *Spreadsheet data management programs.* Practically every computer has an 'office' suite of software designed to handle various tasks such as word processing and data management. Examples include Microsoft Excel, which is part of Microsoft Office, OpenOffice, and Gnumeric. Such programs can generate graphs, tables, and most of the statistical

Box 11.3 How to report inferential statistics

In presenting the results of inferential analysis we should try to be as non-technical as possible, by stating our conclusion in plain words and indicating the practical or theoretical meaning that flows from the results. The inferential statistics should be presented but should not be the focus of the discussion, which should concentrate on the general meaning of the results. We cannot avoid using a little bit of jargon, but we should keep this to a minimum.

To illustrate the way in which we present results, assume that we conduct a sample survey from two separate groups of students. One group has been taught mathematics using traditional methods, while the other has been taught using a new method of team-based teaching. The two samples are asked to sit a standardised test and the mean grades for each group are compared. The starting assumption is that there is no difference between the scores of each group *as a whole*. Do the sample results justify rejecting this assumption?

- We begin by stating in general terms what we are investigating. Thus I might introduce my findings by stating 'We are interested in whether a new method of teaching mathematics based on teacher teams improves student exam performance.'
- I then state the relevant descriptive statistics that summarise the sample results: 'A random sample of 30 students taught under the existing method and another 30 students taught under the new team-based method completed a standard mathematical test. The first group had a mean score of 65, while the second group had a mean score of 73.'
- I then discuss the statistical significance of this result and report the relevant statistics: 'The difference of 8 marks between the two samples is statistically significant ($p < 0.0001$).'
- I then interpret the results with reference, in plain words, to the hypothesis that I have tested and the practical importance of any statistical difference I have discovered: 'We therefore reject the hypothesis that students who receive the new method of teaching perform no better than those who receive the traditional method; the new method does seem to produce higher scores. Moreover, the difference of 8 marks in practical terms represents a substantial improvement in test scores and warrants an expansion of the team-teaching method.'

that we require. Their advantage is their ubiquity. Their disadvantage is that they do not perform more complicated statistical analysis, or if they do it is often through the use of complicated equations that have to be precisely entered.

2. *Comprehensive commercial programs*. There are many commercial programs such as SPSS, GB-Stat, InStat, JMP, Minitab, SAS and StatA. A full list of such packages is available at <www.statistics.com/resources/software/commercial/index.php3>. Such packages often have

the appearance of spreadsheet data management programs, but are specifically designed for statistical analysis. They have a more complete range of options than spreadsheet programs, and the type of analysis desired can be selected from a menu of options rather than by entering equations on the spreadsheet.

3. *Free comprehensive programs.* An exciting development in recent years is the availability of free software, and this includes some useful statistical analysis software. A list of such software is available at <statpages.org> Of these, Epi Info developed by the US Centers for Disease Control, available at <www.cdc.gov/epiinfo>, is particularly worth mentioning as a tool for health researchers. An open source version of Epi Info, called OpenEpi, which runs on all platforms and in a web browser, is available from <www.openepi.com>.

4. *Calculation pages for specific statistical pages.* These are web pages that provide tools for conducting very specific analysis such as calculating ideal sample sizes, rather than comprehensive statistical programs. A listing of these pages is available at <statpages.org>.

Conclusion

This chapter has covered a wide range of tools for quantitative data analysis. A key element determining which of these tools are appropriate is the way in which our variables of interest have been measured. In particular, we need to first determine whether our variables have been measured at the nominal, ordinal, or interval/ratio levels.

We then introduced three broad classes of statistical techniques that help us describe the data that we collect: graphs, tables and numerical calculations, and within each of these broad groups we have further choices. For example, we saw that there are different classes of numerical calculations depending on whether we are trying to identify the central tendency of a distribution or the amount of dispersion it contains.

Once we have described the data we have collected, or when we are presented with such statistics that others have generated, we are then confronted with another problem. This is the problem of inference, which arises when we are dealing with data from a random sample drawn from a population of interest. Inferential statistics help us generalise from the results obtained from a random sample to the population from which it has been taken.

12 Measuring the relationship between variables

George Argyrous

The previous chapter looked at methods for describing the distribution of a single variable. This *univariate analysis* can help address simple questions such as 'what is the language background of service users?' or 'how satisfied are service users with the service?' Each of these questions is interested in only one variable: language background and satisfaction level respectively. This simple analysis may only be a precursor to more complex analysis that asks whether variables such as satisfaction with service and language background are related to each other. Research questions that address the possible *relationship* between two variables requires *bivariate statistical analysis*.

Everyone probably has a commonsense notion of what it means for two variables to be 'related to' each other. We know that as children grow older they also get taller: age and height are related. This example expresses a general concept for which we have an intuitive feel: as the value of one variable changes the value of the other variable also changes in a systematic, predictable way.

If we do believe two variables – such as language background and satisfaction rating of service – are related we need to express this relationship in the form of a *model* before we undertake bivariate analysis to measure this relationship. A model is an abstract depiction of the possible relationships among variables. For this example the model is easy to depict: if there is a relationship it is because a person's language background affects their satisfaction rating. It is not possible for the relationship to 'run in the other direction': a person's language background will not change as a result of a change in how they rate their quality of service. In this instance we say that language background is the *independent variable* and satisfaction rating is the *dependent variable*. Sometimes the dependent variable is referred to as the 'outcome' variable, while independent variables are sometimes called 'predictor' variables.

Once we have specified the model that we believe underpins any relationship between two variables, we then generate appropriate statistics to see if such a relationship does in fact appear in the data we collect. There are two ways we can assess whether a statistical relationship exists between two variables:

1. For each of the groups defined by the independent variable, generate descriptive statistics to summarise the dependent variable and compare the differences.
2. Calculate measures of association and correlation.

The first method is the simplest: we generate the same statistics covered in the previous chapter, but rather than doing so for the whole data set, we *generate these statistics for each of the groups defined by the independent variable*. For example, if I wished to see whether service satisfaction rating is affected by language background, I calculate summary statistics for service satisfaction rating, but I do so separately for English speaking background (ESB) and non-English speaking background (NESB) users. This is illustrated by the *stacked bar chart* in Figure 12.1, where we generate separate stacks for each of the language background groups. The same comparison between ESB and NESB is also made using the *bivariate table* in Table 12.1 (also known as a *contingency table* or *crosstabulation* or '*crosstab*' for short), where we have separate columns for each language group.

Figure 12.1 Stacked bar chart: Satisfaction rating by language background of service users

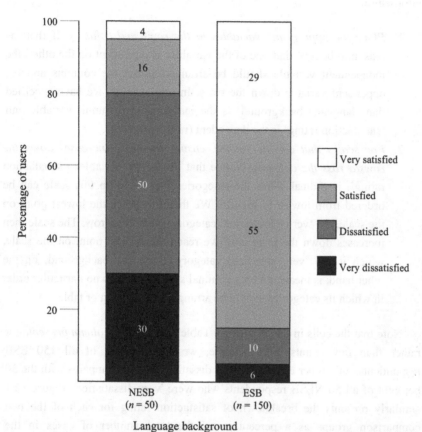

Table 12.1 Crosstab: Satisfaction rating by language background of survey respondents

Satisfaction rating	Language background		
	NESB %	ESB %	Total %
Very dissatisfied	30	6	12
Dissatisfied	50	10	29
Satisfied	16	55	34
Very satisfied	4	29	25
Total	100	100	100
	(n = 50)	(n = 150)	(n = 200)

With crosstabs such as Table 12.1 we follow two rules for arranging the information:

1. *Place the appropriate variables in the rows and columns.* If there is reason to believe that one of the variables is dependent on the other, the independent variable should be arranged across the columns and the dependent variable down the rows. In this example we have specified that 'language background' is the independent (column) variable and 'satisfaction rating' is the dependent (row) variable.
2. *For scales that can be ranked, ensure the scale increases down the rows/across the columns.* Notice that one of the variables, 'satisfaction rating', is ordinal. Thus the categories that make up this scale can be ordered from lowest to highest. We therefore place the lowest point on the scale, the 'very dissatisfied' category, on the first row. The scale then increases down the page until we reach the highest point on the scale, which is the 'very satisfied' category. Language background, on the other hand, is measured on a nominal scale so there is no particular order in which its categories should be arranged in the graph or table.

Note that the cells in the crosstab in Table 12.1 contain *column percentages* rather than raw counts. For example, we can see that of all 150 ESB respondents, only 6 per cent were 'very dissatisfied'. This compares with the 30 per cent of all 50 NESB respondents who were 'very dissatisfied'. Figure 12.1 similarly presents the breakdown of satisfaction rating for each of the two comparison groups as a percentage of the total number of cases in the respective group. In both the crosstab and the bar chart, these percentages adjust for the different total number of ESB and NESB service users in the data and thereby allow for a more valid comparison than using just the raw counts.

The scale for the dependent variable (satisfaction level) in Table 12.1 and Figure 12.1 is made up of broad categories, which is why we displayed the results using a bar chart and crosstab. Where the dependent variable is measured on an interval/ratio scale that has many points, we instead compare the groups in terms of summary statistics such as the mean and median. For example, we may want to compare language groups in terms of number of visits to the service rather than their service satisfaction rating. The scale for measuring number of visits can be collapsed into a discrete number of categories and the comparison made using a crosstab or stacked bar chart.

Alternatively, or in addition to that analysis, we can calculate summary statistics such as the mean and median number of visits on the original data for each language group, as illustrated in Table 12.2.

Table 12.2 Average visits to the service by language background

Measures of average	NESB	ESB
Mean number of visits	3.1	1.2
Median number of visits	3	1

Once we have generated graphs, tables, or summary statistics to compare the relevant groups, the task is then to interpret the differences – to assess whether they reveal a relationship between the two variables. When comparing differences between the relevant groups we look at the *pattern* and *strength* of any relationship that such differences reveal. For example, from the crosstab in Table 12.1 we can say that there is a relationship between satisfaction rating and language background, such that NESB service users are less satisfied with the service they receive than ESB users. From Table 12.2 we can also see that a relationship exists such that NESB service users do not use the service as often as ESB users.

Measures of association and correlation

In the previous section, we detected a relationship between satisfaction rating and language background and also between frequency of service visits and language background. Once we have established that a relationship exists, the next step is to assess the *strength* of this relationship. We can make an arbitrary assessment of a relationship's strength by arguing, for example, that the set of percentages in each column of Table 12.1 are very different to the other and therefore suggest a relationship that is moderate in strength. We can, alternatively, arrive at a more precise and objective measure of the strength of a relationship by calculating numerical *measures of association and correlation*. These measures are descriptive statistics that quantify a relationship between two variables.

Table 12.3 lists the most common measures. Detailing the logic of each of these measures and the methods for calculating them is beyond the scope of this chapter; for a comprehensive guide see Liebetrau (1983). Table 12.3 indicates that a starting point for choosing the appropriate measure, as with most other statistics, is the level at which the variables under analysis have been measured.

Table 12.3 Measures of association and correlation

Measure	Data consideration
Lambda	At least one variable nominal
Goodman and Kruskal's tau	At least one variable nominal
Eta	Independent variable nominal; dependent interval/ ratio
Somer's *d*	Both variables at least ordinal
Gamma	Both variables at least ordinal
Kendall's tau-*b*	Both variables at least ordinal
Kendall's tau-*c*	Both variables at least ordinal
Spearman's rho	Both variables at least ordinal with many points on scale
Pearson's *r*	Both variables interval/ratio with many points on scale
Kappa	Both variables at least ordinal and measured on same scale

The general point to note about these measures is that they give a precise value, on a scale from 0 to 1, indicating the *strength* of any relationship observed between two variables. We can then interpret the value according to the terminology suggested in Table 12.4. Rather than just relying on a visual impression of a crosstab or graph, measures of association thereby provide a single figure for the strength of association. In addition, where both variables are measured at least at the ordinal level, a + or − sign also indicates the *direction* of association: whether an increase in the quantity of one variable is associated with an increase (positive association) or decrease (negative association) in the quantity of the other variable.

Table 12.4 Interpreting values for measures of association and correlation

Range (±)	Relative strength
0	No relationship
0– 0.2	Very weak, negligible relationship
0.2–0.4	Weak, low association
0.4–0.7	Moderate association
0.7–0.9	Strong, high, marked association
0.9–1	Very high, very strong relationship
1	Perfect association

For example, we observed a relationship between language background and satisfaction rating of service in Table 12.1. To give this assessment some quantitative precision we can calculate the relevant measures of association. With at least one of the variables in the crosstab measured on only a nominal scale, the appropriate measures are lambda and Goodman and Kruskal's tau, which have values of 0.32 and 0.35 respectively. In other words, on a scale from 0 to 1, where 0 indicates no association, the quantitative strength of the relationship between language background and satisfaction with the service is weak; a relationship exists but language background does not closely 'track' service satisfaction.

It is important to remember that these measures only detect a *statistical association*; they do not necessarily show whether one variable causes a change in another. We may suspect theoretically that one variable causes a change in the other, but the measures listed in Table 12.3 cannot prove causation, only provide supporting evidence for a model. For example, we may observe a relationship between the number of storks in an area and the birth rate in that area, and we may calculate a measure that quantifies this statistical relationship. However, we cannot conclude from this statistical association that the presence of storks determines the birth rate!

The lesson to draw from this 'theory of the stork', as it has come to be known in the literature, is that we should be very careful drawing conclusions about *causality* from a statistical association between two variables. Box 12.1 discusses how variables that are not present in the analysis may be affecting the statistical relationship we have observed. To uncover more complex relationships, we require more sophisticated statistical methods than bivariate techniques. Such methods are discussed in the next section.

Regression analysis

The simple statistical techniques we have discussed above can take us a long way into data analysis and help address many of the research questions we wish to answer. However, there are many more, and more complicated, methods of analysis that are available to the researcher willing to learn and use them. One such technique you may frequently encounter is *regression analysis*, which seeks to depict the relationship between an independent variable and one or more dependent variable in the form of a *regression equation*. For example, we may be concerned with the level of absenteeism in a government department and wish to identify the factors that determine this variable.

As a starting point we may believe that annual number of days lost (as a measure of absenteeism) is affected by the amount of weekly unpaid overtime an employee is regularly asked to do. In this instance, our model places absenteeism as the dependent variable and unpaid overtime as the independent variable.

Box 12.1 Explaining a statistical association between two variables

As part of its analysis of service use, a public sector agency finds a statistical relationship between the income of users and the frequency of service use: low-income people tend to use the service more frequently than high-income earners. A simple explanation is to take this statistical association at face value and conclude that income level *determines* the frequency of service use. At least three other explanations are, however, possible:

1. *The relationship is spurious.* The underlying causal model may be that income and frequency of service use are each independently determined by a third variable, such as education level. Education level determines people's income, and also independently affects frequency of service use. The bivariate analysis does not take this other variable into account, making it appear that income affects service use, which is not really the case.

2. *There is an intervening variable.* It may be the case that income does indirectly affect service use, but only in so far as income affects health status first, and then health status affects service use. For example, as income increases health improves, and the improvement in health reduces the need to visit the service. Health status, in other words, stands between the two observed variables.

3. *The relationship is conditional.* This occurs when the relationship between the two observed variables changes according to the value of a third, unobserved variable. For example, an observed relationship between income and frequency of service use may only apply to females; for males the relationship may not exist. Thus sex of users determines the nature of the relationship between income and service use. By measuring including all users when measuring the relationship between income and service use, the correlation between these variables is a misleading average of the two different forms this correlation takes according to sex of service users.

The basic problem is that we can rarely explain a variable of any importance with reference to only one other variable. Other variables need to be taken into account for decisions to be based on sound evidence

A survey of 90 employees is conducted, and the number of unpaid hours of work per week is recorded for each employee and matched with the number of days lost in the previous year due to illness. Each of these variables is measured on an interval/ratio scale, which produces a wide spread of data. These data are displayed in the form of scatterplot (Figure 12.2), with the independent variable across the horizontal axis, and the dependent variable along the vertical axis.

Figure 12.2 Scatterplot: Weekly unpaid overtime and annual days lost ($n = 90$)

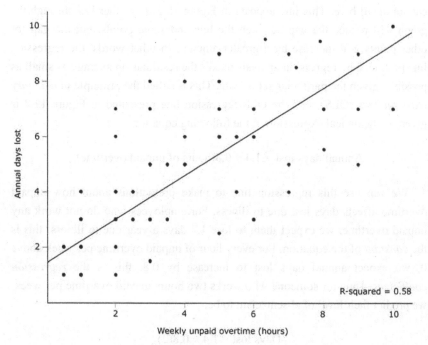

The scatterplot is made up of *coordinates* that represent the combination of scores for each of the 90 cases. In this way, a scatterplot performs the same function as the stacked bar chart and crosstab presented above, in that it depicts the relationship between two variables. But since each variable is measured on an interval/ratio scale, the scatterplot is able to express the quantitative differences between cases for each of the two variables simultaneously. We can immediately see: (a) that there is a relationship between these two variables; (b) that this is a positive relationship; (c) that the relationship is *linear* in that the coordinates of the plot seem to cluster around a straight line; and (d) that the relationship is moderate in strength in that most of the coordinates lie reasonably close together.

Note the subjective nature of some of these judgments about the relationship expressed by the scatterplot. Linear regression analysis overcomes this subjectivity by providing exact quantitative values for aspects of a relationship. The starting point to regression analysis involves determining the line through the scatterplot that 'best fits' the data. This line of best fit is that which minimises the gaps (called the *residual*) between each coordinate and the line. This line is determined by a complex mathematical procedure that we cannot detail here. This line appears in Figure 12.2; any other line through the graph will reduce the gap between the line and some points, but the gap for other points will increase by a greater amount. In other words, the regression line produced by regression analysis makes the residuals on average as small as possible, given the particular set of data. This is called the principle of *ordinary least squares* (OLS), and the OLS regression line presented in Figure 12.2 is given mathematical expression in the following equation:

Annual days lost = 1.4 + 0.8(hours of unpaid overtime)

We can use this regression line to make predictions about how unpaid overtime affects days lost due to illness. For employees who do not work any unpaid overtime, we expect them to lose 1.4 days a year due to illness; this is the *constant* of the equation. For every hour of unpaid overtime per week above 0, we expect annual days lost to increase by 0.8; this is the *regression coefficient*. Thus for someone who works two hours unpaid overtime per week, we predict their level of absenteeism to be:

$$\text{Days lost} = 1.4 + 0.8(2)$$

$$= 1.4 + 1.6$$

$$= 3 \text{ days}$$

Note that we do not expect this *estimate* to be perfectly correct. For any given employee who works on average two hours of unpaid overtime, we expect that they will be absent for three days of work. This is our best 'guess', but we also know that our guess may involve some error. We can see this in the scatterplot, where the regression line does not perfectly capture the spread of scores. Most of the points in Figure 12.2 lie around to the regression line, but only one actually lies on this line. For the rest there is an error between the level of absenteeism this simple model predicts, and the actual amount of absenteeism observed.

The extent to which the coordinates in the scatterplot fall close to the line, and thereby the confidence we have in the accuracy of our estimates of absenteeism, is captured by the *coefficient of determination*, R^2, which measures the amount of the variation in days lost we can explain with reference to unpaid overtime, on a scale from 0 to 1. In this instance, we can explain just over half (0.58) of the variation in days lost by knowing unpaid overtime alone. This coefficient is especially useful because it indicates the predictive power of our model: if we know how much unpaid overtime someone is regularly asked to do we can predict how many days of lost work they will experience, and we can have a reasonable amount of confidence that our prediction will be correct or not too much in error if the value for R^2 is high.

Multiple regression analysis

In the previous section we looked at a simple bivariate relationship and found that one variable (unpaid overtime) explained statistically a reasonable amount of the distribution of another variable (days lost due to illness). However, there is a considerable amount of variation in days lost that is still left unexplained. Complex variables such as absenteeism can rarely be explained solely with reference to one other variable; other factors must also contribute to levels of absenteeism. We can extend the analysis to take into account more than one independent variable, which is the task of *multivariate analysis*. By taking account of these other explanatory variables, we hope to reduce the error 'gaps' and explain a greater proportion of the variation in absenteeism.

We may, for example, elaborate our model of what affects absenteeism; we now believe that absenteeism for any given employee is determined by their length of service, their salary, the amount of unpaid overtime they regularly spend on the job, and their smoking habits. A survey of employees is conducted and data on the number of years of employment (EMP), the number of unpaid hours of work per week (OVER), gross annual salary in the previous year (SAL), and the number of cigarettes smoked per day (CIGS), are recorded for each respondent and matched with the number of days lost in the previous year from illness. A regression analysis of the data produces the following equation.

$$\text{Annual days lost} = 0.5 + 0.3(\text{EMP}) - 0.00002(\text{SAL}) + 0.5(\text{OVER}) + 0.1(\text{CIGS})$$

$$\text{Adjusted } R^2 = 0.72$$

Note that the regression equation is not written 'in full' but rather uses the abbreviations for each variable. This is common when presenting multiple regression results, as space often precludes the full listing of each variable's label. When abbreviations are used it is important to identify somewhere in the report the variable to which each of the abbreviations refers and how it has been measured.

How do we 'read' such an equation? The first thing to note is the explanatory power of the equation overall, which is given by the value for the adjusted R^2 (the reason for the 'adjustment' is a technical matter that is not of material importance). This value of 0.72 indicates that our model with these four variables accounts for nearly three-quarters of the variation in absenteeism. Note that the simple model in the previous section, which explained absenteeism using just hours of unpaid overtime as an explanatory variable, produced an R^2 of 0.58. Thus the extra information provided by the three additional variables in the expanded model does seem to improve our ability to explain absenteeism.

The next thing to look for is the positive or negative sign in front of each independent variable (the items to the right of the equals sign). These signs indicate the direction of the relationship between each independent variable and the dependent variable, and should accord with what we know or expect the direction of the relationship to be. For example, our equation indicates that gross annual salary is negatively related to number of days lost: the more someone is paid the fewer days they spend absent from work. This is a reasonable result based on past research. The other variables are each positively related to absenteeism: an increase in years of employment, unpaid overtime or smoking is associated with an increase in days lost. If the sign in front of smoking was negative rather than positive we might question the validity of the data and how they were gathered and analysed, given that everything we know about health tells us that smokers are less healthy and more prone to sickness than non-smokers.

The other thing to look for is the value in front of each independent variable. These numbers are the *regression coefficients* that quantify the relationship that each of these variables has with the dependent variable. These coefficients allow us to estimate the number of working days lost by an employee, given information about the other 'predictor' variables. If we know that someone has been employed for two years, has an annual salary of $40 000 and spends five hours on average a week doing unpaid overtime, but does not smoke, we expect the number of lost working days to be:

$$\text{Days lost} = 0.5 + 0.3(2) - 0.00002(40000) + 0.5(5) + 0.1(0)$$

$$= 0.5 + 0.6 - 0.8 + 0.25 + 0$$

$$= 2.15 \text{ days}$$

We can use these regression coefficients to predict the dependent variable, given known values for the independent variables. These regression coefficients are therefore very useful for decision-making, because they tell us how much of a change in the target variable a change in any of the predictor variables will 'buy'. For example, the regression coefficient for gross annual salary is –0.00002, which suggests that for every dollar increase in salary we expect number of working days lost to decrease by –0.00002. If a person's salary increased by $10 000 we predict their absenteeism will fall by 0.2 days.

One common mistake when reading regression information is to assume that the relative sizes of the regression coefficients indicate the relative importance of each independent variable in explaining the dependent variable. Thus although the coefficient for unpaid overtime of 0.5 is much higher than that for annual salary (0.00002), we cannot say that unpaid overtime has a greater affect on absenteeism than pay. This is because the units in which the variables are measured affect the coefficients. If we had measured unpaid overtime in number of minutes rather than number of hours, the coefficient will be 0.0083 rather than 0.5. If we wish to determine which variables have the stronger relationship with the dependent variable, we need to present a different set of values called *standardised coefficients*, which range between 0 and 1, regardless of the units in which each variable is measured.

Another common mistake with regression equations is to assume that they predict the impact of changes in the independent variables with perfect certainty. This is never the case. We expect, for example, that a $1 increase in salary will lead to a decrease in absenteeism by a factor of 0.00002, but we also accept that there will be some error in this prediction. At the very least, random factors will mean that absenteeism will never be fully explained by the set of variables we have included in the regression (which is expressed by the fact that R^2 has a value less than one).

Table 12.5 lists the main techniques for *multivariate analysis* (see Argyrous (2005) for a more detailed introduction).

Table 12.5 Types of multivariate analysis

Multivariate techniques	Data considerations
Multiple regression	Interval/ratio independent and dependent variables. Categorical independent variables can be included as dummy variables.
Logistic regression	Dependent variable is categorical and independent variables are interval/ratio.
Loglinear analysis	All variables are categorical.

Inferential statistics for measures of association

The measures we have discussed in the previous sections all describe patterns of statistical association that appear in a set of data that we are analysing. The same issue of inference discussed in chapter 11 arises here: can we generalise from the sample results to the broader population? That is, we may find that two variables exhibit a statistical association with each other, and measure this to be 0.58, but if this comes from sample scores can we generalise to the broader population and argue that a relationship of this strength holds? Is such an inference valid?

We will not go over the logic of inferential statistics again here; the previous chapter discussed this in some detail. Here we present the way that inferential statistics are reported when researchers discuss relationships among variables, and how we make sense of these statistics.

Take, for example, the discussion and results presented in Table 12.6, which extends the discussion of the results discussed in Table 12.1, but now including inferential statistics.

A sample of 50 service users of non-English speaking background and 150 service users of English speaking background were surveyed and asked their satisfaction with the level of service they received. The results of this survey are presented in the following table (Table 12.6).

Table 12.6 Satisfaction rating by language background of survey respondents

Satisfaction rating	Language background		
	NESB %	ESB %	Total %
Very dissatisfied	30	6	12
Dissatisfied	50	10	29
Satisfied	16	55	34
Very satisfied	4	29	25
Total	100	100	100
	($n = 50$)	($n = 150$)	($n = 200$)

The data display a relationship between satisfaction rating and language background, such that NESB users are less satisfied with the service they receive; 80 per cent of NESB users were either dissatisfied or very dissatisfied with the service, while only 16 per cent of ESB users rated the service this poorly. The relationship between language background and service rating is moderate in strength (lambda = 0.32), and statistically significant (chi-square test for independence, $p < 0.01$), suggesting that the sample results can be generalised to the wider population of service users.

Table 12.6 compares the service satisfaction levels of service users by language background. These data come from a random sample of service users so we need to assess whether the difference between language background groups in terms of satisfaction rating is due to sampling error or really reflects a difference that exists in the whole population.

It is common to report the specific test used to make an inference; in this instance it is the chi-square test for independence (sometimes the actual value of this statistic is also presented). The specific test used depends on a number of factors, such as the type of data description used (in this instance a crosstab), and the number of cases included in the sample. Knowledge of these tests is beyond the scope of this chapter, but their general purpose is the same. They measure the likelihood of obtaining the differences we have observed in our sample(s) if there is no difference in the population(s), and this is always reported as the 'significance level'. Here the chance of random sampling error alone producing the differences observed between language groups is less than 1-in-100. We therefore conclude that the sample results reflect a real underlying difference between language background groups in terms of satisfaction levels.

Table 12.6 illustrates one common method for presenting the results of a single test of statistical significance. When several comparisons are summarised in one table, an asterix system is used to signify the comparisons that are statistically significant. In a footnote to the table, the particular tests used and the significance levels (indicated by the number of asterixis), are then presented. This leaves the discussion of the table to be free of overly technical language. To illustrate this method for reporting inferential statistics, we reproduce a table similar to Table 12.2 as Table 12.7, but with the addition of the results of significance tests and the confidence intervals for the means.

Table 12.7 Average age and number of visits to the service by language background

Measures of average	NESB	ESB
Mean age in years*	34.4	32.1
Mean number of visits**	3.1	1.2
95 per cent confidence interval	2.7–3.5	1.0–1.4
Median number of visits†	3	1

* Significant difference at the 0.05 level (independent samples *t*-test)
** Significant difference at the 0.01 level (independent samples *t*-test)
† Significant difference at the 0.05 level (Wilcoxon rank-sum test)

Regression analysis also requires the inclusion of inferential statistics when it is based on random sample data. A regression analysis such as we discussed earlier, but which includes inferential statistics, might read as follows:

A regression analysis assessed the extent to which the number of working days lost due to illness was affected by the following factors: length of employment measured in years (EMP); gross annual salary in whole dollars (SAL); amount of unpaid overtime regularly worked in hours (OVER); and the number of cigarettes smoked on a normal day (CIGS).

The results of this analysis are summarised in the following equation, which indicates the extent to which a change in any given variable will produce a change in absenteeism (*t*-scores in brackets).

$$\text{Days lost} = 0.5 + 0.3(\text{EMP}) - 0.00002(\text{SAL}) + 0.5(\text{OVER}) + 0.1(\text{CIGS})$$
$$(2.58)^* \qquad\qquad (1.13) \qquad\qquad (3.56)^{**} \qquad (3.25)^{**}$$

The overall equation had high explanatory power (adjusted $R^2 = 0.72$, $F = 4.52$, $p < 0.01$), suggesting that it is a reliable model for predicting absenteeism among staff. The correlations for years of employment, amount of unpaid overtime, and cigarette smoking habit were all statistically significantly greater than 0, at either the 0.05 or 0.01 levels (indicated by * and ** respectively). However, while there was some correlation between gross annual salary and absenteeism in the sample data, this was not statistically significant, and therefore we cannot dismiss the possibility that there is no relationship between these two variables.

The relevant parts of this discussion and their meaning are as follows:

- *The equation as a whole* contains predictor variables that are significantly correlated with the dependent variable of annual days lost. This is indicated by the *F*-statistic, which has a probability of less than 0.01 of occurring by chance.
- While the overall equation may be statistically significant, *individual regression coefficients* may not be. In the discussion, an asterix system similar to that in Table 12.7 is used to indicate which regression coefficients are significantly *greater than zero*. Although for the sample data all the regression coefficients are greater than zero (ignoring any minus signs), we need inferential statistics to tell us whether this is due to sampling error alone, or whether it reflects that the variables are statistically correlated for the population as whole. In this example, a correlation is measured between annual salary and absenteeism. But the correlation is not statistically significant, so we cannot dismiss the possibility that it came about as a result of sampling error when sampling from a population where these variables are not related.

Conclusion

This chapter has introduced a range of statistical procedures that allow us to assess whether two or more variables are statistically associated with each other. The focus has been on the general character of these procedures, and their limitations, rather than the detailed nature of each. We now conclude with three concerns that must always be raised when dealing with these and other complex statistical measures.

The first concern is that these procedures only measure statistical association. They tell us that a series of numbers are related to another series of numbers. But this is only a first step. Questions must still be asked about the validity of these numbers and whether they accurately reflect the underlying concept they seek to measure. Statistical association also needs *theoretical explanation*; we need to stand back from the procedures at some point at try to make sense of what they produce in terms of some coherent understanding of how the world operates.

The second concern is that the more complex and advanced the statistical procedure, the more restrictive are the assumptions that justify its use. Whenever we commission or encounter such procedures in decision-making, it is valid to ask what the assumptions are behind the particular analysis used, and the extent to which such assumptions are appropriate in the circumstances. For example, multiple regression analysis such as the one we used as an example assumes that all the independent variables are not correlated with each other; they are each only correlated with the dependent variable. In the example, this means that length of employment, gross annual salary, amount of unpaid overtime, and smoking habit are not correlated with each other. We might thus question including both length of employment and salary in the one regression equation, as it is likely that salary will be affected by the length of time one has been in employment.

The last concern is one we raised in chapter 11 regarding the difference between statistical significance and practical significance, but is worth noting again. If we do measure a relationship among a set of variables, the more important question then arises as to whether this relationship is strong enough for us to base any practical decisions upon it. Statistics feed into a broader decision-making process, but the extent to which they do so is determined outside the field of statistical analysis. A correlation between two variables may be measured at 0.35; whether this is strong enough to form the basis of a new policy relies depends on the specific circumstances of the case.

References

Abelson, P (2003a) *Cost–Benefit Analysis of Proposed New Health Warnings on Tobacco Products*, Report prepared for Commonwealth Department of Health and Ageing, Canberra, viewed 11 February 2008, <www.treasury.gov.au/documents/836/PDF/Cost_Benefit_Analysis.pdf> .
—— (2003b) *Public Economics: Principles and Practice*, Applied Economics, Sydney.
Abrams, P (1968) *The Origins of British Sociology 1834–1914*, University of Chicago Press, Chicago.
Albaek, E (1995) Between knowledge and power: utilization of social science in public policy making, *Policy Sciences*, 28: 79–100.
Alexander, I (1978) The planning balance sheet: an appraisal. In JC McMaster & GR Webb (eds) *Australian Project Evaluation: Selected Readings*, Australia & New Zealand Book Company, Sydney.
Alkin, M (ed.) (2003) *Evaluation Roots.* Sage, Thousand Oaks, CA.
Alkin, MC & Christie, AC (eds) (2005) *Theorists' Models in Action. New Directions for Evaluation,* no. 106, Jossey-Bass, San Francisco, CA.
Argyrous, G (2005) *Statistics for Research*, Sage, London.
Arnstein, S (1969) A ladder of citizen participation, *Journal of the American Institute of Planners*, 35(2): 216–24.
Arrow, K, Solow, R, Portney, PR, Leamer, EE, Radner, R & Shuman, H (1993)

Report of the NOAA Panel on Contingent Valuation, 11 January 1993. <www.darp.noaa.gov/library/pdf/cvblue.pdf>.

Assim, F, Bari, M & Hill, C (1997) *Multicriteria Analysis: Application to the Murrumbidgee Irrigation Area and Districts Land and Water Management Plan*, paper presented to the 42nd Annual Conference of the Australian Agricultural and Resource Economics Society, University of New England, Armidale, New South Wales, 19–21 January.

Auspos, P & Kubisch, A (2004) *Building Knowledge About Community Change: Moving Beyond Evaluations*, Aspen Institute Round Table on Community Change, New York.

Australian Government Solicitor (2002) *Commercial Notes*, 27(6) November, Canberra.

Bass, S (1995) *Participation in Policy Processes*, Forestry and Land Use Program, International Institute for Environment and Development, London.

Bell, S (2004) Appropriate policy knowledge, and institutional and governance implications, *Australian Journal of Public Administration*, 63(1): 22–28.

Benton, T & Craib, I (2001) *Philosophy of Social Science*, Palgrave, Basingstoke, Hampshire.

Bernstein, DJ (1999) Comments on Perrin's 'Effective use and misuse of performance measurement', *American Journal of Evaluation*, 20(1): 85–94.

Bevan, G & Hood, C (2006) Have targets improved performance in the English NHS? *British Medical Journal*, 332: 419–22.

Bickman, L & Rog, D (eds) (1998) *Handbook of Applied Social Research*, Sage, Thousand Oaks, CA.

Bird, S, Kurowski, W & Dickman, G (2005) Evaluating a model of service integration for older people with complex health needs, *Evaluation Journal of Australasia*, 4(1–2): 34–41.

Blake, A (2000) *The Economic Effects of Tourism in Spain*, Discussion Paper 2000/2, Tourism and Travel Research Institute, Nottingham University Business School, Nottingham.

Blake, A, Durbarry, R, Sinclair, M, & Sugiyarto, G (2001) *Modelling Tourism and Travel using Tourism Satellite Accounts and Tourism Policy and Forecasting Models*, Discussion Paper 2001/4, Tourism and Travel Research Institute, Nottingham University Business School, Nottingham.

Blake, A, Sinclair, MT & Sugiyarto, G (2003) Quantifying the impact of foot and mouth disease on tourism and the UK economy, *Tourism Economics*, 9(4): 449–65.

Boardman, AE, Greenberg, DH, Vining, AR & Weimer, DL (2006) *Cost–Benefit Analysis: Concepts and Practice*, third edition, Prentice Hall, New Jersey.

Bobbitt, P (2003) Seeing the futures, *New York Times*, 8 December.

Boyle, JS (1994) Styles of ethnography. In JM Morse (ed.) *Critical Issues in*

Qualitative Research, Sage, Thousand Oaks, CA.

Brealey, RA & Myers, SC (1991) *Principles of Corporate Finance*, fourth edition, McGraw Hill, USA.

Brown, SR (1980) *Political Subjectivity: Applications of Q methodology in Political Science.* Yale University Press, New Haven, CT.

Bryman, A (1988) *Quantity and Quality in Social Research,* Routledge, London.

—— (2004) *Social Research Methods,* Oxford University Press, Oxford.

Buchy, M & Hoverman, S (2000) Understanding public participation in forest planning: a review, *Forest Policy and Economics,* 1: 15–25.

Buchy, M, Ross, H & Proctor, W (2000) *Enhancing the Information Base of Participatory Approaches to Australian Natural Resource Management,* Commissioned Report to the Land and Water Resources Research and Development Corporation, Canberra.

Buhrs, T & Bartlett, R (1993) *Environmental Policy in New Zealand: The Politics of Clean and Green,* Oxford University Press, Oxford.

Bullock, H, Mountford, J & Stanley, R (2001) *Better Policy Making*, Centre for Management and Policy Studies, Cabinet Office, London.

Bulmer, M (1986) The policy process and the place in it of social research. In M Bulmer (ed.) *Social Science and Social Policy*, Allen & Unwin, London.

Bureau of Transport and Regional Economics (2005) *Risk in Cost–Benefit Analysis*, Report 110, Commonwealth of Australia, Canberra.

Business Council of Australia (2004) *Aspire Australia 2025*, Melbourne, <www.bca.com.au>.

Cabinet Office (1999) *Professional Policy Making for the Twenty First Century*, Strategic Policy Making Team, Cabinet Office, London.

—— (2000) *Adding It Up: Improving Analysis and Modelling in Central Government*, Performance and Innovation Unit, Cabinet Office, London.

—— (2001) *A Futurist's Toolbox*, Cabinet Office, London.

—— (2003a) *The Magenta Book: Guidance Notes for Policy Evaluation and Analysis*, Government Chief Social Researcher's Office, Cabinet Office, London.

—— (2003b) *Trying It Out: The Role of 'Pilots' in Policy Making: Report of the Review of Government Pilots*, Government Chief Social Researcher's Office, Cabinet Office, London.

Campbell, D (1969) Reforms as experiments, *American Psychologist*, 24: 409–29.

Cassels, D & Valentine, P (1988) From conflict to consensus: towards a framework for community control of the public forests and wildlands, *Australian Forestry,* 51: 47–56.

CfEBP (2001) *Coalition for Evidence-Based Policy*, sponsored by the Council for Excellence in Government, Washington, DC, <www.excelgov.org>.

Chen, H-T (1990) *Theory-Driven Evaluations*, Sage, Newbury Park, CA.

Chinn, S, & Rona, RJ (2001) Prevalence and trends in overweight and obesity in three cross-sectional studies of British children, 1974–1994, *British*

Medical Journal, 322: 24–26.

Churchman, C, Ackoff, R & Arnoff, E (1957) *Introduction to Operations Research,* Wiley, New York.

Clarence, E (2002) Technocracy reinvented: the new evidence-based policy movement, *Public Policy and Administration,* 17(3): 1–11.

Clark, G & Kelly, L (2005) *New Directions for Knowledge Transfer and Knowledge Brokerage in Scotland,* Office of the Chief Researcher, Scottish Executive, Edinburgh.

Cm 4310 (1999) *Modernising Government White Paper,* The Stationery Office, London.

Commission on Social Sciences (2003) *Great Expectations: The Social Sciences in Great Britain,* Academy of Learned Societies for the Social Sciences, London, <www.the-academy.org.uk>.

Commonwealth of Australia (1998) *The National Landcare Program: What has it Changed? A Compilation of Evaluations of the National Landcare Program 1992–1998,* Agriculture Fisheries Forestry Australia, Canberra.

—— (2004) *Commonwealth Procurement Guidelines – January 2005,* Financial Management Guidance no. 1, Department of Finance and Administration, Canberra.

—— (2006) *Guidance on the Gateway Review Process: A Project Assurance Methodology for the Australian Government,* Financial Management Guidance no. 7, Department of Finance and Administration, Canberra.

Cook, D & Proctor, W (2007) Assessing the threat of exotic plant pests, *Ecological Economics,* 62(2–3): 594–604.

Coote, A, Allen, J & Woodhead, D (2004) *Finding Out What Works: Building Knowledge About Complex, Community-Based Initiatives,* King's Fund, London.

Costanza, R, d'Arge, R, de Groot, R, Farber, S, Grasso, M, Hannon, B, Limburg, K, Naeem, S, O'Neill, R, Paruelo, J, Raskin, R, Sutton, P & van den Belt, M (1997) The value of the world's ecosystem services and natural capital, *Nature,* 387(6630): 253–60.

Court, J, Hovland, I & Young, J (2005) *Bridging Research and Policy in Development: Evidence and the Change Process,* ITDG Publishing, Rugby.

Cousins, JB & Simon, M (1996) The nature and impact of policy induced partnerships between research and practice communities, *Educational Evaluation and Policy Analysis,* 18(3): 199–218.

Cousins, JB & Whitmore, E (1998) Framing participatory evaluation. In E Whitmore (ed.) *Understanding and Practicing Participatory Evaluation. New Directions for Evaluation,* no. 80, Jossey-Bass, San Francisco, CA.

Cropper, M & Laibson, D (1999) The implications of hyperbolic discounting for project evaluation. In PR Portney & JP Weyant (eds) *Discounting and Intergenerational Equity,* Resources for the Future, Washington, DC.

Crosby, N (1999) Using the citizens jury process for environmental decision making. In K Sexton, AA Marcus, KW Easter & TD Burkhardt (eds) *Better Environmental Decisions: Strategies for Governments, Businesses, and*

Communities, Island Press, Washington, DC.

Crotty, M (1998) *The Foundations of Social Research,* Allen & Unwin, Sydney.

Davey Smith, G, Ebrahim, S & Frankel, S (2001) How policy informs the evidence, *British Medical Journal,* 322: 184–85.

Davies, HTO, Nutley, SM & Smith, PC (eds) (2000) *What Works? Evidence-Based Policy and Practice in Public Services,* The Policy Press, Bristol.

Davies, HTO, Nutley, SM & Walter, I (2007) Academic advice to practitioners: the role and use of research-based evidence, *Public Money and Management,* 27(4): 232–35.

Davies, P (2004) *Is Evidence-Based Government Possible?* Jerry Lee Lecture 2004, Paper presented at the 4th Annual Campbell Collaboration Colloquium, Washington, DC, 9 February.

Denzin, NK & Lincoln, YS (eds) (2007a) *The Landscape of Qualitative Research,* third edition, Sage, Thousand Oaks, CA.

—— (2007b) *Strategies of Qualitative Inquiry,* third edition, Sage, Thousand Oaks, CA.

—— (2007c) *Collecting and Interpreting Qualitative Materials,* Sage, Thousand Oaks, CA.

Department of Finance and Administration (2006) *Handbook of Cost–Benefit Analysis,* Financial Management Reference Material no. 6, Commonwealth of Australia, Canberra.

Dey, I (1993) *Qualitative Data Analysis,* Routledge, London.

Dienel, P (1988) *Die Planungszelle: Eine Alternative zur Establishment-Demokratie,* second edition, Westdeutscher Verlag, Opladen, Germany.

Dixit, AK & Pindyck, RS (1994) *Investment Under Uncertainty*, Princeton University Press, Princeton, NJ.

Dixon, P & Rimmer, M (2002) *Dynamic, General Equilibrium Modelling for Forecasting and Policy: A Practical Guide and Documentation of MONASH*, North-Holland, Amsterdam.

Dobes, L (2006) *Managing Consultants: A Practical Guide for Busy Public Sector Managers*, Australian National University E-Press, Canberra.

—— (2007) Turning isolation to advantage in regional cost–benefit analysis, *Economic Papers,* 26: 17–28.

Donaldson, SI (2003) Theory-driven program evaluation in the new millennium. In SI Donaldson & M Scriven (eds.) *Evaluating Social Programs and Problems: Visions for the New Millennium,* Lawrence Erlbaum Associates, Mahwah, NJ.

Donaldson, SI & Christie, CA (2005) The 2004 Claremont debate: Lipsey vs Scriven, *Journal of Multidisciplinary Evaluation,* 2(3): 60–77.

Dwyer, L, Forsyth, P, Madden, J & Spurr, R (2000) Economic impact of inbound tourism under different assumptions about the macroeconomy, *Current Issues in Tourism,* (3)4: 325–63.

Dwyer, L, Forsyth, P, Spurr, R & Ho, T (2005) *The Economic Impacts and*

Benefits of Tourism in Australia: A General Equilibrium Approach, (M2RNSW model), Sustainable Tourism Cooperative Research Centre, Griffith University, Gold Coast Campus, Queensland.

Economic Research Associates (2003) *Aviation in California: Benefits to an Economy and Way of Life*, report prepared for Division of Aeronautics, Department of Transportation, California.

Econtech (2001) *Economic Effects of the Recent Tourism-Related Events on the Tourism Sector of the Economy*, report prepared for the Department of Industry, Science and Resources, Canberra.

Etzioni, A (1968) *The Active Society: A Theory of Societal and Political Processes*, Free Press, New York.

Fagence, M (1977) *Citizen Participation in Planning*, Pergamon Press, Oxford.

Fear, W & Roberts, A (2004) *The State of Policy in Wales: A Critical Review*, Wales Funders Forum, Cardiff.

Ferlie, E (2005) Conclusion: from evidence to actionable knowledge? In S Dopson & L Fitzgerald (eds) *Knowledge to Action? Evidence-Based Health Care in Context*, Oxford University Press, Oxford.

Fernandez, L (1996) *Evaluating Proposed uses of Coral Reefs: Comparison of Economic and Multiple Criteria Approaches*, unpublished PhD thesis, University of Hawaii.

Ferraro, PJ & Taylor, LO (2005) Do economists recognize an opportunity cost when they see one? A dismal performance from the dismal science, *Contributions to Economic Analysis and Policy*, 4(1), article 7, Berkeley Electronic Press, viewed 11 February 2008, <www.bepress.com/bejeap/contributions/vol4/iss1/art7>.

Fetterman, DM (2000) *Foundations of Empowerment Evaluation*, Sage, Thousand Oaks, CA.

Fetterman, DM, Kaftarian, S & Wandersman, A (eds) (1996) *Empowerment Evaluation: Knowledge and Tools for Self-Assessment and Accountability*, Sage, Thousand Oaks, CA.

Finch, J (1986) *Research and Policy: The Use of Qualitative Methods in Social and Educational Research*, Farmer Press, London.

Fitzpatrick, JL, Sanders, JR & Worthen, BR (2004) *Program Evaluation: Alternative Approaches and Practical Guidelines*, third edition, Allyn & Bacon, Boston.

Flick, U (2006) *An Introduction to Qualitative Research*, second edition, Sage, London.

Flyvbjerg, B, Skamris Holm, MK & Buhl, SL (2005) How (in)accurate are demand forecasts in public works projects? The case of transportation, *Journal of the American Planning Association*, 71: 131–45.

Forsyth, P (2005a) *Tourism Benefits and Aviation Policy*, mimeo, Martin Kunz Memorial Lecture, Hamburg Aviation Conference, Hamburg, Germany.

—— (2005b) *Promoting Competition in Trans-Pacific Aviation*, mimeo,

Monash University, Melbourne.

Frank, RH & Bernanke, BS (2007) *Principles of Micro-Economics*, third edition, McGraw Hill Irwin, New York.

Gillis, C (2005) *Economic Impact Model: General Aviation Airports*, presentation to Fall GA/Non-Hub American Association of Airport Executives Meeting, Phoenix, AZ, 3 November.

Gomez, R (2000) *Multicriteria Analysis and Complexity: A Review of the Analytic Hierarchy Process*, unpublished report, Centre for Resource and Environmental Studies, Australian National University, Canberra.

Government Social Research (2002) *Annual Report 2001–02*, Government Social Research Heads of Profession Group, London.

Gramlich, EM (1981) *Benefit–Cost Analysis of Government Programs*, Prentice-Hall, New Jersey.

Gregan, T & Johnson, M (1999) *Impacts of Competition Enhancing Air Services Agreements: A Network Modelling Approach*, Productivity Commission Staff Research Paper, Ausinfo, Canberra.

Haas-Wilson, D (1986) The effect of commercial practice restrictions: the case of optometry, *Journal of Law and Economics*, 29: 165–86.

Hajkowicz, S (2000) *An Evaluation of Multiple Objective Decision Support for Natural Resource Management*, unpublished PhD Thesis, Department of Geographical Sciences and Planning, University of Queensland, Brisbane.

Hall, R (2001) Performance measurement. In J Mitchie (ed.) *Reader's Guide to the Social Sciences,* Fitzroy Dearborn, London.

—— (2008) *Applied Social Research,* Palgrave MacMillan, Melbourne.

Hamel, G & Prahalad, C (1996) *Competing for the Future*, Harvard Business Press, Boston, MA.

Harrington, W, Morgenstern, RD & Nelson, P (2000) On the accuracy of regulatory cost estimates, *Journal of Policy Analysis and Management*, 19: 297–322.

Hatry, HP (1999) *Performance Measurement: Getting Results*, Urban Institute Press, Washington, DC.

Head, BW (2008) Three lenses of evidence-based policy, *The Australian Journal of Public Administration*, 67(1): 1–11.

Heaton, J (1998) Secondary analysis of qualitative data. *Social Research Update*, no. 22, Department of Sociology, University of Surrey, Guildford, <sru.soc.surrey.ac.uk/SRU22.html>.

Home Office (1999) *Reducing Crime and Tackling its Causes: A Briefing Note on the Crime Reduction Programme*, Home Office, London.

Homel, P, Nutley, S, Webb, B & Tilley, N (2004) *Investing to Deliver: Reviewing the Implementation of the UK Crime Reduction Programme*, Home Office Research Study 281, Home Office, London.

Hope, T (2004) Pretend it works: evidence and governance in the evaluation of the reducing burglary initiative, *Criminal Justice*, 4(3): 287–308.

Hoverman, S (1997) *Environmentalism and Social Change: Public*

Participation in Australian Forest Management, unpublished PhD thesis, University of Hawaii.

Howlett, M & Ramesh, M (1995) *Studying Public Policy: Policy Cycles and Policy Subsystems,* Oxford University Press, Oxford.

Huberman, M (1994) Research utilization: the state of the art, *Knowledge and Policy: The International Journal of Knowledge Transfer and Utilization,* 7(4): 13–33.

Hwang, C & Yoon, K (1981) Multiple attribute decision-making. In M Beckman & H Kunzi (eds) *Lecture Notes in Economics and Mathematical Systems*, Springer-Verlag, Berlin.

IMF Independent Evaluation Office (2002) *Evaluation of Prolonged Use of IMF Resources,* International Monetary Fund, Washington, DC.

Industry Commission (1996) *Report on Tourism Accommodation and Training,* Industry Commission, Canberra and Melbourne.

James, R & Blamey, R (1999) *Public Participation in Environmental Decision-making: Rhetoric to Reality?* Paper presented at the 1999 International Symposium on Society and Resource Management, Brisbane, 7–10 July.

Janesick, VJ (2003) The choreography of qualitative research design: minuets, improvisations, and crystallization. In NK Denzin & YS Lincoln (eds) *Strategies of Qualitative Inquiry,* second edition, Sage, Thousand Oaks, CA.

Janowitz, M (1972) *Sociological Models and Social Policy*, General Learning Systems, Morristown, NJ.

Janssen, R & Rietveld, P (1990) Multicriteria analysis and geographical information systems: an application to agricultural land use in the Netherlands. In H Sholten & J Stillwell (eds) *Geographical Information Systems for Urban and Regional Planning,* Kluwer Academic Publishers, Dordrecht.

Jefferson Center (2004) *Citizens Jury Handbook,* <www.jefferson-center.org>.

Jollife, D (2004) Extent of overweight among US children and adolescents from 1971 to 2000. *International Journal of Obesity and Related Metabolic Disorders,* 28 (1): 4–9.

Joubert, AR, Leiman, A, de Klerk, HM, Katua, S & Aggenbach, JC (1997) Fynbos (fine bush) vegetation and the supply of water: a comparison of multi-criteria decision analysis and cost–benefit analysis, *Ecological Economics,* 22(2): 123–140.

JRF (Joseph Rowntree Foundation) (2000) *Findings: Linking research and practice,* September, Joseph Rowntree Foundation, York, <www.jrf.org.uk>.

Jung, T & Nutley, SM (2008) Evidence and policy networks: the UK debate about sex offender community notification, *Evidence & Policy,* 4(2): 233–53.

Kazana, V (1999) A critical overview of multiple criteria decision making methods for natural resource planning and management with reference to practice. In L Sisak, H Jobstl & M Merlo (eds) *Proceedings of the Symposium 'From Theory to Practice: Gaps and Solutions in Managerial*

Economics and Accounting in Forestry, Prague, 13–15 May.

Kirk, J & Miller, ML (1986) *Reliability and Validity in Qualitative Research,* Sage, Newbury Park, CA.

Krutilla, K (2005) Using the Kaldor–Hicks tableau format for cost–benefit analysis and policy evaluation, *Journal of Policy Analysis and Management*, 24: 864–875.

Lai, Y & Hwang, C (1996) Fuzzy multiple objective decision-making. In G Fandel & W Trockel (eds) *Lecture Notes in Economics and Mathematical Systems,* Springer, Berlin.

Latham, M (2001) Myths of the welfare state, *Policy*, 17(3): 40–43.

Lavis, J, Davies, HTO, Oxman, A, Denis, J-L, Golden-Biddle, K & Ferlie, E (2005) Towards systematic reviews that inform health care management and policy-making, *Journal of Health Services Research and Policy*, 10(1): 35–48.

Layard, R (ed.) (1972) *Cost–Benefit Analysis: Selected Readings*, Penguin, UK.

Leicester, G (1999) The seven enemies of evidence-based policy, *Public Money and Management*, 19(19): 5–7.

Lenaghan, J (1999) Involving the public in rationing decisions: the experience of citizens juries, *Health Policy*, 49: 45–61.

Liebetrau, AL (1983) *Measures of Association*, Sage, Beverly Hills, CA.

Lincoln, YS & Guba, E (1985) *Naturalistic Inquiry,* Sage, Newbury Park, CA.

Lind, RC (1999) Analysis for intergenerational decisionmaking. In PR Portney & JP Weyant (eds) *Discounting and Intergenerational Equity*, Resources for the Future, Washington, DC.

Lipsky, M (1979) *Street Level Bureaucracy*, Russell Sage Foundation, New York.

Louviere, J, Hensher, D & Swait, J (2000) *Stated Choice Methods: Analysis and Application*, Cambridge University Press, Cambridge.

Low, SM, Taplin, DH & Lamb, M (2005) Battery Park City: an ethnographic field study of the community impact of 9/11. *Urban Affairs Review,* 40(5): 655–82.

Luskin, D & Dobes, L (1999) *Facts and Furphies in Benefit–Cost Analysis: Transport*, Bureau of Transport Economics Report 100, Commonwealth of Australia, Canberra.

Lyons, E & Coyle, A (eds.) (2007) *Analysing Qualitative Data in Psychology*, Sage, London.

MacCrimmon, KR (1968) *Decisionmaking Among Multiple-Attribute Alternatives: A Survey and Consolidated Approach*, Rand Memorandum, Santa Monica, CA.

McDavid, JC & Hawthorn, LRL (2006) *Program Evaluation and Performance Measurement,* Sage, Thousand Oaks, CA.

McKillip, J (1998) Need analysis process and techniques. In L Bickman & DJ Rog (eds*) Handbook of Applied Social Research Methods*, Sage, Thousand Oaks, CA.

Macquarie Graduate School of Management (2005) *Formulation of a Human*

Resource Development Masterplan for Malaysia: Final Report, June, Macquarie Graduate School of Management, Sydney.

Maguire, M (2004) The Crime Reduction Programme in England and Wales, *Criminal Justice*, 4(3): 213–37.

Mannion, R, Davies, HTO & Marshal, MN (2005) Impact of 'star' performance ratings on English NHS Trusts, *Journal of Health Services Research and Policy*, 10(1): 18–24.

Marston, G & Watts, R (2003) Tampering with the evidence: a critical appraisal of evidence-based policy making, *The Drawing Board: An Australian Review of Public Affairs*, 3(3): 143–63.

Martin, LL & Kettner, PM (1996) *Measuring the Performance of Human Services Programs*, Sage, Thousand Oaks, CA.

Martin, LM (1994) *Equity and General Performance Indicators in Higher Education,* vol. 1, Australian Government Publishing Service, Canberra.

Massam, B (1988) Multi-criteria decision-making techniques in planning. In D Diamond & J McLoughlin (eds) *Progress in Planning*, vol. 30, part 1, Pergamon Press, Oxford.

Maxwell, JA (1998) Designing a qualitative study. In L Bickman & DJ Rog (eds) *Handbook of Applied Social Research Methods,* Sage, Thousand Oaks, CA.

Mays, N, Pope, C & Popay, J (2005) Systematically reviewing qualitative and quantitative evidence to inform management and policy-making in the health field, *Journal of Health Services Research and Policy*, 10(supp 1): 6–20.

Mertens, DM (1999) Inclusive evaluation: implications of transformative theory for evaluation, *American Journal of Evaluation*, 20(1): 1–14.

—— (2003) The inclusive view of evaluation: visions for the new millennium. In SI Donaldson & M Scriven (eds) *Evaluating Social Programs and Problems: Visions for the New Millennium,* Lawrence Erlbaum Associates, Mahwah, NJ.

Miles, MB & Huberman, AM (1994) *Qualitative Data Analysis,* second edition, Sage, Thousand Oaks, CA.

Milewa, T & Barry, C (2005) Health policy and the politics of evidence, *Social Policy and Administration*, 39(5): 498–512.

Millet, I (1997) The effectiveness of alternative preference elicitation methods in the analytic hierarchy process, *Journal of Multi-Criteria Decision Analysis,* 6(1): 41–51.

Mishan, EJ (1988) *Cost–Benefit Analysis: An Informal Introduction*, Unwin Hyman, London.

Mohr, LB (1999) The qualitative method of impact analysis, *American Journal of Evaluation,* 20(1): 69–84.

Morton, S & Nutley, SM (2008) Seminar 1: Types of knowledge for evidence-based policy, Report of Seminar 1, *NORFACE Seminar Series on Evidence & Policy*, University of Edinburgh, 26 November 2007, <www.crfr.ac.uk/norface/publications.html>.

Mulgan, G (2003) Government, knowledge and the business of policy making, *Canberra Bulletin of Public Administration*, 108: 1–5.

Munda, G, Nijkamp, P & Rietveld, P (1994) Qualitative multicriteria evaluation for environmental management, *Ecological Economics*, 10: 97–112.

Murphy, C (2002) *A Guide to Econtech's Industry Model: Murphy Model 600 Plus (MM 600+)*, mimeo, Econtech, Canberra and Sydney, <www.econtech.com.au>.

Musgrave, RA & Musgrave, PB (1976) *Public Finance in Theory and Practice*, second edition, International Student Edition, McGraw-Hill Kogakusha, Tokyo.

Narayan, PK (2004) Economic impact of tourism on Fiji's economy: empirical evidence from the computable general equilibrium model, *Tourism Economics*, 10(4): 419–33.

National Intelligence Council (2005) *Mapping the Global Future: Report of the National Intelligence Council's 2020 Project*. National Intelligence Council, Washington, DC.

NECG (Network Economic Consulting Group) (2002) *Report on the Competitive Effects and Public Benefits Arising from the Proposed Alliance between Qantas and Air New Zealand*, Network Economics Consulting Group Pty Ltd, Canberra.

Neuman, WL (2003) *Social Research Methods*, fifth edition, Allyn & Bacon, Boston.

Newcomer, K (ed) (1997) *Using Performance Measurement to Improve Public and Nonprofit Programs. New Directions for Program Evaluation*, no. 75, Jossey-Bass, San Francisco, CA.

Nicoll, LH & Beyea, SC (1999) Using secondary data analysis for nursing research, *AORN Journal*, 69(2): 428–33.

Niemeyer, SJ & Blamey, RK (2003) *The Far North Queensland Citizens' Jury*, Land and Water Australia, Canberra.

Nijkamp, P (1977) *Theory and Application of Environmental Economics*, North Holland Publishing Company, Amsterdam.

Nijkamp, P, Rietveld, P & Voogd, H (1990) Multicriteria evaluation in physical planning. In J Tinbergen (ed.) *Contributions to Economic Analysis*, 185, Elsevier Science, Amsterdam.

Nordhaus, WD (1991) To slow or not to slow: The economics of the greenhouse effect, *Economic Journal*, July: 920–37.

Nutley, SM (2003) Bridging the policy/research divide: reflections and lessons from the UK, *Canberra Bulletin of Public Administration*, 108: 19–28, <www.ruru.ac.uk>.

Nutley, SM, Bland, N & Walter, IC (2002) The institutional arrangements for connecting evidence and policy: the case of drug misuse, *Public Policy and Administration*, 17(3): 76–94.

Nutley, SM, Davies, HTO & Walter, I (2003) Evidence-based policy and practice: cross-sector lessons from the UK, *Social Policy Journal of New Zealand*, 20: 29–48.

Nutley, SM, Percy-Smith, J & Solesbury, W (2003) *Models of Research Impact: A Cross-Sector Review of Literature and Practice*, Learning and Skills Research Centre, London.

Nutley, SM, Walter, I & Davies, HTO (2007) *Using Evidence: How Research Can Improve Public Services,* The Policy Press, Bristol.

Nutley, SM & Webb, J (2000) Evidence and the policy process. In HTO Davies, SM Nutley & PC Smith (eds) *What Works? Evidence-Based Policy and Practice in Public Services*, The Policy Press, Bristol.

O'Connor, M (2000) The VALSE project: an introduction. *Ecological Economics*, 34(2): 165–74.

Oakley, A, Strange, V, Stephenson, J, Forrest, S & Monteiro, H (2004) Evaluating processes: a case study of a randomized controlled trial of sex education, *Evaluation,* 10(4): 440–62.

Oxford Economic Forecasting (1999) *The Contribution of the Aviation Industry to the UK Economy*, report commissioned by the Airport Operators and British Air Transport Association, mimeo, Oxford Economic Forecasting, Oxford, UK.

Parsons, W (1995) *Public Policy*, Edward Elgar, Cheltenham.

—— (2002) From muddling through to muddling up: evidence based policy making and the modernisation of British government, *Public Policy and Administration*, 17(3): 43–60.

Patton, MQ (1997) *Utilization Focused Evaluation,* third edition, Sage, Thousand Oaks, CA.

Pawson, R, Greenhalgh, T, Harvey, G & Walshe, K (2005) Realist review: a new method of systematic review designed for complex policy interventions, *Journal of Health Services Research and Policy*, 10(supp 1): 21–34.

Perman, R, Ma, Y & McGilvray, J (1996) *Natural Resource and Environmental Economics*, Longman, London.

Perrin, B (1998) Effective use and misuse of performance measurement, *American Journal of Evaluation*, 19(3): 367–79.

Portney, PR & Weyant, JP (eds) (1999) *Discounting and Intergenerational Equity*, Resources for the Future, Washington, DC.

Posavac, EJ & Carey, RG (2007) *Program Evaluation Methods and Case Studies*, Pearson Education, Upper Saddle River, NJ.

Prato, T (1999) Multiple attribute decision analysis for ecosystem management, *Ecological Economics,* 30: 207–22.

Prest, AR & Turvey, R (1965) Cost–benefit analysis: a survey, *The Economic Journal*, December.

Procter, M (1996) Analysing other researchers' data. In N Gilbert (ed.) *Researching Social Life*, Sage, London.

Proctor, W (2001) *Multi-Criteria Analysis and Environmental Decision-Making: A Case Study Of Australia's Forests*, unpublished PhD thesis, Centre for Resource and Environmental Studies, Australian National University, Canberra.

Proctor, W & Drechsler, M (2006) Deliberative multi-criteria evaluation, *Environment and Planning C: Government and Policy – Special Edition in Participatory Approaches to Water Basin Management*, 24(2): 169–90.

Proctor, W, McQuade, C & Dekker, A (2006) Managing environmental and health risks from a lead and zinc smelter: an application of deliberative multi-criteria evaluation. In G Herath & T Prato (eds) *Using Multi-Criteria Decision Analysis in Natural Resource Management*, Kluwer.

Productivity Commission (1998) *International Air Services*, report no 2, Ausinfo, Canberra.

—— (1999) *Australia's Gambling Industries*, Report no. 10 (published in 3 volumes), November, Commonwealth of Australia, AusInfo, Canberra.

Quiggin, J (2005) Risk and discounting in project evaluation, appendix to *Risk in Cost–Benefit Analysis*, Report 110, Bureau of Transport and Regional Economics, Commonwealth of Australia, Canberra.

Quinn, M (2002) Evidence-based or people-based policy making? A view from Wales, *Public Policy and Administration*, 17(3): 29–42.

Qureshi, ME & Harrison, SR (2001) A decision support process to compare riparian revegetation options in the Scheu Creek Catchment in North Queensland, *Journal of Environmental Management*, 62(1): 101–12.

Race, D & Buchy, M (1998) A role for community participation in Australian forest management? *Rural Society*, 9(2): 405–19.

Reichhardt, CS & Rallis, SR (1994) *The Qualitative–Quantitative Debate: New Perspectives. New Directions for Program Evaluation*, no. 61, Jossey-Bass, San Francisco.

Reid, F (2003) *Evidence-Based Policy: Where is the Evidence for it?* School for Policy Studies, University of Bristol, Bristol, viewed January 2005 <www.bristol.ac.uk/sps>.

Rein, L (1976) *Social Science and Public Policy*, Penguin Education, Harmondsworth.

Resource Assessment Commission (1992) *Multi-Criteria Analysis as a Resource Assessment Tool*, RAC Research Paper no. 6, March, Australian Government Publishing Service, Canberra.

Rietveld, P (1980) Multiple objective decision methods and regional planning. In A Andersson & W Isard (eds) *Studies in Regional Science and Urban Economics*, 7, North-Holland, Amsterdam.

Ringland, G (1998) *Scenario Planning: Managing for the Future*, John Wiley & Sons, Chichester, UK.

Robinson, J (1998) *Using a Multiple Criteria Decision Support System to Support Natural Resource Management Decision-Making for Ecologically Sustainable Development*, unpublished PhD thesis, Department of Economics, University of Queensland, Brisbane.

Robinson, J, Clouston, B & Suh, J (2002) *Estimating Preferences for Water Quality Improvements Using a Citizens' Jury and Choice Modelling: A Case Study on the Bremer River Catchment*, South East Queensland Discussion Paper no. 319, School of Economics, University of Queensland, Brisbane.

Rog, D (1994) *The Homeless Families Program: Interim Benchmarks*, Vanderbilt Institute for Public Policy Studies, Washington, DC.

—— (1999) The evaluation of the homeless families program, *American Journal of Evaluation*, 20(3): 558–61.

Rogers, PJ, Hacsi, TA, Petrosino, A & Huebner, TA (eds) (2000) *Program Theory in Evaluation: Challenges and Opportunities. New Directions for Evaluation,* no. 87, Jossey-Bass, San Francisco, CA.

Rossi, PH, Lipsey, MW & Freeman, HE (2004) *Evaluation: A Systematic Approach,* seventh edition, Sage, Thousand Oaks, CA.

Ryan, GW & Bernard, HR (2003) Data management and analysis methods. In NK Denzin & YS Lincoln (eds) *Collecting and Interpreting Qualitative Materials*, second edition, Sage, Thousand Oaks, CA.

Saaty, TL (1982) *The Logic of Priorities,* Kluwer-Nijhoff, Boston.

—— (1996) *Decisions with the Analytic Network Process (ANP)*, Proceedings of the ISAHP, Vancouver, Canada, 12–15 July.

Sabatier, P & Jenkins-Smith, HC (1993) *Policy Change and Learning: An Advocacy Coalitions Approach*, Westview Press, Boulder, CO.

Sackett, DL, Rosenberg, WMC, Gray, JAM, Haynes, RB & Richardson, WS (1996) Evidence based medicine: what it is and what it isn't, *British Medical Journal*, 312: 71–72.

Sanderson, I (2002) Evaluation, policy learning and evidence-based policy making, *Public Administration*, 80(1): 1–22.

—— (2006) Complexity, 'practical rationality' and evidence based policy making, *Policy and Politics*, 34(1): 115–32.

Saul, P (2001) Futures studies: take a good look over the horizon, *Business Review Weekly*, 27 April.

Schelling, TC (1999) Intergenerational discounting. In PR Portney & JP Weyant (eds) *Discounting and Intergenerational Equity*, Resources for the Future, Washington, DC.

Schoemaker, P (1995) Scenario planning: a tool for strategic thinking, *Sloan Management Review*, 36(2): 25–40.

Schwandt, T (2003) Three epistemological stances for qualitative inquiry: interpretivism, hermeneutics and social constructionism. In NK Denzin & YS Lincoln (eds) *The Landscape of Qualitative Research,* second edition, Sage, Thousand Oaks, CA.

Schwartz, P (1991) *The Art of the Long View*, Doubleday, New York.

Scriven, M (1993) *Hard-Won Lessons in Program Evaluation. New Directions for Program Evaluation*, no. 58, Jossey-Bass, San Francisco, CA.

—— (2003) Evaluation in the new millennium: the transdisciplinary vision. In SI Donaldson & M Scriven (eds) *Evaluating Social Programs and*

Problems: Visions for the New Millennium. Lawrence Erlbaum Associates, Mahwah, NJ.

Seddon, N (2004) *Government Contracts: Federal, State and Local,* third edition, The Federation Press, New South Wales.

Seligman, M, Steen, T, Park, N & Peterson, C (2005) Positive psychology progress: empirical validation of interventions, *American Psychologist,* 60(5): 410–21.

Sheldon, T (2005) Making evidence synthesis more useful for management and policy-making, *Journal of Health Services Research and Policy,* 10(supp 1): 1–5.

Shenson, HL (1990) *How to Select and Manage Consultants: A Guide to Getting What You Pay For,* Lexington Books, Boston.

Silverman, D & Marvasti, A (2008) *Doing Qualitative Research,* second edition, Sage, Thousand Oaks, CA.

Slocum, R (ed.) (1995) *Power, Process and Participation: Tools for Change,* Intermediate Technology Publications, London.

Smith, P (1995) On the unintended consequences of publishing performance data in the public sector, *International Journal of Public Administration,* 18: 277–310.

SPEaR (Social Policy Evaluation and Research Committee) (2001) *Terms of Reference,* Wellington, New Zealand, accessed 7 March 2008, <www.spear.govt.nz/about-us/terms-of-reference.pdf>.

Spencer, L, Ritchie, J, Lewis, J & Dillon, L (2003) *Quality in Qualitative Evaluation: A Framework for Assessing Research Evidence,* Cabinet Office, London.

Stern, N (2007) *The Economics of Climate Change: The Stern Review,* Cambridge University Press, Cambridge, UK.

Sterne, JAC & Smith, GD (2001) Sifting the evidence: what's wrong with significance tests? *British Medical Journal,* 322: 226–31.

Stirling, A & Mayer, S (1999) *Rethinking Risk: A Pilot Multi-Criteria Mapping of a Genetically Modified Crop in Agricultural Systems in the UK,* Science and Technology Policy Research Unit, University of Sussex, Brighton.

Sugden, R & Williams, A (1978) *The Principles of Practical Cost–Benefit Analysis,* Oxford University Press, Oxford.

Sugiyarto G, Blake, A & Sinclair, T (2002) *Economic Impact of Tourism and Globalisation in Indonesia,* Discussion Paper 2002/2, Tourism and Travel Research Institute, Nottingham University Business School, Nottingham.

—— (2003) Tourism and globalization: Economic impact in Indonesia, *Annals of Tourism Research,* 30(3): 683–701.

Tashakkori, A & Teddue, C (eds) (2003) *Handbook of Mixed Methods in Social and Behavioral Research,* Sage, Thousand Oaks, CA.

Taylor, AF, Wiley, A, Kuo, FE & Sullivan, WC (1998) Growing up in the inner city: green spaces as places to grow. *Environment and Behavior,* 30: 3–27.

Tedlock, B (2003) Ethnography and ethnographic representation. In NK Denzin

& YS Lincoln (eds) *Strategies of Qualitative Inquiry,* Sage, Thousand Oaks, CA.

The Economist (2006) Too much blubber, 17 June: 13–14.

Tilley, N (2004) Applying theory driven evaluation to the British Crime Reduction Programme: the theories of the programme and its evaluation, *Criminal Justice,* 4(3): 255–76.

Tourism Forecasting Committee (2005) *Forecasts*, Tourism Research Australia, Canberra.

United Kingdom (Her Majesty's) Treasury (2003) *The Green Book: Appraisal and Evaluation in Central Government*, The Stationery Office, London.

Vaile, M (2007) Stopping the cost blowouts on Queensland road projects, Media Release, 120MV/2007, 19 July.

Van Delft, A & Nijkamp, P (1977) Multi-criteria analysis and regional decision-making. In P Nijkamp (ed.) *Studies in Applied Regional Science,* 8, Martinus Nijhoff Social Sciences Division, Leiden.

Van Manaan, J (1988) *Tales of the Field: On Writing Ethnography,* University of Chicago Press, Chicago.

Wack, P (1985) Scenarios: uncharted waters ahead, *Harvard Business Review,* September–October, 73–89.

Walter, I, Nutley, S, Percy-Smith, J, McNeish, D & Frost, S (2004) Improving the use of research in social care, *Knowledge Review*, 7, The Policy Press/Social Care Institute for Excellence, Bristol/ London.

Walter, I, Nutley, SM & Davies, HTO (2003) *Research Impact: A Cross-Sector Review*, Research Unit for Research Utilisation, University of St Andrews, St Andrews, viewed January 2006, <www.ruru.ac.uk/publications.html>.

Weiss, CH (1979) The many meanings of research utilization, *Public Administration Review*, 39(5): 426–31.

—— (1987) The circuitry of enlightenment: diffusion of social science research to policy makers, *Knowledge: Creation, Diffusion, Utilization*, 8(2): 274–81.

—— (1995) The haphazard connection: social science and public policy, *International Journal of Educational Research*, 23(2): 137–50.

—— (1998) *Evaluation,* second edition, Prentice-Hall, Upper Saddle River, NJ.

Weitzman, ML (1999) 'Just keep discounting, but …'. In PR Portney & JP Weyant (eds) *Discounting and Intergenerational Equity*, Resources for the Future, Washington, DC.

Western Australian Department of Infrastructure and Planning (2005) *Citizens' Jury on Community Engagement and Deliberative Democracy*, 27–31 May, Perth, <www.dpi.wa.gov.au/mediafiles/dialogue_conf_citizensjury.doc>.

White, A & Parker, RP (1999), *Cost–Benefit Analysis Concepts for Insensitive Munitions Policy Implementation*, AR-011-169, Commonwealth of Australia, Aeronautical and Maritime Research Laboratory, Defence Science, Melbourne.

Wholey, JS (1987) Evaluability assessment: developing program theory. In L Bickman (ed.), *Using Program Theory in Evaluation. New Directions for*

Program Evaluation, no. 33, Jossey-Bass, San Francisco, CA.

Wilensky, H (1997) Social science and the public agenda: reflections on relation of knowledge to policy in the United States and abroad, *Journal of Health Politics, Policy and Law*, 22(5): 1241–65.

Winston, C (1993) Economic deregulation: days of reckoning for microeconomists, *Journal of Economic Literature*, 36: 1263–89.

Winston, J (1999) Understanding performance measurement: a response to Perrin, *American Journal of Evaluation*, 20(1): 95–100.

Woollett, G, Townsend, J & Watts, G (2002) *Development of QGEM-T: A Computable General Equilibrium Model of Tourism*, Office of Economic and Statistical Research, Queensland Treasury, Brisbane.

WT Grant Foundation (2008) *Studying the Use of Research Evidence in Policy and Practice*, Annual Report Essay, forthcoming, <www.wtgrantfoundation.org>.

Wyatt, T, Carbines, R & Robb, L (2005) Managing stakeholder relations in multi-site, multi-layered evaluations, *Evaluation Journal of Australasia*, 5(1): 33–41.

Yin, R (2002) *Case Study Research*, third edition, Sage, Thousand Oaks, CA.

Yoon, K & Hwang, C (1995) Multiple attribute decision-making: an introduction. In M Lewis-Beck (ed.) *Quantitative Applications in the Social Sciences*, series/no. 07-104, Sage, Thousand Oaks, CA.

Young, K, Ashby, D, Boaz, A & Grayson, L (2002) Social science and the evidence-based policy movement, *Social Policy and Society*, 1(3): 215–24.

Zeleny, M (ed.) (1976) *Multiple Criteria Decision Making*, Springer-Verlag, Berlin.

Zerbe, RO (1991) Does benefit cost analysis stand alone? rights and standing, *Journal of Policy Analysis and Management*, 10: 96–105.

Zhou, DJ, Yangida, Chakravorty, V & Leung, P (1997) Estimating economic impacts from tourism, *Annals of Tourism Research*, 24(1): 76–89.

Zhuang, J, Liang, J, Lin, T, & De Guzman, F (2007) *Theory and Practice in the Choice of Social Discount Rate for Cost–Benefit Analysis: A Survey*, ERD Working Paper 94, Asian Development Bank, Manila.

Zussman D (2003) Evidence-based policy making: Some observations of recent Canadian experience, *Social Policy Journal of New Zealand*, 20: 64–71.

Index

Page numbers followed by *fig* denote figures; those followed by *tab* denote tables.